VIRGINIA WOOLF'S LITERARY
SOURCES AND ALLUSIONS

GARLAND REFERENCE LIBRARY
OF THE HUMANITIES
(VOL. 397)

VIRGINIA WOOLF'S LITERARY SOURCES AND ALLUSIONS

A Guide to the Essays

Elizabeth Steele

GARLAND PUBLISHING, INC. • NEW YORK & LONDON
1983

Library of Congress Cataloging in Publication Data

Steele, Elizabeth.
Virginia Woolf's literary sources and allusions.

(Garland reference library of the humanities ;
v. 397)
Includes index.
1. Woolf, Virginia, 1882–1941—Bibliography.
2. Woolf, Virginia, 1882–1941—Sources. I. Title.
II. Series.
Z8984.2.S74   1983 [PR6045.072]   016.824'912   82-49166
ISBN 0-8240-9169-8

Printed on acid-free, 250-year-life paper
Manufactured in the United States of America

To Beverly Schlack-Randles, Brenda Silver, and Louise DeSalvo, who have assured me this was worth doing and proved it by their own examples.

CONTENTS

ACKNOWLEDGMENTS

To friends and colleagues at the William S. Carlson Library, The University of Toledo, who through their Inter-Library Loan services, fine reference collection, patience and good advice have made this publication possible, I owe my deep gratitude. For the kindnesses shown me by Leila Luedeking, curator of the extensive Woolf collection of books at Washington State University, and her staff, on the several occasions I visited the collection, I again am most grateful.

I am also indebted to Quentin Bell and Angelica Garnett, Executors of the Estate of Virginia Woolf; as well as to the staffs of the Library, University of Sussex, the Beinecke Rare Book and Manuscript Library, Yale University, the Humanities Research Library, University of Texas (Austin), and the Henry W. and Albert A. Berg Collection of the New York Public Library, Astor, Lenox and Tilden Foundations; and to my truly admirable husband, Arthur Steele.

Part I
Virginia Woolf, Literary Scholar

VIRGINIA WOOLF, LITERARY SCHOLAR

"My Own Expression"

Uneducated in the orthodox way, Virginia Woolf was, many would say, a genius. Although she died in 1941, her influence as an author and thinker has grown steadily in recent years. Her best-known work is incontrovertibly in the novel. *Mrs. Dalloway, To the Lighthouse, The Waves, Orlando, Jacob's Room* and the others are names honored wherever modern fiction is honored. But her output of non-fiction is also notable: the two book-length biographies (*Roger Fry* and *Flush*), the two feminist studies (*A Room of One's Own* and *Three Guineas*), and--perhaps her most impressive accomplishment--the hundreds of shorter pieces, including short stories, personal essays, literary critiques, and biographical sketches of authors and their subjects. This monograph is concerned with the last two categories: the critiques and the biographical sketches.

In 37 years Virginia Woolf wrote over 500 critical reviews and essays, the heaviest years being 1918 and 1919 (for a total of 87). By the time of her death she had seen these essays published in some three dozen journals on both sides of the Atlantic: *The Academy and Literature, The Arts* (New York); *The Athenaeum; The Atlantic*

Monthly; The Bermondsey Book; The Bookman (New York; including her longest essay, "Phases of Fiction"); *The Cornhill Magazine; The Criterion; The Daily Herald* (London); *The Daily Worker* (London); *The Dial* (New York); *Folios of New Writing* (London); *The Fortnightly Review; The Forum* (New York); *The Guardian* (London); *Life and Letters; The Listener* (London; including 2 broadcast texts); *The Literary Review* of the *New York Evening Post; The Living Age; The London Mercury; Lysistrata* (Oxford); *The Nation and Athenaeum; The New Republic; The New Statesman; The New Statesman and Nation; New York Herald Tribune Books; The Saturday Review of Literature; The Speaker; The Times* (London); the *TLS; Vogue; Weekly Dispatch* (London); and *The Yale Review.*

Some of the American journals regularly picked up her essays after they were published in England. One such arrangement operated between *The New Republic* in America and *The Nation and Athenaeum* in London. Or the American journal might exercise prior publication rights. *The Yale Review* had this kind of agreement.

How did Virginia Woolf herself feel about her essays? That she took them seriously is shown by, for one thing, the great pains she expended on them. Many that began as book reviews were extensively revised, as often as a half dozen times, before being collected into books. Others, technically speaking not reviews but critical essays from the start, were also carefully written and rewritten.

Although she did not apply the word "criticism" to them publicly until 1927--when she titled a review of Ernest Hemingway's *Men Without Women* "An Essay in Criticism"--for a long time even after becoming a novelist, she considered herself a critic and reviewer rather than a writer of fiction. While working on *Jacob's Room,* her diary records, she "thought of never writing any more--save reviews" (April 8, 1921). "Oddly, for all my vanity," she wrote four years later, "I have not until now had much faith in my novels, or thought them my own expression."[1] The implication is clear: criticism was her "own expression."

Such an attitude can be accounted for partly by certain experiences from her earliest years.

Context of a Career

Before she became Virginia Woolf, she was Virginia Stephen, her father being Leslie Stephen, philosopher, biographer, editor, and literary critic. An essay written by his daughter a few years after his death,[2] discusses the effect of his reading tastes on his children, to whom he frequently read aloud. "At the end of a volume my father always gravely asked our opinion as to its merits, and we were required to say which of the characters we liked best and why. I can remember his indignation when one of us preferred the hero to the far more life-like villain." This was good training. Equally impressive were his poetry recitations, "for as he lay back in his chair and spoke the beautiful words with closed eyes, we felt that

he was speaking not merely the words of Tennyson or
Wordsworth but what he himself felt and knew."

He and her mother taught Virginia and her sister
their basics (while their brothers went to public school
and then Cambridge). Stephen also helped tutor Virginia
in German and Greek. "His method of teaching a language
was always the same. He put all grammar on one side, and
then, taking some classic, made straight for the sense."[3]

For the centenary of Sir Leslie's birth the London
Times commissioned a memoir from his daughter. This second essay[4] tells more about his writing habits. He
"wrote daily and methodically, though never for long at a
time.... He wrote lying almost recumbant in a low rock-
ing chair which he tipped to and fro as he wrote, like a
cradle, and as he wrote he smoked a short clay pipe, and
he scattered books round him in a circle." Interestingly
enough, many of these same observations applied to his
daughter, who also had specific hours for writing, sat in
a low chair surrounded with books and, sometimes, smoked
a pipe.

Best of all was her father's permission, freely giv-
en, to use his "large and quite unexpurgated" library. As
a result, from early years, her diaries and letters are
dotted with references to the books she is reading--some-
times for study--(Letter, March 6, [1896]): "my Virgil
must be looked out"; more frequently to broaden her cul-
tural horizons--

(Letter, Nov. 5, [1901]): "I have been reading
Marlow, and I was so much more impressed by him
than I thought I should be, that I read Cymbeline
just to see if there mightnt be more in the great
William than I supposed. And I was quite upset!
Really and truly I am now let in to [the] company
of worshippers--though I still feel a little op-
pressed by his--greatness I suppose.... I have
spotted the best lines in the play--almost in any
play I should think--[Etc.]."

For her, reading was often inseparable from its physical
context--(Diary, Jan. 6, 1915): "evenings reading by the
fire here--reading [Jules] Michelet [*Histoire de France*]
and *The Idiot* ... --are heavenly."

Best of all, it acted as an impetus to her own
creativity--

(Diary, Feb. 27, 1926): "Beatrice Webb's book [*My
Apprenticeship*] has made me think a little of what
I could say of my own life."

(Letter, [Jan. 11, 1936]): "I'm reading--merely to
pacify myself--all [George] Borrow. And very good
too.... Lord, how I wish I could write that particular racy English eccentric East Anglican non-
conformist style."

In short, "at least let me," as she tells herself in her
diary in 1931, " ... read all there is to be read."[5]

Although she became a member of the London Library
and also leaned heavily sometimes on the British Museum

holdings (in addition to the thousands of volumes owned by
herself and her husband, Leonard), she preserved Sir Leslie's books and years later was still using them, when
occasion arose, to consult for her own writing. (See references in charts to Sir Leslie Stephen, *infra*.) They included the monumental *Dictionary of National Biography*,
for which her father, as its first editor, had written
scores of the brief lives it contains. There and in his
book-length studies, Sir Leslie's and his daughter's choice
of literary subjects sometimes overlapped. Though stylis-
tically and philosophically their essays have little in
common, both, for instance, were particularly attracted
to the eighteenth century.

Her mother, Julia--Sir Leslie's second wife as he
was her second husband--also contributed to the budding
genius of Virginia Stephen. Though less tutored, her
background, like her husband's, was intellectual. As a
girl she had inhabited Little Holland House, a venerable
dwelling outside of London (now in Kensington) occupied by
an aunt and uncle, where Tennyson, Ruskin, Thackeray and
his daughters, Tom Hughes, the painters G.F. Watts, Holman
Hunt and Edward Burne-Jones, and two Prime Ministers, Gladstone and Disraeli, were habitués--as Virginia's nephew
and biographer Quentin Bell calls them.[6]

Shortly after her father died in 1904 (her mother
having died in 1895), Virginia began publishing her personal and literary essays in the London *Guardian*, a news-
paper with a religious orientation. While the Stephens

were self-styled agnostics, the *Guardian* was willing to
pay her something for her work, which did not have to be
religious and was not. Among the other publications that
took her early essays was the prestigious *Cornhill* that her
father had once edited. In 1905 she entered upon an in-
formal arrangement with the *Times Literary Supplement,* for
whom she wrote almost every week, her articles frequently
in the honored "lead" position. This connection lasted
33 years, until 1938.

Unlike many prolific professional writers, Virginia
Woolf seldom used a literary agent. Coming from a
family where such matters were a part of daily living,
she faced without trepidation the necessity of collecting
her own fees. Leonard Woolf, whom she married in 1912,
was a man whose interests, although more political than
hers, were also literary, and in 1917 they started the
Hogarth Press, which gave her books a ready outlet in
Britain. Her American publisher was at first George H.
Doran, and from 1921, Harcourt, Brace.

The first two essay collections, *The Common Reader*
and *The Common Reader: Second Series*, were published during Woolf's lifetime. And it was after her death that
additional essays were gathered into four collections by
her husband, Leonard: *The Death of the Moth* (1942), *The
Moment* (1947), *The Captain's Death Bed* (1950), and
Granite and Rainbow (1958).

The most solid contribution in book form to this
body of literature, however, is the *Collected Essays,* a

quartet of substantial volumes published in 1966-67 whose
contents, some 150 pieces, duplicate those of the six titles named above (with a very few omissions). As Leonard
Woolf explains in his Editorial Note (Volume I), the essays in Vols. I and II are literary and critical, those
in Vols. III and IV, aside from a few personal pieces,
biographical. "The essays follow roughly a chronological
order, i.e., a critical essay on a writer born in, say,
1659 precedes one on a writer born in, say, 1672." Volume I concentrates on specific and important literary
works and figures, in contrast with Volume II, which em-
phasizes theoretical and genre criticism. III and IV are
a pair, IV continuing chronologically from where III con-
cludes. Issued too in paperback in England, the *Collected
Essays* form the basic resource for anyone interested in
exploring some of the most delightful short works in the
genre of critical writing. Three more compilations have
also been published: one before the *Collected Essays,* edited by Jean Guiguet and called *Contemporary Writers* (1965);
the others in (a) 1977, edited by Mary Lyon--*Books and Portraits*--and (b) 1979, edited by Michèle Barrett, *Women and
Writing.*[7] Together, these 7 volumes form the basis for
the study which lies at the heart of this monograph.

I myself first discovered Virginia Woolf's essays
through paperback editions of *Common Reader*s I and II,
and came to value them for three reasons: first was the
delight they give--written with gusto and vigor, they en-
gender enthusiasm; second, the knowledge they impart

about literature, history, and people; third was the
chance they provide to watch a literary scholar and
artist at work, producing a fine piece of art. To illustrate this last aspect is the special intent of the
pages to come.

The Reading Notes

To the question "What factors went into the making
of the collected essays?" one must answer genius, of
course, and imagination and the reasoning powers of Virginia Woolf, as well as her marvelous talent with words.
With most essayists one cannot go farther. They leave
little or no trace of their ramblings on paper prior to
the finished work. Happily, with Virginia Woolf this is
far from the case. Through her reading notes, we can
watch her at work from the moment she begins researching
the subjects of almost half of the collected essays.

There are some sixty-six collections of reading
notes, divided mainly between the Monks House Papers,
University of Sussex library, and the Henry W. and Albert
A. Berg Collection of English and American Literature, New
York Public Library.[8] The notebooks come in various
sizes. Some are commercially manufactured, a few are
composed of loose pages gathered later by Leonard Woolf,
but most were put together by Virginia Woolf herself,
sometimes with decorative bindings.[*]

---

[*]To go into their contents in detail, is not necessary here. For that, one may turn to Brenda Silver's excellent Index to the notes, to be published in 1983. [9]

Reading the notebooks is an awe-inspiring experience--
though it can be frustrating when the reader wants to know
exactly what edition or even what book is being so pa-
tiently eviscerated. Then he or she must turn detective.

As a sample, one might investigate the two sets of
reading notes for the 8-page piece "Oliver Goldsmith"
in Volume I of the *Collected Essays*.[10] Though ostensibly
reviewing a new, combined edition of Goldsmith's *The
Citizen of the World* (1762) and *The Bee* (1759) published
in 1934 by J.M. Dent, as she does in so many of her essays she goes beyond the book under review and surveys the
writer's entire career. The two sets of notes--one mainly
on Goldsmith's own works, the other mainly on works <u>about</u>
Goldsmith (see p. 14)--show the kinds of materials Virginia
Woolf typically consulted before writing such an essay.
The notes on primary sources (now in the Beinecke Rare
Book and Manuscript Library, Yale University),[11] written
on one side of 25 sheets of average-sized two-holed notebook paper and ruled an inch from the left margin, contain a series of page numbers and a corresponding series
of notations. On the first two pages, headed in the upper
right-hand corner "The Bee," one finds (for example):

> 59 | how he tried to become a best seller--a
> | very elegant one.
> 128 | industry the road to health & honesty to
> | happiness--copybook maxims here & there.

Sometimes she circles a page number, apparently to indicate its importance.

After three sheets of notes on Goldsmith's *Essays* and two on the *State of Polite Learning*, the next work taken up is *The Vicar of Wakefield*. Notes from *The Good Humoured Man* continue the pagination. We are now into volume IV of whatever edition of Goldsmith's works Woolf is using; and notes from *The Deserted Village* are followed by ones on *The Traveller* and "Retaliation."[12]

With *Citizen of the World*--the other work besides *The Bee* which she was reviewing--we have new pagination. She identifies it as being from the "Small Edition," then as the "Mod[ern] Edition," but they seem to be the same. After three pages of notes, she switches back, for the last three sheets, to what she calls the "Big Edition."

Those interested in knowing what edition of Goldsmith Virginia Woolf was reading, would find such vague notations disappointing. Book publishing records for 1934 (when the essay was published) show that the Dent edition of *The Bee* and the *Citizen of the World* is part of that publisher's familiar Everyman series of books, comparatively small in size; but Brenda Silver points out that the notes labeled "Small Edition" do not correspond to the Everyman version.[13] The "Big" edition, though, is not particularly hard to trace. When the Woolfs' library was sold (after Leonard Woolf's death), partly to the Bow Windows bookshop in Lewes, Sussex, and partly to Holleyman and Treacher in Brighton, the latter firm compiled a catalogue of the volumes which passed through

their shop on the way to the books' final buyer, Washington State University in Pullman, Washington. In this
catalogue, generally called "Holleyman" (see note 14),
are listed three editions of Goldsmith's works, all octavo size, belonging formerly to Leslie Stephen. But
according to the catalogue, only one of the three, a
4-volume edition published by John Murray in 1837 and
edited by James Prior, has "Paper labels on [the] spines
of Vols. 1, 2 and 4 giving contents by V.W."[14] Since
the reading notes described above skip volume III of
whatever edition Virginia Woolf was reading, this is
probably the one an investigator would start with.

Twenty-five pages of notes meanwhile, and if we look
at Woolf's essay to see what use she made of these primary
sources, we find that she (1) quotes from *The Citizen of
the World*; (2) alludes to *The Bee*, but does not quote from
it; (3) discusses and quotes from *The Vicar of Wakefield*;
(4) quotes at length from "The State of Polite Learning"
but does not identify it; (5) quotes fragments from Goldsmith's poems but does not identify them [see chart in
back, *infra*]; (6) discusses Goldsmith's popular play, *She
Stoops to Conquer*, which she took notes from but does not
quote from in her essay.

As to secondary sources, reading notes for "Oliver
Goldsmith" can be found in the Monks House Papers, University of Sussex Library, under a light blue cover (the
consistency of a university "bluebook") marked, in
Woolf's handwriting, "Goldsmith." Through two holes

punched manually, pieces of blue-green yarn with large
brads on each end secure eleven sheets 6 x 8, ruled down
one side in blue. The notes are labeled, page by page:

> Goldsmith Life. Forster. [2 pp.]
>
> Goldsmith in Cunningham. [1 p.]
>
> Forster. Life. [1 p.]
>
> Prior Life. Anecdotes. (2. 410. Goldsmith).
> [1 note]
>
> Boswell on Goldsmith. [5 pp. Several citations
> from each of 3 volumes]
>
> Goldsmith. Thackeray on. [1 note]

With these titles the catalogue of books belonging to
Virginia and Leonard Woolf would not help us much, except
that James Prior (whose 2-volume *Life of Oliver Goldsmith*
[1837] is designated here) reminds us of the 1837 ("Big")
edition of Goldsmith's works, also edited by Prior.

Of this secondary-source material Virginia Woolf in
her finished essay used, openly at least, only Boswell's
Life of Johnson: "It is only necessary to open Boswell,"
she says (*Collected Essays*, I, 113), and follows this
with a series of revealing quotations describing Goldsmith's personality and habits. Like most scholars,
when Woolf started reading and making notes, she didn't
know what she would use. Gradually the picture formed and
sometimes (though not often), she would jot down in the
reading notebook an outline or "plan for essay." Usually,
however, she waited till she sat down to write with pen or
typewriter. As the points came, she knew where to turn

for quotations--although the notes themselves could do no more than refresh her memory. The real fount of her ideas was the waist-deep immersion in her materials she had undergone in preparing to write.

Of course, the reading notebooks still extant do not cover all the essays (between 30 and 40 percent of those collected); nor, where they exist, do they cover everything she may have used in a particular essay. Sometimes she turned to a book and, employing quote marks, incorporated a passage directly into what she was writing. But the process described above is typical.

Part II
Source, Allusion and Structure in the Collected Essays

SOURCE, ALLUSION AND STRUCTURE IN THE COLLECTED ESSAYS

Purpose of the Charts

The charts following (in Part III) have been pre-
pared as a double service to readers--to document, one,
Woolf's wide breadth of reading and, two, the care she
put into shaping her essays.

Both aspects will be considered in the paragraphs
below.

Reading the Charts for Bibliography

The reader has probably gathered by now that, in her
reading notebooks, Woolf's handling of the bibliographical
details tended to be casual. Of course the notebooks were
not intended for us--only the essays were. Still, this
casualness extended even to the printed essays, for
which there are few footnotes (and some of those are
wrong) and no bibliographies. There are probably at
least three reasons for these omissions. First, as a
published reviewer she was used to having the title and
author of the book printed at the head or foot of the review. Thus accustomed to external identifications provided by editors, Woolf was careless about including them
herself, even when writing "straight" critical pieces.
Second, she may have felt that to be specific about

sources and allusions within the essay itself, might spoil
the flow of argument. Although she includes such details
occasionally (when it can be done with grace), obviously
she does not consider them vital to the reader's enjoy-
ment, and to an extent, of course, she is right.

Also relevant is her undoubted belief that her audi-
ence was already well educated in the lore, titles and
authors of Western and especially English literature.
She may have carried this concept too far.

Unfortunately, even such basic bibliographical details as were printed with the original essay are seldom
carried over to the *Collected Essays,* putting the reader
at a further disadvantage. Reviewers like Donald Hall in
New York and Marghanita Laski in London[15] were quick to
point this out when the four volumes were published in
the late 1960s. "A final word on the editing of these
volumes: it is bad," wrote Hall.   "Some of the essays
bear the date of publication in a footnote. Most do not,
and the lack of a date is frequently annoying.... There
are times when a date will fix the meaning of words."

Marghanita Laski was blunter. "The edition is a
rotten one-- ... the names of the books that give rise to
most of [the essays] are only spasmodically given.... I
should mildly like to read the diary of the Rev. John
Skinner, but here not even the date or provenance of the
essay is given, let alone the name of the book or its
editor. What kind of A-level candidates does the Hogarth
Press think we are?"

Weaknesses in bibliographical editing did not begin with the *Collected Essays,* though. As early as the first *Common Reader* (1925), the same complaints would have obtained. Neither Virginia nor, even more surprisingly, Leonard Woolf had a keen eye for these matters. To be fair, the reason they seldom provided the titles of the books being discussed was probably that neither wished the volumes to look merely like collected book reviews. But ironically, even when such titles were given, they were sometimes wrong. The book on which "Miss Ormerod"[16] is based, for instance, was misnamed in the original printing in *Dial* magazine, and all subsequent printings have perpetuated the error. The book was *not,* as stated "The Life of Eleanor Ormerod, by Robert Wallace Murray" but the *Autobiography and Correspondence of Eleanor Ormerod,* edited by Robert Wallace and published by John Murray. A similar, but worse, mistake occurred in the posthumous collection *Granite and Rainbow* (1958)--and thus in *Collected Essays,* Volume IV--where a footnote to "A Talk About Memoirs"[17] cites "*John Porter of Kingsclere.* An anthology written in collaboration with Edward Monkhouse." But it is "autobiography," not "anthology"; not "Monkhouse," but "Moorhouse." Such details are particularly bothersome when, as Marghanita Laski says, you may want to read the original book. Then "Robert Murray" and "Edward Monkhouse" will not help.[18]

Whether externally, as here, or internally, few of the essays are without their challenges for the bibliog-

rapher. To choose almost at random, the delightful
"Sterne's Ghost" (1925)[19] is among those initially hard
to pin down. The reader, seeing the title, expects the
essay to be mainly about Laurence Sterne, one of Woolf's
favorite writers. In fact, in Volume III of the *Collected Essays*, "Sterne's Ghost" is flanked by two other
essays, both about the novelist himself . But the reader
soon realizes that the main figures in "Sterne's Ghost"
are named Mathews, a young married couple who rented,
cheap, the room in Yorkshire where Sterne once wrote
Tristram Shandy, and which his ghost now "haunted" by
knocking on the wall at midnight.

From what source did Woolf ferret out this offbeat
story? According to her second paragraph Charles Mathews,
actor, began his career at "twenty-five shillings a week
in Tate Wilkinson's company." This last name rings a
bell to anyone who has read another essay in Volume III:
"Jones and Wilkinson," which (according to one of Woolf's
rare footnotes) was "Drawn from the *Memoirs of Tate Wilkinson*, 4 vols., 1790." Can the story of the Mathewses
be from this same source? But before trying to locate a
book dated 1790, one looks for other clues. For instance,
the essay also states that Eliza Mathews was a prolific
though indigent writer: "She wrote every kind of piece--
novels, sonnets, elegies, love songs." Did she write an
autobiography, the searcher wonders. However, in the
essay Eliza dies and Charles remarries. Only a survivor
would have known these facts. At this point the searcher

may notice two small, offhand allusions: one in the
second paragraph, "the second Mrs. Mathews said"; and
more important, near the end of the sixth paragraph:
Eliza "took her husband's hand and kissed it; then took
her friend's [Anne Jackson's] and kissed that too 'in a
solemn manner, which I remember made me tremble all
over'.... " Who is speaking here? Possibly Anne Jackson, who later married Charles Mathews. And so it proves.
A large library may yield the 4-volume *Memoirs of Charles
Mathews, Comedian* written by Anne Mathews, 1838 (2nd ed.,
1839); and in the first volume will be found the story of
Sterne's ghost.

Virginia Woolf's sources, it will be seen, range from
the familiar or obvious, to the unusual or esoteric, as do
the ways in which she employs them--the subject of the
next section. Yet searching is a game that anyone with
enough patience can play, and my hope is that the charts
presented will be scrutinized, corrected if necessary and
added to by others as convenience allows. By supplying,
so to speak, the footnotes she herself omitted, these ta-
bles are meant to reassure the reader that Virginia Woolf,
as scholar, stood on solid ground.

Reading the Charts for Essay Structure

Analyzing an essay structurally is a way of illuminat-
ing the other aspect of Woolf's works that cannot be over-
emphasized: her diversity of approach. Like the variety
of sources, this feature will be found codified in the

charts themselves. Studying them along with their re-
spective essays, will help us document David Daiches' in-
sight that in a Virginia Woolf essay, the pattern "is de-
termined by the particular problem under discussion; the
method shifts with the subject matter."[20]

In general, every chart follows the outline described
below--whereby the 4 categories (1) Main Source, (2) Supportive Source(s), (3) Important Allusion(s) and (4) Passing Allusion(s) are presented for each essay where they
occur.

(1) Main Sources generally are described in one of
two ways:

       (a) "Obvious Source(s)"--indicated editorially,
          outside the body of the essay;

       (b) "Inferred Source(s)"--indicated within the
          body of the essay, whether covertly (e.g., as
          in "Fishing":[21] "Major Hills") or overtly
          (e.g., by title).

A "Stated Impulse" is a Main Source stated editorially,
outside the essay, but which is not in fact a main source
at all, rather a jumping-off point. This can happen when
Woolf, given something to review, prefers to discuss another work by the same author. (See, e.g., "*David Copperfield*," supposed to be a review of three other books by
Charles Dickens.)[22]

(2) "Supportive Source(s)," whether indicated internally or simply used quietly, are almost as germane to the
essay's argument and structure as category (1).

(3) "Important Allusion(s)" highly enrich the argument but are not necessary to its support.

(4) "Passing Allusion(s)" provide graceful tracery that gives the growth its final outline. Marginal comparisons and contrasts, apparently extraneous facts and names far from vital to the essay's argument, are introduced in this guise. This is where one would start if one were pruning the essay.

Whether or not this form of analysis seems artificial and arbitrary, its usefulness for describing relationships among the structural components of Woolf's essays can, I hope, be made apparent as we study the charts on three pieces, each of which represents a different type of essay structure. First is the commemorative essay that draws on all a writer's works, or at least the most important ones (we have seen something like this already in "Oliver Goldsmith"). Second is the review of a current book, where most of Woolf's allusions and subsidiary sources are mentioned by the author being reviewed. Third is the "idea" piece, where Woolf's thesis constitutes the essay's core which the works and authors mentioned help simply to flesh out.

(a) "Addison." An example of a commemorative essay is "Addison,"[23] the subject of the first chart. Although the name of this 18th-century man-of-letters is usually linked with the *Spectator* (along with Sir Richard Steele), we would find if we looked through Woolf's essay that while the *Spectator* is mentioned several times, so are

other works by, or partly by, Addison. In fact, Addison's writings as a whole comprise the main source of the essay. This source is mentioned in passing during the third paragraph, in a key sentence which reveals the framework of much of the essay: "The temptation to read Pope on Addison, Macaulay on Addison, Thackeray on Addison, Johnson on Addison rather than Addison himself is to be resisted, for you will find, if you study the *Tatler* and the *Spectator,* glance at *Cato,* and run through the remainder of the six moderate-sized volumes, that Addison is neither Pope's Addison nor anybody else's Addison.... " Thus Addison's complete canon in six volumes with notes by Bishop Hurd (who's mentioned later in the essay), is to be the main source of the essay, with special emphasis on three works: the *Tatler*, the *Spectator* and *Cato*.

Although more space is given to the two journals, Addison's tragic drama *Cato* is discussed first. Turning next to the *Tatler* and *Spectator*, Woolf retells a story from the *Tatler*; quotes at length from two *Tatler* articles, one on the lute and one on women's clothes; alludes to Addison's defense (in the *Spectator*, though she does not say so) of two classics: the old ballad "Chevy Chase" and Milton's *Paradise Lost*; and discusses at some length Sir Roger de Coverley, that famous country-squire foil to Addison's urbanity.[24]

Three supportive secondary sources are also given prominence by Woolf. A quote from Macaulay's 1843 piece on Addison opens the essay, is quoted again extensively on the first page, alluded to in the key sentence, and discussed again some pages later (rather disapprovingly).

"Johnson on Addison" is mentioned first in the key sentence, quoted briefly in connection with *Cato*, and four pages later praised and quoted from at greater length.

"Pope on Addison" is mentioned first in the key sentence and thereafter in spurts--"the corrosion of Pope's wit," "in spite of Pope"--and quoted from briefly. (For specific sources, see chart.)

Two "Important Allusions" are "Thackeray on Addison," which, though mentioned in the key sentence, is not followed up, and an allusion to Addison's rousing the "illhumour" of Swift with his views on women, which while interesting, is also relatively gratuitous.

Toward the end, Woolf's piece takes briefly another direction that, if we thought of the essay as a "tree" (a familiar structural metaphor), might then be called a "shoot," since if allowed to develop unchecked, it would be capable of starting another organism. Identifying Addison at this point as the "respectable ancestor of an innumerable progeny" of essayists, Woolf asks us to "pick up the first weekly journal, and the article upon the 'Delights of Summer' or the 'Approach of Age' will show his influence. But it will also show," she continues, "unless the name of Max Beerbohm, our solitary essayist, is attached to it, that we have lost the art of writing essays"--a loss she discusses briefly before bringing the subject back to Addison. We find several such offshoots from the parent plant among Woolf's essays. Always under control, they are good breeding-spots for "Passing Allusions."

(b) *"Gothic Romance."* The essay on Addison was written to mark the bicentenary of his death. "Gothic Romance," whose structure we trace next as an example of a different type of essay, was a "review" of *The Tale of Terror: A Study of the Gothic Romance* by Edith Birkhead.[25] The work being reviewed is the main source. Obvious as this sounds, it cannot be taken for granted, as mentioned before. But in "Gothic Romance," a three-page piece, Woolf defers often to Birkhead--"as Miss Birkhead shows," "as Miss Birkhead suggests"--and quotes twice from the book itself.

Presenting the history of the Gothic novel, or terror-tale, from 1764, the year of Horace Walpole's *Castle of Otranto*, up to and into the future, when technology will continue to modify the genre, Woolf devotes most space to the first stage. Besides *The Castle of Otranto* and Ann Radcliffe's *The Mysteries of Udolpho*, the list of famous Gothic romances includes works by Agnes Marie Bennett, Henry James, and Sarah Wilkinson. Additional, more briefly mentioned Gothic novelists and parodists constitute "Important Allusions," as does Coleridge's poem *Kubla Khan*, named as a puzzling mixture of straight and Gothic romance.

There are also "Passing Allusions," having less to do with the subject, except indirectly. These include the works, mostly neo-classic, on our forefathers' shelves when *The Castle of Otranto* was published: Addison's *Cato*, Gray's poems, Johnson's lyric epic *The Vanity of Human Wishes*, Pope's *Essay on Man* and Richardson's *Clarissa*, a list posited by Woolf (surprising in the case of *Clarissa*) to show that the readers of that time might at first have welcomed Gothic fiction with less than open arms. Also quickly dismissed are two authors that, for purposes of comparison, are considered "Romantic" but not Gothic: Spenser and Shakespeare.

(c) "Hours in a Library." So far the patterns outlined here have had either a book or a set of books at their core. What happens when the governing thesis of the essay itself is the mainstem to which all the works mentioned are subsidiary? A good example is "Hours in a Library."[26] At the essay's center stands the idea that during a lifetime of reading, of countless "hours in a library," the reader constantly changes, desiring as s/he gets older, different things from reading.

First of course are the "books we read in childhood, having purloined them from some shelf supposed to be inaccessible.... " And then comes "the great season for reading ... between the ages of eighteen and twenty-four. The bare list of what is read then," Woolf declares, "fills the heart of older people with despair." To illustrate this stage she gives (but seldom names their

authors) most of the specific titles mentioned in the essay: two Meredith novels, Fielding's *Tom Jones*, a novel by
Hardy, Dewey's *Psychology*, the Book of Job, William
Webbe's *Discourse of Poesie*, and two Elizabethan plays.
A typical reader whom she knows, between January and
June of his twentieth year read, she reports, not only
all of the above but a "great deal" of poetry by Browning, Shelley and Spenser, Congreve's dramas, Peacock
"from start to finish; and most of Jane Austen's novels
two or three times over." In addition, according to
lists he kept, "He read the whole of ... Ibsen, and a
little of Bernard Shaw.... Euripides in wooden boards,
and Voltaire in eighty-nine volumes octavo."[27]

After twenty-four, readers are more interested in
their contemporaries--from a sense of fellow-feeling, if
nothing else. This stage is again followed by another as
readers mature and find themselves returning to the
classics: *Comus, Lycidas, Urne Burial, Anthony and Cleopatra*--the final paragraph enlarges on Woolf's own
pleasure in this literary heritage.

To show how variously, meanwhile, "Miscellaneous
Writers" are used by her in passing: she cites Carlyle,
Tennyson and Ruskin as Victorian models; Pope as a
possible "hero" for a bookish young man, and Racine as
someone to "pit against" Shakespeare in a friendly literary tiff.

In discussing "Hours in a Library" I have obviously
put more emphasis on theme than in discussing "Addison"

and "Gothic Romance," whose structures depend heavily on the use of primary and secondary printed sources. Even in these essays, of course, most important are the"ideas" which the sources illuminate and illustrate. But where allusions--however vague--to such printed sources exist, as they do in most of Virginia Woolf's essays, I consider that they strongly influenced her concept of how she should put the essay together. In sum, the sources Virginia Woolf employed in her essays are used liberally (if obliquely) and gracefully. With the evidence of her reading notebooks before us, it is also clear that such sources and allusions acted as a basis for her structural approach--analyzable now and in the future with the following charts as guides.

Some Final Notes About the Charts

(1) The *HEADING* of each chart contains: (a) the title of the essay followed by (b) the volume of the *Collected Essays* or abbreviated indication of the other recent collection(s) involved: *Contemporary Writers, Books and Portraits, Women and Writing*; (c) the date of composition or, more often, date and place of original publication; (d) further provenance of essay; (e) indication of existing variants (whether few or many); and finally, (f) the volume title of the reading notes, where applicable (numbers apply to the Berg collection, New York Public Library, and letters to the Monks House Papers, University of Sussex).

(2) *DATES* of book publication are never given by
Woolf or her editors, and *PUBLISHERS' NAMES* almost never;
nor does B.J. Kirkpatrick's *Bibliography of Virginia
Woolf*, even for the many titles it provides, help with
these data. Aside from their scholarly value, my own
reason for including them is to enable the reader, again,
to better follow the path Virginia Woolf took when writing her essays. In the charts the *PLACE* of publication
is London unless otherwise shown.

(3) In the case of works with *MORE THAN ONE EDITION:*
(a) "Indicated by the reading notes" means that the actual source has been sought out, and that the reading notes
do indeed refer to that edition. (b) "Prob. ed." means
either that the edition(s) sought was/were unavailable,
despite diligent searching; or that the reading notes
contained no page numbers to aid the search. (c) "Listed
in the reading notes" refers only to the title, not to
the edition, whether the latter is multiple or single.

(4) *Re* the fact, mentioned in many charts, that a
book is "*LISTED IN HOLLEYMAN*" (the catalogue of books, described earlier, owned by Virginia and Leonard Woolf),
this is meant to help show what works she had on hand or
at least available when she was writing, as she usually
did, at home. But the Woolfs' actual library was of
course much larger, as the Introduction to Holleyman em-
phasizes. The Woolfs themselves sold or gave away many
of their books, especially review copies; the Blitz de-
stroyed others; and after Leonard's death, the executors

of the estate rightly had first choice of the remainder. Thus, "Holleyman" itself is necessarily incomplete. Not only so but Holleyman and Treacher, Ltd., Brighton, had the selling of only a portion of the Woolfs' library when it passed from England to the United States bought by Washington State University, where it is now housed. The other was purchased by Washington State at the same time through the Bow Windows Bookshop, Lewes. And the Bookshop did not issue a catalogue.

Thus it seemed advisable to go to Pullman, as I first did in the spring of 1976, and compile a list of the books there relating to literature which had belonged to the Woolfs but were not covered in Holleyman. Later, learning that the Bow Windows Bookshop had sold yet another batch of the Woolfs' books (formerly on more or less permanent loan to Leonard's nephew Cecil Woolf for some years) to Washington State, I journeyed to Pullman again, in summer 1980. The *"HOLLEYMAN ADDENDUM"* noted in the charts, refers to the composite list of books on literature drawn up as a result, and included in this study: see Appendix B.[28]

(5) Both Holleyman itself (though it does not list publishers) and the Addendum have been extremely helpful in assembling the following charts. Most useful of all, however--that is, where *READING NOTES* are involved--, is the superb study *Virginia Woolf's Reading Notebooks*, by Brenda Silver. Woolf's reading notes, as mentioned, were recently deciphered by Professor Silver, an impressive

paleographical task, for publication, with bibliographical details, by Princeton University Press. Professor
Silver's study provides notes--where they exist,--not
only from Woolf's basic sources, but also from what
amount to some of the "extra" works composing her reading environment: the "hidden springs" which fed her
imagination and increased her fund of knowledge as she
wrote. I am grateful to Ms. Silver and Princeton University Press for the chance to see a Xerox copy of the
page proofs before the volume itself was published. A
PLUS SIGN (+), wherever it occurs, shows that for a particular bibliographical item, I defer to this excellent
work.

(6) As a rule--except where prompted by Brenda
Silver's study--I have not collated the standard 18th-
and 19th-century *NOVELS* mentioned in the essays, with
Holleyman. Most of them are found there in profusion,
and Woolf also had many other editions available to her
through the British Museum and the London Library, both
of which she relied on to furnish her with books to supplement her own holdings.

(7) Due to their lack of specific literary allusions,
9 non-personal essays in the *Collected Essays* are absent
from the charts: "The Artist and Politics"; "The Cinema";
"Memories of a Working Women's Guild"; "Middlebrow"; "The
Patron and the Crocus"; "Professions for Women"; "Roger
Fry"; "Walter Sickert," and "Why?"

Citations for the Foreword:

1. *The Diary of Virginia Woolf*, ed. by Anne Olivier Bell (New York and London: Harcourt Brace Jovanovich, 1978, 1980), II, 106; III, 12. The second entry is dated April 20, 1925.

2. Pp. 474-76 in Frederick William Maitland, *The Life and Letters of Leslie Stephen* (London: Duckworth, 1907).

3. *Ibid.*

4. "Leslie Stephen," *Collected Essays* [hereinafter called *C.E.*] (New York: Harcourt, Brace and World, 1967), IV, 76-80; orig. in *The Times* (London), Nov. 28, 1932, pp. 15-16; repr. in *The Captain's Death Bed*.

5. Diary quotations are from *The Diary of Virginia Woolf, op. cit.*, I (1977), 10; III (1980), 62; IV (1982), 12, February 17, 1931. Letter quotations are from *The Letters of Virginia Woolf*, ed. by Nigel Nicolson and Joanne Trautmann (New York and London: Harcourt Brace Jovanovich, 1975-80), I:2, 45; VI:3-4.

6. *Virginia Woolf, A Biography* (London: Hogarth, 1973), I, 15.

7. See Appendix A, *infra*, for specific contents. *Women and Writing* contains only 3 essays previously uncollected.

8. An exception are the notes on "Oliver Goldsmith" at Yale University. (See discussion later.)

9. *Virginia Woolf's Reading Notebooks* (Princeton, N.J.: Princeton University Press).

10. Pp. 106-14; orig. in *TLS*, March 1, 1934, pp. 133-34; repr. in *The Captain's Death Bed*.

11. This is the only set of Woolf's reading notes owned by Yale University. Purchased in June 1956 from Hamill and Barker, book dealers, they were given to the library by friends of Helen McAfee, editor of *The Yale Review* when Virginia Woolf was writing for that journal.

12. Another set of notes on *The Traveller* and *The Deserted Village*, from the same source, is found in reading notebook #23 (Berg).

13. See note 9.

14. "Victoria Square Catalogue," Sec. 1, p. 32, in ... *Books from the Library of Leonard and Virginia Woolf* (Brighton: Holleyman and Treacher, 1975).

15. Marghanita Laski, "Lofty Intimations," *The Listener*, Oct. 20, 1967; Donald Hall, "Who Else Is Afraid of Virginia Woolf?" *New York Times Book Review*, Dec. 24, 1967. Hall also complained about the lack of an index. One is provided with the present study, as Appendix C.

16. Not in *C.E.*; orig. in *The Dial*, Dec. 1924, pp. 466-74; repr. in *The Common Reader* (Am. ed. only).

17. *C.E.*, IV, 216-20; orig. in *The New Statesman*, March 6, 1920, pp. 642-43; repr. in *Granite and Rainbow*.

18. B.J. Kirkpatrick, *A Bibliography of Virginia Woolf*, 3rd ed. (Oxford: Clarendon, 1980), gives the correct titles, though not dates and publishers, of the books which Woolf reviewed. It also gives date(s) and original place(s) of publication for each essay--facts which Laski

and Hall (see note 15) would have liked to find footnoted in the *Collected Essays*.

19. *C.E.*, III, 94-99; orig. in *The Nation and Athenaeum*, Nov. 7, 1925, pp. 207-09; repr. in *The Moment*.

20. David Daiches, *Virginia Woolf*, 2nd ed. (Norfolk,
Conn.: New Directions, 1963), p. 140.

21. *C.E.*, II, 301-04; orig. printed in *The Moment*.

22. See chart. *"David Copperfield,"* *C.E.*, I, 191-95;
orig. in *The Nation and Athenaeum,* Aug. 12, 1925, pp. 620-
21; repr. in *The Moment*.

23. *C.E.*, I, 85-94; orig. in *TLS,* June 19, 1919, pp.
329-30; repr. in *Common Reader: Second Series*.

24. Sir Roger of course was not created solely by
Addison. See chart for statistics.

25. *C.E.*, I, 131-33; orig. in *TLS,* May 5, 1921, p.
288; repr. in *Granite and Rainbow*.

26. *C.E.*, II, 34-40; orig. in *TLS,* Nov. 30, 1916,
pp. 565-66; repr. in *Granite and Rainbow* and published by
Harcourt, Brace as a pamphlet, 1958.

27. The mention of Voltaire, especially, suggests
that the "notebook" Virginia Woolf says she took this
list from had been Leonard's as a young man: see chart.

28. Washington State University itself plans to
issue the entire catalogue of its holdings from the libraries of Virginia and Leonard Woolf.

Part III
Compilation: Sources and Allusions Used in Writing the Collected Essays

C O M P I L A T I O N

SOURCES AND ALLUSIONS USED IN WRITING THE COLLECTED

ESSAYS

(Arranged alphabetically by essay title)

ADDISON (I)--*TLS,* June 19, 1919, pp. 329-30; first collected in *C.R. I* (w/var.)   Reading notes
#2

Inferred Source:

"the six moderate-sized volumes"; "Bishop Hurd and
his notes"

Joseph Addison, *The Works of,* w/notes by Richard
Hurd. New ed.+ 6 vol. T. Cadell and W. Davies,
1811.

This is indicated by the reading notes and is listed
in Holleyman; it belonged to Leslie Stephen.

Supportive Sources:

(1) Thomas Babington Macaulay, "The Life and Writings
of Addison," orig. in *Edinburgh Review,* 1843;
repr. in Macaulay, *Critical and Historical Essays,* edited by A.J. Grieve.+ (Orig. 1843)
Everyman's Ed. 2 vol. J.M. Dent, 1907. Vol.
II.

This is indicated by the reading notes and is
listed in Holleyman.

(2) Repr. in Addison, *Works* (see above)

(a) *The Tatler* (periodical, 1709-11). Vol. II
of *Works.*+

(i) a "little fable ... [in] one of the
early numbers": #108, Dec. 17, 1709.

All quotes, except the last, on p. 89
are from here; "the country" should
read "their country."

(ii) Addison "count[ed] ... women['s] ...
follies": #116, Jan. 5, 1709.

(iii) Addison "described himself in the character of the lute": #153, Apr. 1, 1710.

This is indicated by the reading notes.+

(b) *The Spectator* (periodical, 1711-12). Vols.
IV and V of *Works.*+

(i) Addison's "defence of *Chevy Chase*" [a
16th-century ballad]: #s70 and 74, May
21 and 25, 1711.

(ii) Addison "rediscover[ed] ... *Paradise
Lost*": 17 papers on John Milton's
Paradise Lost [orig. 1667], in #s267 to
369, Jan. 5 to May 3, 1712, *passim.*

This is indicated by the reading notes (along
with notes from Addison, *Works,* edited by
Hurd. New ed. 6 vol. Bohn British Classics
ser. Bohn, 1854-85. Vols. II and III).+

    (c) *Cato* (orig. 1713).   Vol. I of *Works*.+

        This is indicated by the reading notes.+

        Quote, p. 88: II:vi:51-57.

(3) "Pope on Addison"

    (a) "Pope's wit" (last quote, p. 89)

        Alexander Pope, "Satire on Mr. Addison."
        (Orig. 1723)   Quoted in W.J. Courthope,
        Joseph Addison.   English Men of Letters ser.
        Macmillan, 1884.

        Courthope is listed in the reading notes.

    (b) "said Pope" (p. 91)

        Joseph Spence, *Anecdotes, Observations, and
        Characters ... ,* w/notes by Samuel Weller
        Singer. W.H. Carpenter, 1820.

        This is indicated by the reading notes.

(4) "[Samuel] Johnson on Addison"

    In *Lives of the English Poets*. (Orig. in Vol. V,
    1781).   Vol. X of Johnson, *The Works of,* edited
    by A. Chalmers. 12 vol. J. Johnson, 1806.

    This is indicated by the reading notes and is
    listed in Holleyman; it belonged to Leslie Ste-
    phen.

(5) "the Sir Roger de Coverley papers": 35 pieces
    (23 by Addison, others by Sir Richard Steele
    and Eustace Budgell), orig. in *The Spectator,*
    #s2 to 553, March 2, 1711 to Dec. 4, 1712,
    passim.

    Sir Roger de Coverley. By the Spectator.
    Longman, Brown, Green, and Longmans, 1850.

    This is indicated by the reading notes.+

Important Allusions:

(1) "Thackeray on Addison"

    William Makepeace Thackeray, *The English Humour-
    ists of the Eighteenth Century*.   (Orig. 1853)
    Prob. ed.: Smith, Elder, 1877.

    This is listed in Holleyman Addendum.

(2) Addison "roused the ill-humour of Swift"

    Jonathan Swift, note to "Stella" (Esther John-
    son), Feb. 8, 1711. Quoted in Courthope (see
    above).

    [Cf. "Swift's *Journal to Stella*."]

(3) "[Addison] wrote" (first quote, p. 94)

  Spectator, #445, July 31, 1712

(4) "[Addison] thought" (2nd and 3rd quotes, p. 94)

  Spectator, #435, July 19, 1712

Passing Allusions:

  Miscellaneous writers:

  (1) Mentioned by Macaulay: Francois Marie Arouet de Voltaire

  (2) Max Beerbohm, Miguel de Cervantes Saavedra, William Shakespeare

- -

ALL ABOUT BOOKS (II)--*New Statesman and Nation,* Feb. 28, 1931, pp. 14-15; repr. in *New Republic* (w/var.), Apr. 15, 1931, pp. 226-28; first collected in *C.D.B.* (text in *C.D.B.* and *C.E.* from *New Statesman and Nation*)

Supportive Sources:

  (1) "the diary of ... Cole"

  William Cole, *A Journal of My Journey to Paris in the Year 1765* ... , edited by Francis Griffin Stokes, w/introduction by Helen Waddell. Constable, 1931.

  (2) *Scrutinies,* compiled by Edgell Rickword. 2nd vol. of 2. Wishart, 1931. (First vol. 1928)

Important Allusions:

  (1) "Your last letter"

  The letter quoted was from Clive Bell (n.d. given); I am grateful to Nigel Nicolson and Joanne Trautmann, editors of *The Letters of Virginia Woolf,* IV, 294n, for this identification.

  (2) Grand Duchess Marie of Russia, *Things I Remember.* Cassell, 1930.

(3) *"The Diary of a Somersetshire Parson"* [sic]

John Skinner, *Journal of a Somerset Rector,* edited by Howard Coombs and Arthur Bax. John Murray, 1930.

[Cf. "The Rev. John Skinner."]

(4) William Guy Carr, *By Guess and By God.* Hutchinson, 1930.

Passing Allusions:

(1) Walter Scott, *Guy Mannering.* (Orig. 1815)

(2) Miscellaneous writers:

(a) Jane Austen, Thomas Carlyle, Charles Dickens, Thomas Babington Macaulay, Alexander Pope, Anthony Trollope, William Wordsworth

(b) Mentioned by Cole: Jean Jacques Rousseau, Horace Walpole

(c) Some contributors to or subjects of *Scrutinies:* Alex Brown, Mary Butts, T.S. Eliot, Bertram Higgins, Aldous Huxley, James Joyce, D.H. Lawrence, Jack Lindsay, Peter Quennell, Christopher Saltmarshe, Edith Sitwell, Lytton Strachey, Sherard Vines

(3) William Shakespeare, *Henry IV.* (Orig. 1600)

- -

AMERICAN FICTION (II)--*Sat. Rev. of Lit.,* Aug. 1, 1925, pp. 1-3; first collected in *M.*

Supportive Sources (prob. eds.):

(1) Sherwood Anderson, *A Story Teller's Story.* Jonathan Cape, 1925.

(2) Sherwood Anderson, *The Triumph of the Egg.* Jonathan Cape, 1922.

(3) Sinclair Lewis, *Babbitt,* w/introduction by Hugh Walpole. Jonathan Cape, 1922.

(4) Sinclair Lewis, *Main Street.* Jonathan Cape, 1926[?]. (Orig. 1914)

(5) Sinclair Lewis, *Our Mr. Wrenn.* Jonathan Cape, 1923. (Orig. 1920)

(6) Ring Lardner, *You Know Me Al*. New York and London: Scribner's, 1925. (Orig. 1916)

On Jan. 26, 1925, in response to a request from Woolf (see Vol. III of her *Letters*), Logan Pearsall Smith, an American critic living in England, wrote: "I am making enquiries about American fiction, and will let you know the results. In the meantime I am sending you two books of Sherwood Anderson, who is regarded, and rightly, I think, as the best of the new school. I should look at the Autobiography first, and especially the Epilogue, and then at the volume of stories. He impresses me as having a real talent, and real desire to get closer to the texture of life, though style and charm are wanting, and I find the uneasy national consciousness and inferiority complex a bore." Pearsall Smith also suggests Willa Cather and "Miss" Thurber. "Henry James used to say that the best story-writer in America was a negro, William Dubois, but the fact was hushed up on account of Colour-prejudice." (Pearsall Smith's letter is in the Woolf files at the University of Sussex. I am grateful to copyright owner John Russell for permission to quote from it.)

Important Allusion:

Walt Whitman, *Leaves of Grass*. (Orig. 1855)

Passing Allusions:

Miscellaneous writers: Arnold Bennett, James Branch Cabell, Dorothy Canfield, Willa Cather, Anton Chekhov, Theodore Dreiser, Ralph Waldo Emerson, Henry Fielding, Nathaniel Hawthorne, Joseph Hergesheimer, Fanny Hurst, Henry James, James Russell Lowell, Edgar Lee Masters, William Makepeace Thackeray, H.G. Wells, Edith Wharton

- -

THE ANATOMY OF FICTION (II)--*Athenaeum*, May 16, 1919, p. 331; first collected in *G.R.*

Obvious Source
(stated in *Athenaeum* with essay and in footnote):

Clayton Hamilton, *Materials and Methods of Fiction*, w/introduction by Brander Matthews. Rev. and enl. ed. G. Allen and Unwin, 1918.

Important Allusions:

(1) Jane Austen, *Emma*. (Orig. 1816)

(2) Mentioned by Hamilton

    (a) George Eliot, *Middlemarch*. (Orig. 1872-73)

    (b) William Makepeace Thackeray, *Vanity Fair*. (Orig. 1848)

    (c) Quotes, pp. 139-40

        (i) Alfred, Lord Tennyson, *The Princess*. (Orig. 1847)

        (ii) John Keats, "Ode to a Nightingale." (Orig. 1819)

        (iii) Sir Thomas Browne, *Urne Burial*. (Orig. 1658)

Passing Allusions:

Miscellaneous writers: Matthew Arnold, Henry James

- -

THE ANTIQUARY (I)--*Nation and Athenaeum,* Nov. 22, 1924, pp. 293-94; repr. in *New Republic* (w/var.), Dec. 3, 1924, pp. 42-43; first collected in *M.* (w/var.)   Reading notes #26

Obvious Source:

Sir Walter Scott, *The Antiquary*. (Orig. 1816)

This is listed in the reading notes.

Important Allusion:

Robert Louis Stevenson, *Kidnapped*. (Orig. 1886)

Passing Allusions:

(1) Miscellaneous writers: Anton Chekhov, Gustave Flaubert, Henry James, Marcel Proust, William Shakespeare, Stendhal, Leo Tolstoy

(2) Various characters

    (a) In Shakespeare: Falstaff, Hamlet

    (b) In Scott: *The Antiquary*--Jonathan Oldbuck, [Major Neville] Lovel, Isabella Wardour, Edie Ochiltree, Mrs. Maggie Mucklebackit,

the Earl of Glenallan; *Redgauntlet* (1824)--
Darsie Latimer; *Old Mortality* (1817)--Edith
Ballenden, Henry Morton; *Guy Mannering*
(1815)--Dandy Dimmont

- -

ARCHBISHOP THOMSON (IV)--*Athenaeum,* May 9, 1919, pp. 299-
                        300; first collected in *C.R. I*
                        (w/var.)   Reading notes B3f
                        and "Modern Novels ... , Holo-
                        graph Notebook, Unsigned and Un-
                        dated" (Berg)+

Obvious Source
(stated in *Athenaeum* with essay):

   Ethel H. Thomson, *The Life and Letters of William
   Thomson, Archbishop of York.*   John Lane, 1919.

   This is listed in the reading notes.

Supportive Source (quoted by E. Thomson):

   "Sir Henry Taylor described [Thomson]"

   Taylor to Aubrey De Vere, Dec. 1854-Jan. 1855; repr.
   in *Henry Taylor's Autobiography.* 2 vol. Longmans,
   1885. Vol. II. (Taylor spelled it "Thompson.")

Important Allusions (mentioned by E. Thomson):

   (1) William Thomson, *Outline of the Laws of Thought.*
       London: n.p., 1842.

   (2) "[Thomson] had been exhorted"

       Canon A.W. Thorod to William Thomson, Jan. 10,
       1861

   (3) *Aids to Faith,* edited by William Thomson.   Lon-
       don: n.p., 1861.

   (4) "he asked"; "he replied"; "he said" (quotes,
       top of p. 118)

       Thomson, speech at Working Men's Congress, Shef-
       field, Oct. 3, 1878

Passing Allusions (mentioned by E. Thomson):

   (1) Miscellaneous writers: Victor Cousin, Charles
       Dickens, William Makepeace Thackeray

(2) "the authors of *Essays and Reviews*"

> I.e., Frederick Temple, Rowland Williams, Robert
> Baden Powell, Henry Bristow Wilson, C.W. Good-
> win, Mark Pattison, Benjamin Jowett. London:
> J.W. Parker, 1860.

- -

THE ART OF BIOGRAPHY (IV)--*Atlantic Monthly,* Apr. 1939,
                              pp. 506-10; first collected in
                              D.M.

Supportive Sources:

> (1) Lytton Strachey, *Eminent Victorians*. (Orig.
>   1918)

> (2) Lytton Strachey, *Queen Victoria*. (Orig. 1921)

> (3) Lytton Strachey, *Elizabeth and Essex*. (Orig.
>   1928)

Important Allusions:

> Miscellaneous biographers and subjects: James Bos-
> well, Thomas Carlyle, J.A. Froude, Edmund Gosse,
> Samuel Johnson, John Lockhart, Sir Walter Scott

Passing Allusions:

> (1) Miscellaneous writers: Geoffrey Chaucer, Henry
>   James, William Shakespeare

> (2) Various characters:

>> (a) In Shakespeare: Cleopatra, Falstaff

>> (b) In Dickens: Belinda Bates (in "The Haunted
>>   House" [1859], repr. in *Christmas Stories*
>>   [orig. 1871; see *"David Copperfield"*]);
>>   Micawber (in *David Copperfield* [1850])

- -

THE ART OF FICTION (II)--*New York Herald Tribune Books,*
                        Oct. 16, 1927, pp. 1, 5-6; repr.
                        in *Nation and Athenaeum* (w/var.),
                        Nov. 12, 1927, pp. 247-48; first
                        collected in *M*. (text in *M*. and
                        C.E. from *Nation and Athenaeum*)
                        Reading notes #25

Obvious Source
(stated in *New York Herald Tribune Books* with essay and
in footnote):

    E.M. Forster, *Aspects of the Novel*. E. Arnold, 1927.

    This is listed in the reading notes.

Important Allusions:

    (1) Henry James, *The Golden Bowl*. (Orig. 1904)

        Woolf reviewed this for *The Guardian* (London),
        Feb. 22, 1905, p. 339.

    (2) Mentioned by Forster:

        (a) Laurence Sterne, *The Life and Opinions of
            Tristram Shandy*. (Orig. 1759-67)

        (b) Leo Tolstoy, *War and Peace*. (Orig. 1868)

        (c) Fyodor Dostoevsky, *The Brothers Karamazov*.
            (Orig. 1880)

        (d) Marcel Proust, *A la Recherche du Temps Perdu*.
            8 vol. Paris: Bernard Grasset and La Nou-
            velle Revue Francaise, 1914-27.

        (e) Miscellaneous novelists: Charles Dickens, Gus-
            tave Flaubert, Thomas Hardy, George Meredith,
            Samuel Richardson, H.G. Wells

    (3) Miscellaneous critics and writers: Percy Lubbock,
        Walter Raleigh (modern), Sir Walter Scott, An-
        thony Trollope

- -

AURORA LEIGH (I and WW)--*Yale Review,* June 1931, pp. 677-
                        90; repr. in *TLS* (w/var.), July
                        2, 1931, pp. 517-18; first col-
                        lected in *C.R. II* (w/var.)
                        Reading notes "[Flush] Holograph
                        and Typewritten ... Notes, Un-
                        signed and Undated" (Berg)+

Obvious Source:

>Elizabeth Barrett Browning, *Aurora Leigh*. (Orig.
>1857) Prob. ed.: 13th ed. Smith, Elder, 1873.

>This is listed in Holleyman; it belonged to Leslie
>Stephen. "Thirteen editions" and "1873" are men-
>tioned in the 3rd paragraph.

Supportive Sources:

>"Her letters"; "the *Letters*"

>(1) Robert Browning and Elizabeth Barrett, *Let-
>ters: 1845-1846*, edited by Robert W.B. Browning.
>2 vol. Smith, Elder, 1879.+

>Quotes, pp. 210 and 212, are from here:

>>(a) Elizabeth to Robert, Feb. 27, 1845; there
>>should be ellipses between "truth" and "of."

>>(b) Same to same, March 20, 1845; there should be
>>ellipses between "reveries" and "And."

>(2) Elizabeth Barrett Browning, *The Letters of,*
>edited by Frederic G. Kenyon. 2 vol. 3rd ed.
>Smith, Elder, 1898. (Orig. 1897)

>Quote, p. 213, is from here: to John Kenyon, May
>1, [1848].

>This is listed in Holleyman Addendum.

>Both are indicated by the reading notes.

Important Allusions:

>(1) Elizabeth Barrett, "Lady Geraldine's Courtship."
>(Orig. 1844)

>(2) "the primers dismiss her"

>Cannot locate

>(3) Coventry Patmore, *The Angel in the House*. (Orig.
>1854, 1856)

>(4) Arthur Hugh Clough, "The Bothie of Toper-na-
>Fuosich: A Long-Vacation Pastoral." (Orig.
>1848)

Passing Allusions:

  (1) Miscellaneous writers:

    (a) . Edwin Arnold, Thomas Beddoes, Robert
        Bridges, the Brontës, Eliza Cook, Mrs. [Eliz-
        abeth] Gaskell, Mrs. [Felicia] Hemans, Jean
        Ingelow, Robert Montgomery, Christine Rosset-
        ti, Alexander Smith, Henry Taylor, Alfred Lord
        Tennyson, Anthony Trollope

    (b) Mentioned by E. Browning: Aeschylus, Honoré
        de Balzac, David Hume, Plato, George Sand
        [pseud. of Amadine Aurore Lucie Dupin, Baron-
        ess Dudevant]

  (2) Charlotte Brontë, *Jane Eyre.* (Orig. 1847)

  (3) William Makepeace Thackeray, *Vanity Fair.* (Orig.
      1848)

  (4) Charles Dickens, *David Copperfield.* (Orig. 1850)

  (5) George Meredith, *The Ordeal of Richard Feverel.*
      (Orig. 1859)

  (6) Character: the Ancient Mariner

- -

BEAU BRUMMELL (III)--*Nation and Athenaeum,* Sept. 28, 1929,
                pp. 824-26; repr. in *New York Herald
                Tribune Books* (w/var.), Sept. 29,
                1929, pp. 1, 6; in *The Listener* (w/var.),
                Nov. 27, 1929, pp. 720-21; and as pam-
                phlet (w/var.) by Remington and Hooper,
                N. Y., 1930; first collected in *C.R. II*
                (text in *C.R. II* and *C.E.* from pam-
                phlet)   Reading notes #20

Inferred Source:

    William Jesse, *The Life of Beau Brummell* ... (Orig.
    1844) 2 vol. Nimmo, 1886.

    This is indicated by the reading notes.+

Supportive Sources:

 (1) "Harriette Wilson had heard"

 Harriet Wilson, *Memoirs of Herself and Others,* edited by James Laver. Peter Davies, 1929. (Orig. 1825)

 This is indicated by the reading notes.+

 (2) "According to Lady Hester Stanhope" (quoted by Jesse)

 (See "Lady Hester Stanhope.")

Important Allusions:

 (1) "Cowper ... predicted"

 William Cowper to the Rev. John Newton, May 31, 1783; repr. in Cowper, *Correspondence*

 (See "Cowper and Lady Austen.")

 (2) "[George Brummell's] verses, called 'The Butter-fly's Funeral'"

 In MS; quoted by Jesse.

- -

BEFORE MIDNIGHT (CW)--*TLS,* March 1, 1917, p. 104

 Obvious Source
 (stated in *TLS* with essay and in headnote):

 Elinor Mordaunt [pseud. of Evelyn May Clowes], *Before Midnight*. Cassell, 1917.

 Important Allusions:

 Specific stories mentioned:

 (1) "Pan"

 This is quoted from, pp. 54-55.

 (2) "the first story in the book ... the last"

 I.e., "The Weakening Point" and "Parentage," respectively

- -

BODY AND BRAIN (BP)--*New Statesman,* June 5, 1920, pp. 254,
                256

   Obvious Source
   (stated in *New Statesman* with essay and in footnote):

      William Roscoe Thayer, *Theodore Roosevelt.* Consta-
      ble, [1920].

- -

BOOKS AND PERSONS (CW)--*TLS,* July 5, 1917, p. 319

   Obvious Source
   (stated in *TLS* with essay and in headnote):

      Arnold Bennett, *Books and Persons.* Chatto and Wind-
      us, 1917.

   Supportive Sources:

      Specific quotes from *Books and Persons:*

      (1) P. 61

          (a) "W.W. Jacobs and Aristophanes" (orig. in
              The New Age, Oct. 24, 1908), pp. 53-56,
              espec. p. 56.

          (b) "Artists and Critics" (orig. in *The New Age,*
              Oct. 21, 1909), pp. 158-59, espec. p. 158.

      (2) P. 62

          (a) "The British Academy of Letters" (orig. in
              The New Age, Aug. 18, 1910), pp. 228-34,
              espec. pp. 229-30.

          (b) "The Length of Novels" (orig. in *The New Age,*
              Sept. 22, 1910), pp. 248-49, espec. p. 249.

   Important Allusions:

      (1) *The New Age,* [n.s.] (Periodical, 1907-1938)

      (2) Specific paper in *Books and Persons:* .

          "Neo-Impressionism and Literature" (orig. in *The
          New Age,* Dec. 8, 1910), pp. 280-85.

(3) Miscellaneous writers (mentioned by Bennett):
Joseph Conrad, E.M. Forster, John Galsworthy,
Elinor Glyn, W.H. Hudson, John Masefield, C.E.
Montague, Mrs. Humphry Ward (*née* Mary Augusta Arnold)

(4) Quote from Canon Lambert [of Hull] (p. 62)

Quoted by Bennett in "Censorship of the Libraries" (orig. in *The New Age,* Feb. 24, 1910), pp.
185-89, espec. p. 186.

(5) Quote from Dr. William Francis Berry (p. 62)

Quoted by Bennett in "Unclean Books" (orig. in
The New Age, July 8, 1909), p. 143.

Passing Allusions:

(1) Mentioned by Lambert (see above):

H.G. Wells, *Ann Veronica*. (Orig. 1909)

(2) Mentioned by Bennett :

Fyodor Dostoevsky, *Crime and Punishment*. (Orig.
1867)

- -

A BORN WRITER (CW)--*TLS,* July 29, 1920, p. 485

Obvious Source
(stated in headnote and first paragraph):

"After many years *Esther Waters* appears again, entirely revised, and with an introduction"

George Moore, *Esther Waters*. W. Heinemann, 1920.
(Orig. 1894)

Important Allusions:

(1) Sir Walter Scott, *Waverley*. (Orig. 1814)

(2) Charles Dickens, *The Pickwick Papers*. (Orig.
1837)

(3) Charlotte Brontë, *Jane Eyre*. (Orig. 1847)

Passing Allusions:

(1) Mentioned by Moore in his introduction:
Miguel de Cervantes Saavedra, *Don Quixote de la Mancha*. (Orig. 1605, 1615)

(2) Miscellaneous English writers: William Shakespeare, Mrs. Henry Wood (Ellen Price Wood)

- -

THE CAPTAIN'S DEATH BED (I)--*TLS*, Sept. 26, 1935, pp. 585-86; first collected in *C.D.B.* Reading notes #10

Inferred Source:

"the two little volumes ... in which his daughter ... wrote his life"

Florence Marryat, *Life and Letters of Captain Marryat*. 2 vol. Bentley, +1872.

This is listed in the reading notes.

Supportive Sources:

(1) Frederick Marryat, *Peter Simple,* w/biographical essay by Michael Sadleir. 2 vol. Constable, 1929. (Orig. 1834)

This is listed in Holleyman and is indicated by the reading notes.

(2) Frederick Marryat, *Jacob Faithful,* w/introduction by George Saintsbury. 2 vol. Constable, 1928. (Orig. 1834)

This is listed in Holleyman Addendum.

Woolf (p. 175) names these editions.

Important Allusions (mentioned by F. Marryat):

(1) John Marshall, *Royal Naval Biography*. 8 vol. London: n.p., 1823-35.

(2) "the six volumes in which [Marryat] recorded his opinion of America"

Frederick Marryat, *A Diary in America, with Remarks on Its Institutions*. 6 vol. Longman, 1839.

Passing Allusions:

    Miscellaneous English novelists: Jane Austen, Daniel Defoe, Henry Fielding, Tobias Smollett

- -

CAUTION AND CRITICISM (CW)--*TLS*, Oct. 3, 1919, p. 467

Obvious Source
(stated in *TLS* with essay and in headnote):

    Harold Williams, *Modern English Writers*. 2 vol. Sidgwick and Jackson, 1918.

Important Allusions (mentioned by Williams):

    (1) Two periodicals:

        (a) *The Yellow Book*. (1894-1897)

        (b) *The Savoy*. (Jan.-Dec. 1896)

    (2) Miscellaneous British writers of the '90s: W.E. Henley, George Meredith, Oscar Wilde

Passing Allusions (mentioned by Williams):

    (1) Laurence Binyon, *Auguries*. (Orig. 1813)

    (2) Miscellaneous writers: Arnold Bennett, Joseph Conrad, Heinrich Heine, John Keats, Henry Dawson Lowry, Alice Milligan, Seumas O'Sullivan [pseud. of James Sullivan Starkey], William E. Tirebuck

    (3) Last quote, p. 19:

        "Her" refers to Dora Sigerson Shorter.

- -

THE CLAIM OF THE LIVING (CW)--*TLS*, June 13, 1918, p. 275

Obvious Source
(stated in *TLS* with essay and in headnote):

    W[alter] L[ionel] George, *A Novelist on Novels*. W. Collins, [1918].

Important Allusions (mentioned by George):

    (1) Novels by E.M. Forster:

        (a) *A Room with a View*. (Orig. 1908)

        (b) *The Longest Journey*. (Orig. 1907)

        (c) *Howards End*. (Orig. 1910)

    (2) Miscellaneous contemporary British novelists: J. D. Beresford, Gilbert Cannan, D.H. Lawrence, Compton Mackenzie, Oliver Onions, Frank Swinnerton

Passing Allusions (mentioned by George):

    (1) H.G. Wells, *Tono-Bungay*. (Orig. 1908)

    (2) Miscellaneous writers: Joseph Conrad, Leigh Hunt

- -

CLEVERNESS AND YOUTH (CW)--*TLS,* Feb. 5, 1920, p. 83

Obvious Source
(stated in *TLS* with essay and in headnote):

    Aldous Huxley, *Limbo*. Chatto and Windus, 1920.

Important Allusions:

    Specific pieces mentioned:

    (1) "Farcical History cf Richard Greenow"

        Quote, p. 150, is from here; "who" should be in brackets.

    (2) "Happily Ever After"

    (3) "a description of an interview"

        "The Bookshop"

        Quote, p. 151, is from here.

    (4) "Happy Families"

- -

COLERIDGE AS CRITIC (BP)--*TLS,* Feb. 7, 1918, p. 67
          Reading notes "Holograph Note-
          book. November 16 [actually
          Jan. 14], 1918-Jan. 24, 1919"
          (Berg)+

Obvious Source
(stated in *TLS* with essay and in footnote):

Samuel Taylor Coleridge, *The Table Talk and Omniana
of,* w/note ... by Coventry Patmore [and Preface by
H.N. Coleridge]. Oxford U. Pr., 1917. (Orig. 1884)

This is indicated by the reading notes (along with
notes from Coleridge, *Omniana.* In *The Literary Remains of,* edited by Henry Nelson Coleridge. 4
vol. W. Pickering, 1936-39. Vol. I).+

Vols. I and II are listed in Holleyman Addendum;
III and IV, in Holleyman. It belonged to Leslie
Stephen.

Supportive Source:

Samuel Taylor Coleridge, *Anima Poetae,* w/preface by
Ernest Hartley Coleridge. William Heinemann, 1895.

This is listed in Holleyman; it belonged to Leslie
Stephen.

Important Allusions:

(1) the "portraits" of Coleridge by Hazlitt

   (See "William Hazlitt.")

(2) the "portraits" of Coleridge by DeQuincey

   (See, e.g., "The Man at the Gate.")

(3) the "portrait" of Coleridge by Carlyle

   In Thomas Carlyle, *The Life of John Sterling.*
   (Orig. 1851)

(4) Miscellaneous writers (mentioned by S.T. Cole-
   ridge): Edumnd Burke, William Cobbett, Homer,
   Samuel Johnson, Rabelais, William Shakespeare,
   Jonathan Swift

Passing Allusions:

(1) Quote *re* Percy Bysshe Shelley (p. 32)

   Matthew Arnold, "Byron," *Essays in Criticism,
   Second Series.* (Orig. 1888)

(2) Miscellaneous English poets: John Keats, John
   Milton

- -

THE COMPROMISE (BP and WW)--*Nation and Athenaeum,* Sept.
29, 1923, pp. 810-11; repr.
in *New Republic* (w/var.), Jan.
9, 1924, pp. 180-81 (text in
BP and WW from *New Republic*)
Reading notes #25

Obvious Source
(stated in *New Republic* with essay and in footnote):

  Janet Penrose Trevelyan, *The Life of Mrs. Humphry
  Ward.* Constable, 1923.

  This is listed in the reading notes.

Important Allusions (mentioned by Trevelyan):

  (1) Works by Mrs. Ward (*née* Mary Augusta Arnold):

    (a) "one of her first pieces of writing"

      A Morning in the Bodleian. Privately print-
      ed, 1871.

      Quote, middle of p. 143, is from here (quoted
      also by Trevelyan)

    (b) *Plain Facts on Infant Feeding.* Privately
      printed, 1874(?).

    (c) *Robert Elsmere.* (Orig. 1888)

  (2) Sir William Smith and Henry Wace, *Dictionary of
    Christian Biography.* 4 vol. John Murray, 1877-
    87.

Passing Allusions (mentioned by Trevelyan):

  (1) Miscellaneous English writers: John Richard
    Green, Mark Pattison

  (2) 2nd quote, p. 143 (quoted also by Trevelyan)

    Mary Augusta Arnold Ward to Bishop Mandell
    Creighton, Aug. 9, 1898 (in MS)

- -

CONGREVE'S COMEDIES (I)--*TLS,* Sept. 25, 1937, pp. 681-82;
first collected in *M.*   Read-
ing notes B2h

Inferred Source:

> *Comedies of William Congreve,* edited by Bonamy Do-
> brée. Oxford U. Pr., 1925.
>
> This is indicated by the reading notes.+ Woolf
> reviewed it for *Nation and Athenaeum,* Oct. 17, 1925,
> p. 124.

Supportive Sources:

   (1) "Sir Edmund Gosse informs us"

> Edmund Gosse, *The Life of William Congreve.*
> Rev. and enl. ed. Heinemann, 1924. (Orig.
> 1888)
>
> This is indicated by the reading notes.+
> Woolf reviewed it for *Nation and Athenaeum,* Oct.
> 18, 1924, p. 122.

   (2) "Dr. Johnson's dictum"

> Samuel Johnson, *Lives of the English Poets.*
> (Orig. 1779-81) Poss. ed.: see "Addison."

   (3) "as the gossips observed [Congreve]"

> Anon., *Animadversions on Congreve's Amendments*
> ... (1698)
>
> Quoted by Gosse (see above).

   (4) "Voltaire left a dubious anecdote" (mentioned by
Gosse)

> Francois Marie Arouet de Voltaire, *Letters Con-
> cerning the English Nation.* (Orig. trans. 1733)
> No. 19.

   (5) "The Duchess of Marlborough, it is said"

> Thomas Davies, *Dramatic Miscellanies.* (Orig.
> 1784)
>
> This is mentioned in the *DNB* article on Congreve
> by Leslie Stephen, which Woolf was reading at
> the time. (See Woolf, *A Writer's Diary,* June
> 23, 1937.)
>
> For *DNB,* see "White's Selborne."

   (6) "[Congreve's] few discreet letters"

(a) First quote, p. 83:

To Joseph Keally, Nov. 29, 1708

(b) Second quote, p. 83:

To same, June 8, 1706

Both are repr. in Congreve, *The Mourning Bride, Poems, and Miscellanies,* edited by Bonamy Dobrée. World's Classics ser. Oxford U. Pr., 1928.

This is listed in Holleyman.

Important Allusions:

(1) "[Congreve] replies" (quotes, pp. 76, top of 77)

Congreve to John Dennis, July 10, 1695; repr. in Congreve, *Letters on Several Occasions* (1696) and in *Comedies,* edited by Dobrée (see above).

(2) Various Congreve characters: *The Old Batchelor* (1691)--Vainlove, Fondlewife; *Love for Love* (1695)--Miss Prue, Sir Sampson Legend, Angelica, Foresight, Tattle, Ben; *The Way of the World* (1700)--Lady Wishfort

(3) Various plays by Congreve (from Dobrée edition [see above], as indicated by the reading notes):

(a) "Mr. Brisk's comment"

The Double Dealer (publ. 1694): V:xxiv:12

(b) Congreve "strikes off a picture in a flash"

Ibid.: III:v:32-33

(c) Congreve "conveys a whole chapter"

The Way of the World: V:i:4-8

(d) "says Valentine in *Love for Love*"

I:ii:23-24

(e) "as Scandal says" (p. 81)

Ibid.: I:ii:25--"Rail? At whom? the whole World?"

(f) "Mellefont's ... hint"

    The Double Dealer: II:ii:57-59

(g) "a sudden phrase" (p. 81)

    Ibid.: II:vii:10-11

(h) "one such comment" (p. 81)

    Ibid.: IV:iii:76-77

(i) "we exclaim with Scandal" (p. 82)

    Love for Love: IV:v:4-5

(j) "[Millamant's] words"; "Mirabell's reply" (p. 82)

    The Way of the World: V:xiv:30-31, 32

(k) Congreve "brings us to the edge of poetry"

    Love for Love: IV:xvi:76-77

    Quoted by Dobrée in introduction to *Comedies* (see above)

(4) Congreve's "one attempt at fiction"

    I.e., *Incognita* (1692)

Passing Allusions:

Miscellaneous writers:

(1) Mentioned by Congreve: Menander, Terence

(2) Oliver Goldsmith, George Meredith, William Shakespeare, Richard Brinsley Sheridan, Oscar Wilde

- -

THE COSMOS (IV)--*Nation and Athenaeum,* Oct. 9, 1926, p. 26; first collected in *C.D.B.*   Reading notes #25

Obvious Source
(stated in *Nation and Athenaeum* with essay and in footnote):

> *The Journals of Thomas James Cobden-Sanderson, 1879-
> 1922.* 2 vol. R. Cobden-Sanderson, 1926.

> As shown in the reading notes, the idea of the "Kos-
> mos" is taken up in Vol. II.

Passing Allusions:

> Miscellaneous writers (mentioned by Cobden-Sanderson):
> William Morris, Charles Algernon Swinburne

- -

THE COUNTESS OF PEMBROKE'S ARCADIA (I)--c. 1930(?); first
                              published in
                              C.R. II   Read-
                              ing notes B2p and
                              #s8, 11,+ 20

Obvious Source:

> Philip Sidney, *The Countess of Pembroke's Arcadia*.
> (Orig. 1593) 10th ed. William DuGard, 1655.
> 1655.

> This is indicated by the reading notes+ and is listed
> in Holleyman.   "1655" is mentioned in the first
> paragraph.
Passing Allusion:

> "Dorothy Osborne's *Letters*"

> (See essay by same name.)

- -

COWPER AND LADY AUSTEN (III)--*Nation and Athenaeum,* Sept.
                              21, 1929, pp. 793-95; repr.
                              in *New York Herald Tribune
                              Books* (w/var.), Sept. 22,
                              1929, pp. 1, 6; first col-
                              lected in *C.R. II* (w/var.)
                              Reading notes #9

Inferred Source:

"Never had Cowper written more enchantingly ... to his friends"

William Cowper, *The Correspondence of,* arranged by Thomas Wright. 4 vol. Hodder and Stoughton, 1904. Espec. Vols. I and II.

This is listed in Holleyman and in the reading notes.

Specific letters quoted from:

(1) "[Cowper] cried aloud" (p. 183)

   To the Rev. John Newton, Apr. 20, 1783 and Jan. 13, 1784

(2) "Cowper's first impressions" (2nd and 3rd quotes, p. 183)

   To same, July 7, 1781

(3) "Cowper wrote" (top of p. 184)

   To the Rev. William Unwin, Feb. 9, 1782

(4) "as [Cowper] said himself" (p. 184)

   To same, Oct. 6, 1781

(5) Quote, middle of p. 184

   To same, March 21, 1784

(6) 3rd quote, p. 184

   To Frances Maria Cowper, July 20, 1780

(7) "[Cowper] wrote" (first quote, p. 185)

   To the Rev. John Newton, July 27, 1783

(8) 2nd quote, p. 185

   To the Rev. William Unwin, Nov. 10, 1783

(9) Quote, bottom of p. 185

   See (3) above; ellipses should be <u>after</u> "and"

(10) "wrote Cowper" (top of p. 186)

   To the Rev. William Unwin, Jan. 19, 1783

(11) "so Cowper said" (2nd quote, p. 186)

   Cannot locate

(12) 3rd quote, p. 186

   To Joseph Hill, Oct. 25, 1765; a paraphrase, not
   a quote

(13) 4th quote, p. 186

   To the Rev. William Unwin, Feb. 24, 1782

Important Allusion:

   "a poem about a sofa"

   William Cowper, *The Task*. (Orig. 1785) Rivingtons,
   1874.

   This is indicated by the reading notes.

Passing Allusions:

   (1) "the story of John Gilpin"

   William Cowper, "The Diverting History of John
   Gilpin." (Orig. 1782)

   (2) Miscellaneous writers (mentioned by Cowper in
   Letters): George Anson, James Cook, Homer, Virgil

- -

CRABBE (IV)--c. 1933;[*] first published in *C.D.B.*   Read-
              ing notes #10

Inferred Source:

   "the life of Crabbe"

   Prob. ed.: George Crabbe, *Life and Poetical Works,*
   edited by his son [George]. "New and complete" ed.
   John Murray, 1901. (Orig. 1854)

   This is listed in Holleyman; it belonged to Leslie
   Stephen.

Passing Allusions:

   Miscellaneous English writers (mentioned by Crabbe):
   Edmund Burke, John Milton, Edward Young

* On Sept. 26, 1933, Woolf wrote in her diary: "Why not, one of these days, write a fantasy on the theme of Crabbe?--a biographical fantasy--an experiment in biography."

- -

CRAFTSMANSHIP (II)--*Listener,* May 5, 1937; first collected in *D.M.*

Important Allusions:

(1) William Shakespeare, *Antony and Cleopatra.* (Orig. 1606-07)

(2) John Keats, "Ode to a Nightingale." (Orig. 1819)

Quotes, p. 246, are from here.

(3) Jane Austen, *Pride and Prejudice.* (Orig. 1813)

(4) Charles Dickens, *David Copperfield.* (Orig. 1850)

- -

DAVID COPPERFIELD (I)--*Nation and Athenaeum,* Aug. 22, 1925, pp. 620-21; first collected in *M.* Reading notes #5+

Stated Impulse
(stated in *Nation and Athenaeum* with essay):

(1) Charles Dickens, *The Uncommercial Traveller.* Prob. ed.: T. Nelson, 1925. (Orig. 1860)

(2) Charles Dickens, *Reprinted Pieces,* w/introduction by G.K. Chesterton. J.M. Dent, 1921.

(3) Charles Dickens, *Christmas Stories.* T. Nelson, 1925. (Orig. 1871)

Obvious Source:

Charles Dickens, *David Copperfield.* (Orig. 1850)

Important Allusions:

(1) Daniel Defoe, *Robinson Crusoe.* (Orig. 1719)

(2) *Grimm's Fairy Tales*. (Orig. 1812-22; trans. 1823)

(3) Charles Dickens, *Pickwick Papers*. (Orig. 1837)

Passing Allusions:

Miscellaneous writers: Honoré de Balzac, Lord Byron, Sir Walter Scott, William Shakespeare, William Wordsworth

- -

DEFOE (I)--*TLS,* Apr. 24, 1919, pp. 217-18; first collected in *C.R. I* (w/var.)   Reading notes #3

Supportive Sources (all are listed in the reading notes):

(1) Various works by Defoe:

(a) ... *Moll Flanders*. (Orig. 1732)

In Daniel Defoe, *The Novels and Miscellaneous Works of*. 7 vol. Bohn, 1854-67. Vol. III.

This is indicated by the reading notes+

(b) *Roxana*. (Orig. 1724)

In *ibid*. Vol. IV.

This is indicated by the reading notes+ (#3).

(c) "Education of Women" [i.e., "An Academy for Women"] in Defoe, *An Essay Upon Projects*. (Orig. 1694) Repr. in *Later Stuart Tracts,* w/introduction by G.A. Aitken. Vol. XII of *An English Garner,* edited by Edward Arber, rearranged by T. Seccombe. 12 vol. Constable, 1903. (Orig. 1877-96)

This is indicated by the reading notes+

(2) "Mr. Wright, the biographer of Defoe"

Thomas Wright, *The Life of Daniel Defoe*. Cassell, 1894.

Important Allusions:

Various works by Defoe:

(1) ... *Robinson Crusoe*. (Orig. 1719) Poss. ed.: edited by Austin Dobson.

(See "*Robinson Crusoe*.")

(2) ... *Captain Singleton*. (Orig. 1720)

In Defoe, *The Novels* (see above). Vol. I.

This is indicated by the reading notes+

(3) ... *Colonel Jack*. (Orig. 1722-23)

In *ibid.* Vol. I.

This is indicated by the reading notes

(4) "[Defoe] wrote" (p. 63)

    (a) First quote: from *Serious Reflections During the Life and Surprising Adventures of Robinson Crusoe.* (Orig. 1720)

    (b) Second quote: from Preface to Vol. VIII (1711) of *The Review* ... (periodical edited by Defoe, 1704-13); repr. in *Later Stuart Tracts* (see above).

    This is indicated by the reading notes+

Both are quoted by Wright (see above).

Passing Allusions:

(1) Miscellaneous writers: George Crabbe, Henry Fielding, George Gissing, Homer, Henrik Ibsen, George Meredith, Samuel Richardson

(2) Quote, p. 62

    Cannot locate

(3) "Borrow's apple-woman" (mentioned by Wright [see above])

    In George Borrow, *Lavengro.* (Orig. 1851)

    This is listed in the reading notes (#3).

- -

DE QUINCEY'S AUTOBIOGRAPHY (IV)--date unknown; first published in *C.R. II*
Reading notes B2p

Obvious Source:

Thomas DeQuincey, *Autobiographic Sketches.* 2 vol. In *Works. Selections Grave and Gay.* 14 vol. Edinburgh: James Hogg, 1853-60.

This is indicated by the reading notes.+

Important Allusions (mentioned by DeQuincey):

Miscellaneous 17th-century English writers: Sir Thomas Browne, John Milton, Jeremy Taylor

Passing Allusions:

Miscellaneous writers: Jane Austen, Lord Byron, Thomas Carlyle, Jean Jacques Rousseau, John Ruskin, Sir

Walter Scott, Alfred Lord Tennyson

- -

THE DIARY OF A LADY IN WAITING (BP)--*TLS,* July 23, 1908

Obvious Source
(stated in *TLS* with essay and in footnote):

Lady Charlotte [Campbell] Bury, *The Diary of a Lady in Waiting,* edited by A. Francis Steuart. 2 vol. John Lane, 1908. (Orig. 1838; Lady Charlotte's dates were 1775-1861.)

Passing Allusions (mentioned by Bury):

(1) "The Parting of the Ships" [*sic*]

I.e., Thomas Moore, "A Canadian Boat-Song" (orig. 1806; publ. also as sheet music, by James Carpenter, London, 1805)

(2) Miscellaneous British writers: William Blake, Matthew ("Monk") Lewis, Sir Walter Scott, Charles K. Sharpe

- -

DONNE AFTER THREE CENTURIES (I)--1931; first published in
C.R. II   Reading
notes #s8, 11+, 19, 20
and B2e, B2p

Inferred Sources:

"the poems of Donne"

(1) John Donne, *Poems,* edited by E.K. Chambers. 2 vol. The Muses' Library, n.d. [1896?].

This is listed in the reading notes (#8) and in Holleyman; it belonged to Leslie Stephen.

(2) John Donne, *Poems,* edited by Sir Herbert Grierson. 2 vol. Oxford: Clarendon, 1912.

This is indicated by the reading notes (#s8,+ 11,+ 19).

Supportive Sources:

(Dates in parens., from Grierson, indicate first publication)

    (1) Specific poems quoted from:

        (a) P. 32: "Love's Deitie" (1633); "The Broken
            Heart" (1633); "A Lecture Upon the Shadow"
            (1635); "The Relique" (1633)

        (b) P. 34: ["grave Divines ... "] "Satyre I"
            (1633); ["I tell him of new playes"] "Satyre
            IIII" [*sic*] (1633); *ibid.*

        (c) P. 35: "Satyre IIII"; "Elegie VIII. The Com-
            parison" (1633)

        (d) P. 37: ["love's sweetest"] "The Indifferent"
            (1633); ["Of music"] "Elegie III. Change"
            (1633)--the line should read: "Change is the
            nursery/Of ... "; ["who held plurality"] "El-
            egie XVII. Variety" (1650); *ibid.*; ["cag'd"]
            "Elegie I. Jealousie" (1633)

        (e) P. 38: "Elegie XII. His Parting from Her"
            (1635); "Song. Sweetest Love, I Do Not Goe"
            (1633); "The Canonization" (1633); "The Ex-
            tasie" (1633)

        (f) P. 41: "To the Countesse of Bedford. Madame,
            Reason is" (1633)

        (g) P. 42: ["satyrique fires"] "To Mr. R.W.
            Kindly I envy" (1912); ["My muse"] "To Mr.
            B.B." (1633); "The First Anniversary" (1612)

        (h) P. 43: "The Second Anniversarie" (1612)

        (i) P. 44: ["Since she"] "Holy Sonnet XVII"
            (1899); ["little world"] "Holy Sonnet V"
            (1635); "Holy Sonnet XIX" (1899); "Satyre
            III" (1633); ["My devout"] "Holy Sonnet XIX"

        (j) P. 45: "The Dampe" (1633)

    (2) "if we turn to his biography"

        Sir Edmund Gosse, *The Life and Letters of John
        Donne.*

        (See "Dorothy Osmund's *Letters.*")

        This is listed in the reading notes (#sll,+ 20
        and B2e).

    (3) Specific poems mentioned but not quoted from:

        (a) "[To His Mistress] Going to Bed" (1654)

        (b) "Love's Warr" (1802)

        (c) "Hee and Shee" [*sic;* reference to first line of 7th section of "Epithalamion, or Marriage Song on ... St. Valentines Day" ("Here lyes a shee Sunne, and a hee Moone here")?] (1633)

        (d) "An Anatomie of the World" (1611)

        (e) "Progresse of the Soul" (1633)

Important Allusions:

    (1) "Dekker sets out to tell us"

        Thomas Dekker, *The Wonderful Years.* (Orig. 1603) Bodley Head, 1924.

        This is indicated by the reading notes+ (#19; exact quote in B2p) and is listed in Holleyman.

    (2) Miscellaneous women writers, friends of Donne: Lady Bedford (Lucy Russell), Lady Pembroke (Mary Herbert)

    (3) "Lady Ann Clifford ... her diary"

        The Diary of the Lady Anne Clifford, w/introduction by Vita Sackville-West. William Heinemann, 1923.

        This is listed in the reading notes (#19) and in Holleyman.

Passing Allusions:

    (1) Miscellaneous English poets: Robert Browning, Ben Jonson, Christopher Marlowe, George Meredith, William Shakespeare

    (2) "Sidney's *Arcadia*"

        (See "*The Countess of Pembroke's Arcadia.*")

    (3) *Paradise of Dainty Devices,* compiled by Richard Edwards. (Orig. 1576)

    (4) "Lyly's *Euphues*"

    (a) John Lyly, *Euphues, the Anatomy of Wit.*
        (Orig. 1579)

    (b) John Lyly, *Euphues and His England.* (Orig.
        1580)

  (5) Mentioned by Lady Clifford (see above):

    (a) Geoffrey Chaucer, *The Canterbury Tales.*
        (Orig. 1387-1400)

    (b) Edmund Spenser, *The Faery Queen.* (Orig.
        1590, 1596, 1609)

    (c) Michel de Montaigne

  (6) Alfred Lord Tennyson, *Idylls of the King.* (Orig.
      1859-85)

- -

DOROTHY OSBORNE'S *LETTERS* (III)--*New Republic,* Oct. 24,
                                    1928, pp. 278-79;
                                    repr. in *TLS* (w/var.),
                                    Oct. 25, 1928, p. 777;
                                    first collected in
                                    C.R. II (w/var.)
                                    Reading notes
                                    B2p, B3c

Obvious Source
(stated in *TLS* with essay):

    The Letters of Dorothy Osborne to William Temple,
    edited by G.C. Moore Smith. Oxford: Clarendon, 1928.
    (Orig. 1888; Dorothy Osborne Temple's dates were 1627-
    94.)

    This is listed in the reading notes.

Supportive Source:

    "Swift called her"

    Jonathan Swift, "[Ode] Occasioned by Sir William Tem-
    ple's Late Illness and Recovery" (1693); quoted in
    T.P. Courtenay, *Memoirs of the Life, Works and Cor-
    respondence of Temple.* 2 vol. Longman, 1836.

    Courtenay is mentioned in the reading notes (B2p)
    as "Life of Temple," 2 vol.

Passing Allusions:

(1) "Donne, says Sir Edmund Gosse"

   Sir Edmund Gosse, *The Life and Letters of John Donne.* 2 vol. W. Heinemann, 1899.

   This is listed in the reading notes (#s11,+ 20,, and B2e) of "Donne After Three Centuries," *q.v.* ries," *q.v.*

(2) Miscellaneous writers: Lady Bedford (Lucy Russell; mentioned by Donne); James Boswell; the Duchess of Newcastle (Margaret Cavendish; mentioned by Osborne); Horace Walpole

(3) Fanny Burney, *Evelina.* (Orig. 1778)

(4) Jane Austen, *Pride and Prejudice.* (Orig. 1813)

- -

DOROTHY WORDSWORTH (III)--*Nation and Athenaeum,* Oct. 5, 1929, pp. 46-48; repr. in *New York Herald Tribune Books* (w/var.), Oct. 27, 1929, pp. 1, 6; first collected in *C.R. II* (w/var.) Reading notes #20 and B2d

Inferred Source:

   "the diary"

   Journals of Dorothy Wordsworth, edited by W. Knight. 2 vol. Macmillan, 1897.

   This is indicated by the reading notes (#20).

Supportive Source:

   "DeQuincey said"

   Thomas DeQuincey, "William Wordsworth," *Recollections of the Lakes and the Lake Poets.* (Orig. 1839-40).

   Quoted in Edmund Lee, *Dorothy Wordsworth* (James Clarke, 1886) and in George Harper, *William Wordsworth* (2 vol. J. Murray, 1916).

   Lee and Harper are listed in the reading notes (#20 and B2d, respectively).

Important Allusions:

"made [Mary Wollstonecraft] say" (p. 200); "the
passionate cry of Mary Wollstonecraft" (p. 206)

Both quotes are from Wollstonecraft, *Letters Written
During a Short Residence in Sweden, Norway, and Denmark*. (Orig. 1796) 2nd ed. Joseph Johnson, 1802.

This is listed in Holleyman Addendum and indicated
by the reading notes for "Mary Wollstonecraft," *q.v.*

Passing Allusions (mentioned by D. Wordsworth):

(1) "a poem on a Butterfly"

William Wordsworth, "To a Butterfly."

There were two of these, one dated March 1802,
the other Apr. 20, 1802. (Both orig. publ.
1807.) The context in Dorothy's diary suggests
the first.

(2) William Wordsworth, "The Leech Gatherer" (1802).

(3) Samuel Taylor Coleridge, "Christabel" (1816).

- -

DOSTOEVSKY IN CRANFORD (BP)--*TLS,* Oct. 23, 1919, p. 386

Obvious Source
(stated in *TLS* with essay and in footnote):

Fyodor Dostoevsky, *An Honest Thief and Other Stories,*
trans. by Constance Garnett. Heinemann, 1919.

This is listed in Holleyman.

Supportive Source:

Specific story mentioned:

"Uncle's Dream" (orig. 1849)

Quote, p. 121, is from here.

Important Allusions:

(1) "Cranford"

Reference to Elizabeth Gaskell, *Cranford*. (Orig.
1853)

(2) Specific stories mentioned but not quoted from:

    (a) "The Crocodile" (orig. 1865)

    (b) "An Unpleasant Predicament" (orig. 1862)

Passing Allusions:

Miscellaneous English writers: Jane Austen, William Wycherley

- -

DOSTOEVSKY THE FATHER (BP)--*TLS,* Jan. 12, 1922, p. 25

Obvious Source
(stated in *TLS* with essay and in footnote):

Aimée Dostoevsky, *Fyodor Dostoevsky.* William Heinemann, 1921.

Important Allusions:

(1) Miscellaneous writers (mentioned by A. Dostoevsky): Charles Dickens, Count Joseph Arthur de Gobineau, Sir Walter Scott, Ivan Turgenev

(2) Fyodor Dostoevsky, *The Idiot.* (Orig. 1882)

Passing Allusion:

"Matthew Arnold ... deplored the ... Shelley set"

In "Byron," *Essays in Criticism. Second Series.* (Orig. 1888)

- -

DR. BENTLEY (IV)--date unknown;[*] first published in
               C.R. I   Reading notes #25 and B2q

Inferred Source
(stated in first paragraph):

"*Life of Dr. Bentley,* by Bishop Monk"

James Henry Monk, *The Life of Richard Bentley, D.D.* (Orig. 1830) 2nd ed., rev. 2 vol. J.H. and F. Rivington, 1833.

This is listed in Holleyman and is indicated by the
reading notes+ (B2q).

Important Allusion (mentioned by Monk):

John Milton, *Paradise Lost,* edited by Richard Bentley. Jacob Tonson, 1732.

Passing Allusions:

Miscellaneous writers (mentioned by Monk): Callima-
chus, Joannes de Pauw, James Gronovius, Homer, Horace, Manilius, Phalaris, Pindar, Sophocles

*
Quentin Bell, *Virginia Woolf,* II, 99n., connects this
essay with the writing of "On Not Knowing Greek," *q.v.*

- -

DR. BURNEY'S EVENING PARTY (III)--*New York Herald Tribune
                                   Books,* July 21, pp. 1,
                                   6, and July 28, pp. 1,
                                   5-6, 1929; repr. in *Life
                                   and Letters* (w/var.),
                                   Sept. 1929, pp. 243-63;
                                   first collected in
                                   C.R. II (w/var.)
                                   Reading notes #13 and
                                   B2n

Inferred Sources:

(1) "Fanny Burney, from whom we get much of our in-
    formation ... [later] Madam D'Arblay"

    (a) *Diary and Letters of Madame d'Arblay [(1778-
        1840)],* edited by [Charlotte Barrett].
        2nd ed. 7 vol. Henry Colburn, 1854. (Orig.
        1842-46)

        This is indicated by the reading notes (#13).

    (b) [Frances Burney d'Arblay, ed.], *Memoirs of
        Doctor [Charles] Burney, Arranged from His
        Own MSS, from Family Papers, and from Per-
        sonal Recollections.* 3 vol. Edward Moxon,
        1832.

        As shown by Woolf's reading notes (#13), the
        party is described in Vol. II.

    (2) "Fanny's early diary"

       The Early Diary of Frances Burney, 1768-1778
       ... , edited by Annie Raine Ellis. 2 vol. G.
       Bell, 1889.

       As shown by Woolf's reading notes (#13), the
       party is described in Vol. II.

    (3) "Mrs. Thrale ... her anecdotes"

       Hester Lynch Thrale [Piozzi], *Anecdotes of the*
       Late Samuel Johnson ...

       2 eds., as indicated by the reading notes (B2n
       and #13 respectively):

       (a) T. Cadell, 1786.

       (b) In James Boswell, *The Life of Samuel John-*
          son, edited by John Wilson Croker. 9 vol.
          Murray, 1839. Vol. IX.+

Important Allusions:

    (1) Samuel Johnson, *Rasselas*. (Orig. 1759)

    (2) William Fulke Greville, *Maxims, Characters and*
       Reflections. London: n.p., 1756.

Passing Allusions:

    (1) Miscellaneous English writers: Jane Austen, James
       Boswell, Sir Philip Sidney (mentioned by F. Bur-
       ney)

    (2) "Ode to Indifference" [*sic*] (mentioned by F. Bur-
       ney)

       Frances Macartney Greville, *A Prayer for Indif-*
       ference. (Orig. 1759)

- -

THE DREAM (IV)--*Listener,* Feb. 15, 1940, p. 333; first
          collected in *G.R.*

  Obvious Source
  (stated in *The Listener* with essay and in footnote):

    George Bullock, *Marie Corelli: The Life and Death of*
    a Best-seller. Constable, 1940.

  Important Allusions (mentioned by Bullock):

    (1) Marie Corelli, *Ardath*. (Orig. 1889)

    (2) Marie Corelli, *Barabbas*. (Orig. 1893)

Passing Allusions:

Miscellaneous writers:

(1) Florence Barclay, Ella Wheeler Wilcox

(2) Mentioned by Bullock: George Meredith, Oscar Wilde, Edmond Rostand

- -

THE DUCHESS OF NEWCASTLE (III and WW)--date unknown;
first published in
C.R. I

Stated Sources
(stated in footnote; cf. p. 54: "there [her writings] stand, in the British Museum, volume after volume"):

(1) Margaret Cavendish, Duchess of Newcastle, *The Life of William Cavendish, Duke of Newcastle,* edited by C.H. Firth. (Orig. 1667, with subtitle: "Some Few Notes of [and About] the Authoresse"). Prob. ed.: 2nd ed., rev. G. Routledge, [1906].

This is listed in Holleyman; it belonged to Virginia.

Quotes, pp. 51-53, and first quote, p. 54, are from here (quoted also by Longueville [see below]).

(2) Margaret Cavendish, *Poems and Fancies.* (Orig. 1653)

Quotes, p. 56, are from here:

(a) "[The Queen of Fairies] Descending Down"

(b) "The Claspe"

(c) "The City of the Fairies"

(3) Margaret Cavendish, *The World's Olio.* (Orig. 1655)

(4) Margaret Cavendish, *Orations of Divers Sorts Accommodated to Divers Places.* (Orig. 1662)

(5) Margaret Cavendish, *Female Orations*

   In *Orations of Divers Sorts*. (Orig. 1662)

(6) Margaret Cavendish, *Play[e]s Written by ... the Lady Marchioness of Newcastle*. (Orig. 1662)

(7) Margaret Cavendish, *Philosophical Letters*. (Orig. 1664)

Inferred Source:

   Thomas Longueville, *The First Duke and Duchess of Newcastle*. Longmans, 1910.

   Woolf reviewed this for *TLS,* Feb. 2, 1911, p. 40.

Supportive Sources:

(1) "Horace Walpole sneered"

   Walpole, *A Catalogue of the Royal and Noble Authors of England*. (Orig. 1758)

   The episode about John [Rolleston], p. 54, is from here.

(2) Quotes, bottom of p. 54, top of p. 55

   Cannot locate

(3) Margaret Cavendish, *Philosophical and Physical Opinions*. J. Martin and J. Allestrye, 1655.

   Quotes, 2nd paragraph, p. 55, are from here.

(4) "her first volume"

   (See [2] under "Stated Sources," above.)

(5) Margaret Cavendish, *CCXI Sociable Letters*.

   Quotes, pp. 57 and 58, are from here.

(6) "Sir Egerton Brydges ... complained"; there should be ellipses between "Coarseness" and "as"

   Margaret Cavendish, *Select Poems of ... ,* edited by Sir Egerton Brydges. Lee Prior, Kent: Johnson and Warwick, 1813.

(7) Samuel Pepys, *Diary* (quoted also by Longueville)

   (See "Papers on Pepys.")

   Quote from Apr. 26, 1687; see also Apr. 11 and May 1 and 30, 1867.

Important Allusion:

"[Charles] Lamb scattered . . . phrases . . . upon her tomb"

(1) Mentioned by Longueville (see above)

    (a) "The Two Races of Men," orig. in *London Magazine,* Dec. 1820; repr. in Lamb, *Essays of Elia.* (Orig. 1823)

    (b) "Mackery End," orig. in *London Magazine,* July 1821; repr. in *Essays of Elia.*

(2) "A Complaint of the Decay of Beggars in the Metropolis," orig. in *London Magazine,* June 1822; repr. in *Essays of Elia.*

(3) "Detached Thoughts on Books and Reading," orig. in *London Magazine,* July 1822; repr. in *Last Essays of Elia.* (Orig. 1833)

Passing Allusions:

(1) Mentioned by the Duchess (see [3] under "Stated Sources," above)

    (a) "Mr. Stanley's account of ... the old philosophers"

    Thomas Stanley, *The History of Philosophy.* (1655-62)

    (b) "Des Cartes['] . . . work on Passion"

    René Descartes, *The Passions of the Soul.* (1649; first trans. 1650)

    (c) Thomas Hobbes, *De Cive.* (1642)

(2) "'My Lady Sanspareille'" (pp. 56-57)

    Character in Margaret Cavendish, *Youth's Glory and Death's Banquet.* (1662?)

- -

EDMUND GOSSE (IV)--*Fortnightly Review,* June 1, 1931, pp. 766-73; repr. in *New York Herald Tribune Books* (w/var.), July 26, 1931, pp. 1, 4; first collected in *M.* (text in *M.* and *C.E.* from *Fortnightly Review*)

"Eliza and Sterne"

Obvious Source
(stated in *Fortnightly review* with essay and in 2nd
paragraph):

> Evan Charteris, *The Life and Letters of Sir Edmund
> Gosse.* William Heinemann, 1931.

Important Allusions (mentioned by Charteris):

> (1) "one severe review by Churton Collins"
>
>> John Churton Collins," English Literature at the
>> Universities," *Quarterly Review,* 172 (Oct. 1886),
>> 289-329.
>
> (2) Edmund Gosse, *Father and Son.* (Orig. 1907)
>
> (3) Gosse "wrote of Andrew Lang"
>
>> Edmund Gosse, *Portraits and Sketches.* William
>> Heinemann, 1912. Pp. 200-08.

Passing Allusions:

> (1) Miscellaneous writers:
>
>> (a) Arnold Bennett, Francois Arouet de Voltaire
>>
>> (b) Mentioned by Gosse: Matthew Arnold, Mrs.
>> [Catherine] Gore, Edward Bulwer Lytton,
>> Paladin Müller, Plumer Read, Oscar Wilde,
>> André Gide
>
> (2) James Boswell, *The Life of Samuel Johnson, LL.D.*
> (Orig. 1791)
>
> (3) Various novels mentioned by Gosse:
>
>> (a) E.M. Forster, *Howards End.* (Orig. 1910)
>>
>> (b) Benjamin Disraeli, *Coningsby.* (Orig. 1844)

- -

ELIZA AND STERNE (III)--*TLS,* Dec. 14, 1922, p. 839; first
                        collected in *G.R.*   Reading
                        notes B2q and #25

Obvious Source
(stated in *TLS* with essay):

> Arnold Wright and William Lutley Sclater, *Sterne's
> Eliza.* William Heinemann, 1922.
>
> This is listed in the reading notes (B2q).

Supportive Sources:

(1) Letters quoted from (in MS: quoted by Wright and Sclater [see above]):

    (a) "as her sister called it" (p. 101)

        Mary Boddam to Thomas Pickering, Nov. 18, 1760

    (b) Quote, bottom of p. 101

        Elizabeth Draper to Thomas Sclater, March 4, 1772

    (c) First quote, p. 102

        Same to same, Nov. 29, 1767; "the appellation of" should be in brackets

    (d) "she had been told" (p. 102)

        Same to same, Apr. 10, 1769; "assign to" should read "assign for"

    (e) 2nd quote, p. 103

        No date or recipient given; there should be ellipses before "good"

    (f) 4th and 5th quotes, p. 103

        Elizabeth Draper to Thomas Sclater, Apr. 5 1771 and May 1769

    (g) Quote, top of p. 104

        Elizabeth Draper to Daniel Draper, Jan. 1773

(2) *"Journal to Eliza"*

    Laurence Sterne, unpublished MS in the British Museum, described by, e.g., Wilbur Cross, *Life and Times of Laurence Sterne.* (See "Sterne.")

    First and 3rd quotes, p. 103, are from here (quoted also by Wright and Sclater [see above]): entry of June 17, 1767

Important Allusions (mentioned by Wright and Sclater):

(1) Laurence Sterne, *A Sentimental Journey Through France and Italy.* (Orig. 1768) In Sterne, *The Novels of.* George Newnes, 1905.

    This is indicated by the reading notes+ (#25).

(2) Abbé Raynal "addressed Anjengo [village in India]"

Abbé Guillaume Raynal, *Histoire ... des Européens dans les deux Indes.* (Orig. 1780)

Passing Allusions:

Miscellaneous writers: Lord Byron, Percy Bysshe Shelley

- -

ELIZABETH LADY HOLLAND (BP)--*Cornhill Mag.*, 1908, pp. 794-
802; repr. in *Living Age*,
Jan. 2, 1909, pp. 8-13

Obvious Sources
(stated in *Cornhill Magazine* with essay and in footnote):

(1) *The Journal of Elizabeth Lady Holland* [Elizabeth Vassall Fox], edited by the Earl of Ilchester [Giles Stephen Holland Fox]. 2 vol. Longmans, 1908. (Lady Holland's dates were 1770-1845.)

(2) Lloyd Sanders, *The Holland House Circle*. Methuen, 1908.

Supportive Source:

"Macaulay describes a breakfast party"

Thomas Babington Macaulay to Hannah M. Macaulay, June 1, 1831; repr. in G. Otto Trevelyan, *The Life and Letters of Lord Macaulay.* (Orig. 1876)

Important Allusion:

Lord Holland's poem to his wife (p. 191)

Lord Holland [Henry Richard Vassall Fox], "To a Lady on Her Birthday, ... 1795"; repr. in *Journal* (see above)

Passing Allusions:

(1) Miscellaneous writers:

(a) Mentioned by Lady Holland: Pierre Bayle, William Cowper, Herodotus, Juvenal, Michel de Montaigne, Francois Duc de La Rochefoucauld, Francois Arouet de Voltaire, William Wordsworth

  (b) Lord Byron, Percy Bysshe Shelley, Edward
      John Trelawny

(2) Various works (mentioned by Lady Holland):

  (a) "Pope's *Illiad*"

      Homer, *The Iliad,* trans. by Alexander Pope.
      (Orig. 1715-18, 1720)

  (b) Thomas Moore, *Sheridan.* (Orig. 1825)

- -

THE ELIZABETHAN LUMBER ROOM (I)--date unknown;[*] first
                                   published in *C.R. I*
                                   Reading notes #sl9, 21,
                                   25, and B2o

Stated Source
(stated in footnote and referred to in first paragraph):

   "These magnificent volumes"

   [Richard Hakluyt, ed.] *Hakluyt's Collection of the
   Early Voyages, Travels, and Discoveries of the Eng-
   lish Nation.* New ed. 5 vol. R.H. Evans, 1809-12.
   (Orig. 1598-1600)

   (See "Reading" for actual edition used, as indicated
   by reading notes [B2d].)

Supportive Sources (all listed in the reading notes):

  (1) "says Froude"

      (See "Reading.")

  (2) "says Harrison"

      William Harrison, *Harrison's Description of Eng-
      land in Shakespeare's Youth,* edited by Frederick
      J. Furnivall. (Orig. 1577 as Vols. II and III
      of Harrison's *Description of Britain and England*)
      3 vol. New Shakespere Society, 1877-1908.

      Vol. I is listed in the reading notes (#sl9 and
      21) and Vols. I and II are in Holleyman Addendum;
      they belonged to Virginia.

  (3) "the Verneys"

      (See "Reading.")

(4) Philip Sidney, *Defense of Poesie*. (Orig. 1595) Incl. in *The Countess of Pembroke's Arcadia*. 10th ed. (See essay by same name.)

This is listed in Holleyman and is indicated by the reading notes (B2o).

(5) Michel de Montaigne, *Essais*.

(See "Montaigne.")

(6) Ben Jonson, *Epicoene, or the Silent Woman*: I:i:81-87, 99-106. (Orig. 1609)

Poss. ed.: *The Best Plays of the Old Dramatists* [Vol. III]: *Ben Jonson*. Mermaid ser. T. Fisher Unwin, 1894.

This is listed in the reading notes (#19) and in Holleyman Addendum; it belonged to Leonard.

(7) Sir Thomas Browne, *Religio Medici*. (Orig. 1642) In *Works*, edited by Simon Wilkin. 4 vol. William Pickering, 1835-36. Vol. II.

This is indicated by the reading notes+ ($25) and is listed in Holleyman; it belonged to Virginia.

(8) Sir Thomas Browne, ... *Urn Buriall*. (Orig. 1658) Waltham, St. Lawrence: Golden Cockerell Pr., 1923.

This is indicated by the reading notes (#25; along with notes from ... *Urn Burial*, edited by Sir John Evans. Chiswick Pr., 1898+).

The 1898 edition is listed in Holleyman Addendum.

Woolf reviewed the 1923 edition for *TLS*, June 28, 1923, p. 436.

Important Allusions:

Specific quotes from Hakluyt:

(1) Middle of p. 46:

(a) Richard Hakluyt, letter to a prospective merchant in Constantinople. Vol. II.

(b) Voyage of Richard Chancelor, written by Clement Adams. Vol. I.

(2) Bottom of p. 46-top of p. 47: Exploits of John Fox. Vol. II.

(3) Middle of p. 47: Master Hore's voyage, described by Richard Hakluyt. Vol. III.

(4) Bottom of p. 47: Sir Humphrey Gilbert, urging discovery of a Northwest Passage. Vol. III.

(5) Top of p. 48: Richard Hakluyt, letter to a
prospective merchant in Constantinople. Vol. II.

(6) Middle of p. 48 ("One of them ... saw"): Anthony Jenkinson, describing Russia. Vol. I.

(7) Bottom of p. 48:

    (a) William Hareborne's ambassage to Constantino-
    ple. Vol. II.

    (b) Letter from Sultan Murad Can to Queen Eliza-
    beth. Vol. II.

Passing Allusions:

(1) Quote, top of p. 49

    Robert Greene, *Friar Bacon and Friar Bungay:* [Sc.
    viii], ll. 53-54. (Orig. publ. 1594). Prob. ed.:
    *Dramatic and Poetical Works of Robert Greene
    and George Peele,* w/notes by Alexander Dyce. G.
    Routledge, 1883.

    This is listed in Holleyman Addendum and in the
    reading notes (#19).

(2) Quote, middle of p. 49 ("O my America ...")

    John Donne, "Elegie XIX. To His Mistress Going
    to Bed." (1654)

    (See "Donne After Three Centuries.")

(3) John Dryden

* Cf. "Reading" (1919).

- -

ELLEN TERRY (IV)--*New Statesman and Nation,* Feb. 8, 1941,
                   pp. 133-34; first collected in *M*.

Inferred Source:

    "[her] autobiography"

    Ellen Terry, *The Story of My Life.* (Orig. 1908;
    2nd ed. [1922])

Supportive Sources:

    (1) "Her son, Gordon Craig, insists"

        [Edward] Gordon Craig, *Ellen Terry and Her Secret Self*. Sampson Low, Marston, 1931.

    (2) "[she] scribbled page after page to Bernard Shaw"

        Ellen Terry and Bernard Shaw, edited by Christopher St. John. Prob. ed.: 2nd ed. Constable, 1931.

        This is listed in Holleyman Addendum.

Important Allusions:

    (1) George Bernard Shaw, *Captain Brassbound's Conversion*. (Orig. publ. 1901; Terry played Lady Cicely in 1906, 1907, and 1908)

    (2) Various female characters in Shakespeare (mentioned and played by Terry):

        Cleopatra--*Antony and Cleopatra;* Desdemona--*Othello;* Imogen--*Cymbeline;* Ophelia--*Hamlet;* Portia--*The Merchant of Venice;* Lady Macbeth

    (3) "Walt Whitman's words" (quoted by Terry)

        Whitman, "When I Read the Book." (Orig. 1847)

        In Terry, *The Story of My Life,* epigraph to Introduction.

    (4) "[Terry] quotes [from Anne Oldfield (1683-1730), English actress]" (p. 71)

        In *ibid.*

Passing Allusions:

    Miscellaneous writers: Gustave Flaubert, Henrik Ibsen, Alfred Lord Tennyson (mentioned by Terry)

- -

EMERSON'S JOURNALS (BP)--*TLS,* March 3, 1910, pp. 69-70
                            Reading notes "Holograph ... ,
                            Jan. 1909-March 1911" (Berg)+

Obvious Source
(stated in *TLS* with essay and in footnote):

    Ralph Waldo Emerson, *Journals of ... [1820-32],* edited by E[dward] W[aldo] Emerson and W. Emerson

Forbes. 2 vol. Boston and N.Y.: Houghton Mifflin, 1909-10.

Important Allusions:

(1) Quotes, p. 67 and bottom of p. 68

James Elliot Cabot, *A Memoir of Ralph Waldo Emerson.* 2 vol. Boston: Houghton Mifflin, 1887.

This is indicated by the reading notes.+

First and 3rd quotes, p. 67, are attributed to Mary Emerson; in 2nd quote, p. 67, "influences" should read "atmospheres."

(2) "rough sketches of men of genius in the family"

In *ibid.*

(3) "the strange correspondence [of Mary Emerson]"

See, e.g., *Journals* (above), *passim.*

(4) Quote, top of p. 68

Emerson, *Journals,* Jan. 1820. "He" was Socrates.

(5) 2nd quote, p. 68

"For use--PHRASES POETICAL," *Journals.* Vol. I.

(6) Quote, middle of p. 68

Editors' footnote, *Journals,* Aug. 8, 1820.

Passing Allusions:

Miscellaneous English poets: Percy Bysshe Shelley, William Wordsworth

- -

THE ENCHANTED ORGAN (IV)--*Nation and Athenaeum,* March 15, 1924, p. 836; repr. in *New Republic,* Aug. 6, 1924, pp. 304-05; first collected in *M.*

Obvious Source
(stated in *Nation and Athenaeum* with essay and in footnote):

Letters of Anne Thackeray Ritchie, selected and edited by Hester Ritchie. John Murray, 1924.

Supportive Sources (quoted by H. Ritchie):

   (1) "her diary" (p. 73)

      Journal (in MS)

        (a) Aug. 14, 1855

        (b) "Tuesday night" [n.d., July-August], 1857;
            "Tomkins" should read "Tompkins"

        (c) *Ibid.*; "it is wrong" should read "it wrong";
            "it is right" should read "it right"

        (d) *Re* Edward Fitz Gerald and James Spedding

            "Wednesday" [n.d., March-Sept.], 1854

        (e) *Re* Arthur Prinsep

            March 3, 1859

        (f) *Re* Thomas Carlyle (pp. 73-74)

            Nov. 28, 1873

        (g) *Re* Charles Darwin

            [n.d.], 1882

   (2) Specific letters quoted from

        (a) 4th and 5th quotes, p. 73

            To William Makepeace Thackeray, [1852]

        (b) *Re* the Hon. Mrs. Norton

            To Lady Emily Tennyson, [1870]

        (c) Quotes and allusions, p. 74

          (i) *Re* George Eliot

              To Richmond Ritchie, [1873]

          (ii) *Re* Herbert Spencer

              To same, Jan. 10, [1899]

         (iii) *Re* John Ruskin

              To George M. Smith, July [1876]

(iv) *Re* Benjamin Jowett and Caroline Stephen (First and 2nd quotes *re* letter)

To Walter Senior, [Easter 1865]

(v) *Re* Julia Margaret Cameron and Caroline Stephen (3rd quote *re* letter)

To George M. Smith, [Easter 1865]

(vi) *Re* "her novel *Angelica"* [*sic;* i.e., Anne Thackeray, *Miss Angel* (1875)]

To Mrs. Douglas Freshfield, [1875]

(vii) *Re* Thomas Carlyle (p. 74, bottom)

To Reginald J. Smith, July 25, [1902]

(d) Quotes, p. 75

(i) First quote

To Gerald Ritchie, [1887]; "my fisherman" should be in brackets

(ii) 3rd quote

To Richmond Ritchie, Jan. 10, [1899]

(iii) 4th quote

To Lady Robert Cecil, Oct. 1, [1908]

(iv) 5th quote

To Richmond Ritchie, March [1899]

(3) Anne Ritchie, "Notes of Happy Things" (n.d. [1902-05]; in MS

2nd quote, p. 75, is from here; there should be ellipses between "jolly" and "nun"; "hung with" should be in brackets

- -

ENGLISH PROSE (BP)--*Athenaeum,* Jan. 30, 1920, pp. 134-35

Obvious Source
(stated in *Athenaeum* with essay and in footnote):

A Treasury of English Prose, edited by Logan Pearsall Smith. Constable, 1919.

Important Allusions:

    (1) Writers and selections included by Smith (see above):

        (a) Miscellaneous writers: Joseph Conrad, John Donne, Laurence Sterne, Jeremy Taylor

        (b) Stevenson's "reflections upon Happiness"

            Robert Louis Stevenson to Sidney Colvin, March 19, 1891; repr. in Stevenson, *Vailima Letters ... November 1890-October 1894.* (Orig. 1895)

            Quote, p. 15, is from here.

        (c) 2 passages from Walter Pater

            (i) "the famous one"

                Pater, "Epilogue," *Studies in the History of the Renaissance.* (Orig. 1873)

            (ii) "about a red hawthorn tree"

                Pater, "The Child in the House." (Orig. 1878)

        (d) 2 passages from Ralph Waldo Emerson

            Both are from Emerson, "Love," *Essays: First Series.* (Orig. 1841)

    (2) Miscellaneous novelists omitted by Smith: Fyodor Dostoevsky, Thomas Hardy, Ivan Turgenev

Passing Allusions:

    Miscellaneous British writers omitted by Smith: Jane Austen, the Brontës, William Cowper, John Dryden, George Meredith, Thomas Love Peacock, Daniel Defoe, Sir Walter Scott

- -

AN ESSAY IN CRITICISM (II)--*New York Herald Tribune Books,* Oct. 9, 1927, pp. 1, 8; first collected in *G.R.*

Obvious Source
(stated in *New York Herald Tribune Books* with essay):

> Ernest Hemingway, *Men Without Women*. N.Y.: C. Scrib-
> ner's, 1927.

> Specific stories mentioned: "In Another Country," "A
> Canary for One," "The Undefeated," "Fifty Grand,"
> "Hills Like White Elephants"

Supportive Source:

> Ernest Hemingway, *The Sun Also Rises*. Prob. ed.: N.
> Y.: C. Scribner's, 1927. (Orig. 1925)

> This is listed in Holleyman Addendum.

Important Allusions:

> Miscellaneous fictionists: Norman Douglas, James
> Joyce, D.H. Lawrence, Guy de Maupassant, Prosper
> Mérimée, Anton Tchekov

- -

THE FAERY QUEEN (I)--date unknown;[*] first published in *M*.
                    Reading notes B2m

Obvious Source:

> Edmund Spenser, *The Faery Queen*. (Orig. 1590, 1596)
> In *The Works of Edmund Spenser*, edited by J. Payne
> Collier. 5 vol. Bell and Daldy, 1862. Vols. I-IV.

> This is indicated by the reading notes.

> Quote, p. 16: Book I, Canto viii, verse 48, line 2

Passing Allusions:

> (1) John Milton, *Paradise Lost*. (Orig. 1667)

> (2) "Tennyson's Arthur"

> > E.g., Alfred Lord Tennyson, *Idylls of the King*.
> > (Orig. 1869-89)

> (3) William Morris

[*] The reading notes are dated Jan. 20, 1935. After taking notes on Books 1-4, Woolf writes on March 11: "I
have decided to stop reading FQ. at the end of the 4th

book because I am completely out of the mood. I have
read I suppose 2 or 3 large volumes of it since Jan.
20th and it strikes me that I have absorbed that keen
desire I had. Now I shall wait and see how long it
takes to come back.... It may be that the first books
in the FQ. are in fact the best. But I think the ebb
and flow of my feeling is also at the back of it." (I
am grateful to copyright owners Quentin Bell and Angelica Garnett for permission to quote.) On June 13,
Woolf's diary records her intention to "finish" the
Faery Queen: "The mood has come back." (*Diary,* Vol. IV,
edited by Anne Olivier Bell. N.Y. and London: Harcourt
Brace Jovanovich, 1982)

- -

FANNY BURNEY'S HALF-SISTER (III)--*TLS,* Aug. 28, 1930, pp.
                                   673-74; repr. in *New
                                   York Herald Tribune
                                   Books* (w/var.), Sept.
                                   14, pp. 1, 6, and Sept.
                                   21, pp. 1, 6, 1930;
                                   first collected in *G.R.*
                                   (text in *G.R.* and *C.E.*
                                   from *TLS*)   Reading
                                   notes #13

Assumed Impulse
(stated in first sentence):

   Fanny Burney, *Evelina,* edited by Sir Frank D. Mac-
   kinnon. Oxford: Clarendon, 1930. (Orig. 1778)

Inferred Source:

   "A packet of letters survives ... doled out by an
   editor in the eighties"; "in 1770 Fanny was impart-
   ing to her diary"

   The Early Diary of Frances Burney ... , *with a Selection from Her Correspondence* ... , edited by An-
   nie Raine Ellis.

   (See "Dr. Burney's Evening Party.")

Passing Allusions:

   (1) Mentioned by Maria Allan:

       James Fordyce, *Sermons to Young Women.* (Orig.
       1765)

   (2) Hester Lynch Thrale [Piozzi]

(3) Mentioned by Fanny:

> Edmund Spenser, *The Faery Queen*. (Orig. 1590, 1596)

N.B. Maria Allan Rishton was Fanny's *step*-sister, in American parlance.

- -

FISHING (II)--1936(?); first published in *M*.

Inferred Source:

> "Major Hills"

> John Waller Hills, *My Sporting Life*. Philip Allan, 1936.

Passing Allusions:

(1) "as Mr. Yeats said the other day"

> William Butler Yeats, "Modern Poetry." Broadcast from the B.B.C. in October, 1936.

(2) Miscellaneous writers: Charles Dickens, George Eliot, Gustave Flaubert, Andrew Lang (mentioned by Hills), Sir Walter Scott

(3) Mentioned by Hills: Genesis (O.T.; orig. c. 700-600 B.C.)

- -

FLUMINA AMEM SILVASQUE (BP)--*TLS*, Oct. 11, 1917, p. 489

Obvious Source
(stated in *TLS* with essay and in footnote):

> Edward Thomas, *A Literary Pilgrim in England*. Methuen, 1917.

Important Allusions:

(1) "Flumina Amem Silvasque" [Let Me Adore the Rivers and the Woods]

(2) Quoted by Thomas

> (a) William Blake (top of p. 163)

(i) "Milton." (Orig. 1804)

(ii) Annotation (1827) by Blake, made in copy of William Wordsworth, *Poems*. 2 vol. London: n.p., 1815. Vol. I, p. 44.

(b) Quote, middle of p. 163

Matthew Arnold, "Thyrsis." (Orig. 1866)

(3) Miscellaneous writers mentioned by Thomas:

(a) English poets: John Keats, George Meredith, Percy Bysshe Shelley

(b) English prose writers: George Borrow, Emily Brontë, Thomas Hardy, Gilbert White

(4) Alfred Lord Tennyson, "Maud." (Orig. 1855)

Quote, p. 164, is from here.

Passing Allusion (mentioned by Thomas):

John Ruskin

- -

FREUDIAN FICTION (CW)--*TLS,* March 25, 1920, p. 199

Obvious Source
(stated in *TLS* with essay and in headnote):

J[ohn] D[avys] Beresford, *An Imperfect Mother*. W. Collins, 1920.

Important Allusion:

Sigmund Freud

Passing Allusion:

The Lancet (periodical, 1823-present)

- -

A FRIEND OF JOHNSON (III)--*TLS,* July 29, 1909, p. 276; first collected in *G.R.*

Obvious Source
(stated in *TLS* with essay and in footnote):

Lacy Collison-Morley, *Giuseppe Baretti and His Friends:*

with an Account of His Literary Friendships ...   John
Murray, 1909.

Important Allusions (mentioned by Collison-Morley):

   (1) Baretti's "'account of Italy'"

       An Account of the Manners and Customs of Italy.
       2 vol. Davies, 1768.

   (2) "said Johnson" (p. 127); "as Boswell ... told
       it"

       James Boswell, *The Life of Samuel Johnson, LL.D.*
       (Orig. 1791)

   (3) "A dissertation upon the Italian poets"

       Baretti, *A Dissertation Upon the Italian Poetry*
       ... R. Dodsley, 1753.

   (4) *The Rambler.* (Periodical edited by Samuel John-
       son, 1750-51)

   (5) *La Frustra letteraria* ["The Literary Whip"].
       (Periodical edited by Baretti, 1763-65)

   (6) "the Italian dictionary"

       Baretti, *A Dictionary of English and Italian
       Languages.* 2 vol. Hitch and Hawes, 1760.

   (7) "says Johnson" (p. 130)

       G. Birkbeck Hill, ed. *Johnsonian Miscellanies.*
       2 vol. Oxford: Clarendon, 1897.

   (8) "as ... Mrs. Thrale told it"

       Hester Lynch Thrale [Piozzi], *Letters to and
       from Samuel Johnson, LL.D.* (Orig. 1788)

Passing Allusions:

   (1) "what Carlyle has to say about [Charles] Lamb"

       Thomas Carlyle, *Reminiscences,* edited by James
       Anthony Froude. 2 vol. Longmans, Green, 1881.

   (2) Miscellaneous writers (mentioned by Collison-
       Morley): Henry Fielding, Carlo Goldoni, Oliver
       Goldsmith, Charlotte Lennox, John Milton

- -

GAS AT ABBOTSFORD (I)--*New Statesman and Nation,* Jan. 27,
                      1940, pp. 108-09; first collected
                      in *M.*   Reading notes #24

Stated Source
(stated in *New Statesman and Nation* with essay and mentioned in first paragraph):

   "*Sir Walter Scott's Journal,* Vol. I"

   The Journal of Sir Walter Scott, 1825-26, edited by
   J.G. Tait.   Oliver and Boyd, 1939.

Inferred Source:

   "Bewick's ... account"

   William Bewick, *Artist. Life and Letters ... ,*
   edited by Thomas Landseer.   2 vol. Hurst and Black-
   ett, 1871.

   This is listed in the reading notes.

Supportive Sources:

   (1) "as Lockhart tells us"

       J[ohn] G[ibson] Lockhart, *Memoirs of the Life of
       Sir Walter Scott.* (Orig. 1836) Prob. ed.: 10
       vol. Edinburgh: A. & C. Black, 1882.

       This is listed in Holleyman; it belonged to Vir-
       ginia.

       2nd quote, p. 134, is from here; there should be
       ellipses between "was" and "constantly"

   (2) "Did not Haydon say"; "Did not [Haydon] add"

       *The Autobiography and Memoirs of Benjamin Robert
       Haydon,* w/introduction by Aldous Huxley and com-
       piled by Tom Taylor. 2 vol. Peter Davies, 1926.
       (Orig. 1853)

       Quotes from Haydon's Journal, Dec. 31, 1821, and
       June 3, 1840, respectively. (He spells it "Be-
       wicke.")

       [Cf. "Genius."]

Passing Allusions:

   (1) Miscellaneous writers:

       (a) the Brontës, Charles Dickens, Henry James,
           Leo Tolstoy, Anthony Trollope

(b) Mentioned by Scott: Jane Austen, Lord Byron

(c) Mentioned by Bewick: Niccolo Foscolo, William Hazlitt, William Makepeace Thackeray, William Wordsworth

(2) "Sir Patrick Spens" (14th-century ballad; mentioned by Bewick)

- -

GENIUS: B.R. HAYDON (IV)--*Nation and Athenaeum,* Dec. 18, 1926, pp. 419-21; repr. in *New Republic* (w/var.), Dec. 29, 1926, pp. 157-79; first collected in *M.* (text in *M.* and *C.E.* from *Nation and Athenaeum*)

Obvious Source
(stated in *Nation and Athenaeum* with essay and mentioned in first paragraph):

"Haydon's diaries ... now reprinted, with a brilliant introduction by Mr. Huxley"

(See "Gas at Abbotsford.")

Passing Allusions (mentioned by Haydon):

(1) *"Reid on the Human Mind"*

Thomas Reid, *An Inquiry into the Human Mind.* (Orig. 1764)

(2) Miscellaneous writers: Homer, John Keats, Charles Lamb, Pliny, Walter Scott, William Shakespeare, William Wordsworth

- -

THE GENIUS OF BOSWELL (BP)--*TLS,* Jan. 21, 1909, p. 25

Obvious Source
(stated in *TLS* with essay and in footnote):

James Boswell, *Letters of ... to the Rev. W.J. Temple,* w/introduction by Thomas Seccombe. Sidgwick and Jackson, 1909.

Supportive Sources (mentioned by Seccombe):

> "[Boswell] has had the eyes of Carlyle and Macaulay fixed upon him"

> (1) Thomas Carlyle, "Boswell's Life of Johnson," *Fraser's Magazine*, V (May 1932), 378-413; repr. in *Critical and Miscellaneous Essays*. (Orig. 1839) Prob. ed.: Carlyle, *The Collected Works of ...* 16 vol. Chapman and Hall, 1957-58. Vol. IV.
>
> This is listed in Holleyman; it belonged to Leslie Stephen.
>
> Quote, p. 149, is from here.

> (2) Thomas Babington Macaulay's "famous paradox"
>
> Macaulay, "Essay on Boswell's Life of Johnson," *Edinburgh Review*, 1831; repr. in *Critical and Historical Essays*. (Orig. 1843) Poss. ed.: See "Addison."

Important Allusions (mentioned by Seccombe):

> (1) Earlier edition of Boswell, *Letters* (see above):
>
> *Letters of James Boswell, Addressed to the Rev. W.J. Temple,* [edited by Philip Francis]. Richard Bentley, 1857.

> (2) "'*The Times* devoted six entire columns to a review [of the above]'"
>
> Jan. 3-8, 1857. *passim.*

> (3) Samuel Johnson

Passing Allusions (mentioned by Boswell):

> (1) Various literary avatars for himself: Don Juan, Don Quixote

> (2) William Shakespeare

- -

GEORGE ELIOT (I)--*TLS*, Nov. 20, 1919, pp. 657-58; first
          collected in *C.R. I* (w/var.)   Reading notes B2i

Inferred Source:

> "the first volume of her life ... in which Mr. Cross
> condemned her to tell the story"

*George Eliot's Life as Related in Her Letters and
Journals,* arranged and edited by J.W. Cross. (Orig.
1884) 3 vol. Edinburgh: Blackwood, 1885.

This is indicated by the reading notes.+

Supportive Sources:

(1) "George Meredith, with his phrase"

Meredith to Leslie Stephen, Aug. 18, 1902; repr.
in Meredith, *Letters* ... , edited by [William
Maxse Meredith].+ 2 vol. Constable, 1912.

This is listed in Holleyman.

(2) "Lord Acton ... said"

Sir John Acton to Mary Gladstone, Dec. 27, 1880;
repr. in *Letters of Lord Acton to Mary Gladstone,*
edited by Herbert Paul. George Allan, 1904.

(3) "Herbert Spencer exempted her novels"

Woolf may have gotten this through oral tradi-
tion. Herbert Spencer was elected to the London
Library Committee, as were Sir James Stephen,
Virginia's uncle, and her father, Leslie Stephen.

(4) "Mr. Gosse has lately described her"

Edmund Gosse, "George Eliot," *London Mercury,*
1919.

(5) "Lady Ritchie ... has left a ... portrait"

Anne Isabella Ritchie, *From the Porch.* Smith,
Elder, 1913.

This is listed in Holleyman.

(6) George Eliot, *The Mill on the Floss.* (Orig.
1860)

This is listed in the reading notes.

Quote, top of p. 203, is from here.

(7) George Eliot, *Middlemarch.* (Orig. 1871-72) 3
vol. In Eliot, *Works.* "Cabinet Ed." 24 vol.
Edinburgh: W. Blackwood, 1878-85.

This is indicated by the reading notes+ and is
listed in Holleyman Addendum.

Important Allusions:

(1) "a note in [Eliot's] fine clear hand"

Eliot to Leslie Stephen, Jan. 7, 1878

(In MS; first published in 1955, the letter is
now in the Huntington Library, California.)

(2) "'Poor thing,' wrote a friend" (quoted in *George Eliot's Life* [see above])

Mrs. Charles [Caroline] Bray to Sara Hennell, Feb. 14, 1846

(3) "toiling through Strauss"

David Friedrich Strauss, *The Life of Jesus ...* , trans. [by Mary Ann Evans, a.k.a. "George Eliot"]. 3 vol. London: n.p., 1846.

(4) George Henry Lewes

(5) George Eliot, *Scenes of Clerical Life* (including "Janet's Repentance"). (Orig. 1858) In Eliot, *The Novels of.* Edinburgh: Blackwood, n.d. Vol. IV.

This is indicated by the reading notes.+

(6) George Eliot, *Adam Bede.* (Orig. 1859) 2 vol. In Eliot, *Works.* "Standard Ed." 21 vol. Edinburgh: W. Blackwood, 1895.

This is indicated by the reading notes.+

(7) George Eliot, *Romola.* (Orig. 1863)

(8) Various Eliot characters: *The Mill on the Floss*--Maggie Tulliver; *Middlemarch*--Dorothea Causabon; "Janet's Repentance"--Janet

Passing Allusions:

(1) Miscellaneous writers: Dante (mentioned by Acton), Pierre Carlet de Marivaux (mentioned by Eliot)

(2) Various characters:

(a) Jane Eyre; Jane Austen, *Emma*--Mr. Knightley, Emma Woodhouse

(b) In Eliot: *Adam Bede*--the Poysers, Totty, Dinah; *Middlemarch*--Will Ladislaw; *The Mill on the Floss*--the Dodsons, Philip Wakem, Stephen Guest; *Scenes of Clerical Life*--the Gilfils, the Bartons

(3) "a highly intellectual London review"

   The Westminster Review (periodical, 1824-1914)

- -

GEORGE GISSING (I)--*Nation and Athenaeum,* Feb. 26, 1927,
                    pp. 722-23; repr. in *New Republic*
                    (w/var.), March 2, 1927, pp. 49-50;
                    first collected in *C.R. II* (text in
                    C.R. II and *C.E.* from *Nation and Ath-
                    enaeum)**

Obvious Source
(stated in *Nation and Athenaeum* with essay):

   Letters of George Gissing to Members of His Family,
   edited by Algernon and Ellen Gissing. Constable,
   1927.

Supportive Sources:

   Various novels by Gissing:

   (1) *Demos.* (Orig. 1886)

      Quote, pp. 300-01, is from here.

   (2) *New Grub Street.* (Orig. 1891)

   (3) *The Nether World.* (Orig. 1889)

Passing Allusions:

   (1) Miscellaneous writers:

      (a) Charles Darwin, Charles Dickens, George Eliot,
          Thomas Hardy

      (b) Mentioned by Gissing: Edward Gibbon, Thu-
          cydides

   (2) Various Dickens characters: *David Copperfield*
       (1850)--Micawber; *Martin Chuzzlewit* (1844)--
       Mrs. Gamp

*
This essay was later published as the Introduction to
the "Travellers' Library" edition of George Gissing, *By
the Ionian Sea.* Cape, 1933. (Orig. 1901)

- -

GEORGE MOORE (I)--*Vogue* (London), early June 1925, pp. 63,
                   84; first collected in *D.M.*

Obvious Source
(stated in *Vogue* with essay and mentioned in second paragraph):

   "in its new and stately form *Hail and Farewell* (Heinemann)--the two large volumes"

   George Moore, *Hail and Farewell*. 2 vol. Heinemann,
   1925. (Orig. 1911-14)

Important Allusions:

   Various works by Moore:

   (1) *Esther Waters*. (Orig. 1894)

   (2) *Evelyn Innes*. (Orig. 1898)

   (3) *The Lake*. (Orig. 1905)

Passing Allusions:

   (1) Miscellaneous writers:

       (a) Mentioned by Moore: Seumas O'Sullivan [pseud.
           of James Sullivan Starkey], William Butler
           Yeats

       (b) Leo Tolstoy

   (2) Various Tolstoy characters: *Anna Karenina* (1878)
       --Levin; *War and Peace* (1868)--Natasha, Pierre

- -

GERALDINE AND JANE (IV)--*TLS,* Feb. 28, 1929, pp. 149-50;
                         repr. in *Bookman* (w/var.), Feb.
                         1929, pp. 612-20; first collected
                         in *C.R. II* (w/var.)   Reading
                         notes #13

Stated Impulse
(stated in *TLS* with essay):

   (1) Geraldine Jewsbury, *Zoe*. 3 vol. Chapman and
       Hall, 1845.

       This is indicated by the reading notes (cf.
       "the three little yellowish volumes"--10th para-
       graph).

(2) Geraldine Jewsbury, *The Half Sisters*.   2 vol.
Chapman and Hall, 1848.

Inferred Sources:

(1) "Mrs. Ireland, [Jewsbury's] biographer"

*Selections from the Letters of Geraldine Endsor
Jewsbury to Jane Welsh Carlyle,* edited by Mrs.
A. Ireland.   Longmans, Green, 1892.

This is listed in the reading notes.

(2) "Mrs. Carlyle ... reflected" (last quote, p. 29,
and first 2 quotes, p. 30)

Jane Welsh Carlyle to Jeannie Welsh, Jan. 18.
1843; repr. in J. Carlyle, ... *Letters to Her
Family, 1839-1863,* edited by Leonard Huxley.
John Murray, 1924.

This is listed in the reading notes.

4th quote, p. 30, is also from here; 3rd quote,
p. 30, is a paraphrase.

(3) "Mrs. Carlyle ... wrote" (quotes 5-7, p. 30)

To Jeannie Welsh; in *ibid.*

(a) Feb. 24, 1843

(b) March 12, 1843

(c) Apr. 18, 1843

(4) "Mrs. Carlyle herself admitted" (p. 30); "very"
should read "extremely"

To same, March 4, 1850; in *ibid.*

(5) "Jane commented" (p. 31)

To Helen Welsh, Dec. 1843; in *ibid.*

(6) "[Thomas] Carlyle called them" (p. 31); "wrote
Carlyle" (p. 33)

Thomas Carlyle and J.A. Froude, eds., *Letters
and Memorials of Jane Welsh Carlyle.* Longmans,
1883. 3 vol. I, 196n.

This is listed in the reading notes.

(7) P. 32, quotes *re* Elizabeth Mudie

   Jane Welsh Carlyle to Helen Welsh, Dec. 1843; in
   Letters to Her Family (see above); "thrown"
   should be in brackets, "is the result" should
   read "was the result"

(8) 2nd quote, p. 33

   To Jeannie Welsh, Feb. 24, 1843; in *ibid.*; "the"
   should be in brackets

(9) 3rd quote, p. 33

   To same, June 21, 1843; in *ibid.*; "taken" should
   be in brackets, "the" should read "this"

(10) "Mrs. Carlyle ... wrote" (4th and 5th quotes, p.
   33)

   To same, March 16, 1844; in *ibid.*; "for" should
   be in brackets

(11) 6th and 7th quotes, p. 33

   To same, Dec. 25, 1842; in *ibid.*; "ever" should
   read "even"

(12) "Mrs. Carlyle complained" (p. 33)

   Ibid.; there should be ellipses between "reserve"
   and "in"

(13) 10th quote, p. 33

   To same, Feb. 26, 1845; in *ibid.*; "into" should
   read "in"

(14) 2nd quote, p. 35

   To same, June 21, 1843; in *ibid.*; ellipsis is J.
   Carlyle's

(15) 3rd quote, p. 35

   Jane Welsh Carlyle to Thomas Carlyle, July 12,
   1844; repr. in *New Letters and Memorials of Jane
   Welsh Carlyle,* edited by Alexander Carlyle. 2
   vol. John Lane, 1903.

   This is listed in Holleyman and in the reading
   notes. Woolf reviewed it for *Guardian,* Aug. 2,
   1905, p. 1295.

(16) 4th quote, p. 35

To same, July 15, 1844; in *ibid*.

(17) 5th and last quotes, p. 35

To same, Aug. 20, 1845; in *ibid*.

(18) Quote, middle of p. 37

To same, Sept. 12, 1860; in *ibid*.

(19) Quote, middle of p. 38

Jane Welsh Carlyle to Jeannie Welsh, Dec. 25, 1842; in ... *Letters to Her Family* (see above); should read "will either 'make a spoon or spoil a horn'"

(20) "writes Froude"

J.A. Froude, *Thomas Carlyle: A History of His Life in London, 1834-1881*. 2 vol. Longmans, 1884.

This is listed in Holleyman.

Passing Allusions:

(1) Jewsbury "had read Cudworth through"

I.e., Ralph Cudworth, theologian (1617-1688). His works were collected in 1829, edited by Thomas Birch.

(2) Miscellaneous writers (mentioned by J. Carlyle): John Keats, George Sand [pseud. of Amadine Aurore Lucie Dupin, Baroness Dudevant]

- -

A GIANT WITH VERY SMALL THUMBS (BP)--*Nation and Athenaeum*, Apr. 2, 1927, pp. 928, 930

Obvious Source
(stated in *Nation and Athenaeum* with essay and in footnote):

Avrahm Yarmolinsky, *Turgenev: The Man, His Art, and His Age*. N.Y. and London: Century, [1926].

Important Allusions:

  (1) Miscellaneous Russian writers: Anton Chekhov,
      Fyodor Dostoevsky

  (2) Ivan Turgenev, *Fathers and Sons*. (Orig. 1862)

- -

THE GIRLHOOD OF QUEEN ELIZABETH (BP)--*TLS,* Dec. 30, 1909,
p. 516

Obvious Source
(stated in *TLS* with essay and in footnote):

  The Girlhood of Queen Elizabeth, edited by Frank A.
  Mumby, w/introduction by R.S. Rait. Constable, 1909.

Supportive Source:

  "Froude's History"

  James Anthony Froude, *History of England from the
  Fall of Wolsey to the Defeat of the Spanish Armada.*
  (Orig. 1856-70) Prob. ed.: 12 vol. Longmans, Green,
  1870-75(?).

  This is listed in Holleyman Addendum; it belonged to
  Leslie Stephen.

Important Allusions (mentioned in *Girlhood* ...):

  (1) Elizabeth's translation, *A Godly Medytacion of
      the Christen Sowle* (orig. publ. 1548), of "The
      Mirror, or Glass, of the Sinful Soul" [i.e.,
      Margaret, Queen of Navarre, *Le Miroir de l'Ame
      Pécheresse.* (1531)]

  (2) Miscellaneous writers: Roger Ascham, who mentions:
      Cicero, Livy, Sophocles

- -

A GLANCE AT TURGENEV (BP)--*TLS,* Dec. 8, 1921, p. 813

Obvious Source
(stated in *TLS* with essay and in footnote):

  Ivan Turgenev, *The Two Friends and Other Stories,*
  trans. by Constance Garnett. Heinemann, 1921.

Supportive Sources:

>   Specific stories quoted from:

>>   (1) Not identified by Woolf

>>>   (a) "The Two Friends" (orig. 1853)

>>>>   Quotes, p. 206, are from here.

>>>   (b) "A Quiet Backwater" (orig. 1854)

>>>>   Quote, bottom of p. 107, is from here.

>>   (2) "Three Meetings" (orig. 1851)

>>>   Quote from, pp. 107-08, identified by Woolf

- -

GOLD AND IRON (CW)--*TLS,* Dec. 25, 1919, p. 780

>   Obvious Source
>   (stated in *TLS* with essay and in headnote):

>>   Joseph Hergesheimer, *Gold and Iron.* William Heine-
>>   mann, 1919.

>   Important Allusions:

>>   (1) Specific stories mentioned:

>>>   (a) "Wild Oranges"

>>>   (b) "the two stories that follow ['Wild Oranges']"

>>>>   (i) "The Dark Fleece"

>>>>   (ii) "Tubal Cain"

>>   (2) Joseph Hergesheimer, *Java Head.*

>>>   (See "Java Head.")

>   Passing Allusions:

>>   Miscellaneous writers: Joseph Conrad, Henrik Ibsen

- -

GOTHIC ROMANCE (I)--*TLS,* May 5, 1921, p. 288; first collected in *G.R.*

Obvious Source
(stated in TLS with essay and in footnote):

> Edith Birkhead, *The Tale of Terror: A Study of the
> Gothic Romance.* Constable, 1921.

Supportive Sources (mentioned by Birkhead):

(1) Horace Walpole, *The Castle of Otranto.* (Orig.
1764)

(2) Agnes Maria Bennett, *The Beggar Girl and Her Ben-
efactors.* (Orig. 1797)

(3) Quote, pp. 132-33 (quoted also by Birkhead but
not identified)

> Sarah Wilkinson, *Adeline; or, The Victim of Seduc-
> tion.* "Trans. from the French." Date obscure;
> Am. ed.: N.Y.: S. King, 1828.

(4) Ann Radcliffe, *The Mysteries of Udolpho.* (Orig.
1794)

(5) Henry James, *The Turn of the Screw.* (Orig. 1898)

Important Allusions (mentioned by Birkhead):

(1) Miscellaneous Gothic romancers: Matthew ("Monk")
Lewis, Charles Maturin, Clara Reeve

(2) Miscellaneous Gothic parodists: Jane Austen, Thomas Love Peacock, Sir Walter Scott

(3) Samuel Taylor Coleridge, *Kubla Khan.* (Orig. 1797)

Passing Allusions:

(1) Miscellaneous "Romantic" writers: William Shakespeare, Edmund Spenser

(2) Various 18th-century works:

(a) Samuel Johnson, *The Vanity of Human Wishes.*
(Orig. 1749)

(b) Thomas Gray, *Poems.* (Orig. 1768)

(c) Samuel Richardson, *Clarissa Harlowe.* (Orig.
1747-48)

(d) Joseph Addison, *Cato.* (Orig. 1713)

(e) Alexander Pope, *An Essay on Man*. (Orig.
1732-34)

- -

THE GREEN MIRROR (CW)--*TLS,* Jan. 24, 1918, p. 43

Obvious Source
(stated in *TLS* with essay and in headnote):

Hugh Walpole, *The Green Mirror*. Macmillan, 1918.

Important Allusions:

Miscellaneous British novelists: Jane Austen, Arnold
Bennett, E.M. Forster, John Galsworthy, Sir Walter
Scott

- -

HALF OF THOMAS HARDY (not in *C.E.*)--*Nation and Athenaeum,*
Nov. 24, 1928, pp.
289-91; repr. in *New
Republic* (w/var.),
Dec. 5, 1928, pp. 70-
72; collected in *C.D.B.*
(text in *C.D.B.* from
Nation and Athenaeum)
Reading notes #14

Obvious Source
(stated in *Nation and Athenaeum* with essay and in footnote):

Florence Emily Hardy, *The Early Life of Thomas Hardy,
1840-1891*. Macmillan, 1928.

This is listed in the reading notes.

Important Allusions:

Various Hardy novels (mentioned in *Early Life*):

Desperate Remedies (1871); *Under the Greenwood Tree*
(1872); *The Woodlanders* (1887); *The Hand of Ethel-
berta* (1876); *Far from the Madding Crowd* (1874);
The Mayor of Casterbridge (1886); *Tess of the D'Urbervilles* (1891)

Passing Allusions (mentioned in *Early Life*):

    (1) Quote, p. 65

        "The Western Tragedy" (also known, according to
        T. Hardy, as "May Colvine" or "The Outlandish
        Knight"); a version of the popular ballad "Lady
        Isabel and the Elf-Knight"--see, e.g., *The Eng-
        lish and Scottish Popular Ballads,* edited by
        Francis James Child. (Orig. 1857-59)

    (2) Miscellaneous writers: Matthew Arnold, Lord By-
        ron, Daniel Defoe, Henry James, George Meredith,
        Anne Thackeray (later Lady Ritchie)

    (3) "*The Spectator* said" (quoted also in *Early Life*)

        Unsigned review of *Desperate Remedies,* Apr. 22,
        1871, pp. 481-83

    (4) *The Graphic* (periodical, 1869-1932)

- -

HARRIETTE WILSON (III)--*Nation and Athenaeum,* June 13,
                               1925, pp. 32-22; repr. in *New
                               Republic* (w/var.), June 24, 1925,
                               pp. 122-23; first collected in *M.*
                               (text in *M.* and *C.E.* from *Nation
                               and Athenaeum*)

Obvious Source
(stated in *Nation and Athenaeum* with essay):

    The Memoirs of Harriette Wilson, Written by Herself.
    (Orig. 1825) 2 vol. Navarre Society, 1924.

Supportive Sources:

    (1) "Thomas Seccombe in the *Dictionary of National
        Biography*" [*re* Harriette Wilson]

        (For *DNB*, see "White's Selborne.")

    (2) "said Sir Walter Scott" (as cited and quoted in
        DNB [see above])

        J.G. Lockhart, *The Life of Sir Walter Scott,
        Bart.* Edinburgh: A. and C. Black, 1893.

Passing Allusions:

    (1) Miscellaneous English writers (mentioned by Wil-
        son): Lord Byron, William Shakespeare, Laurence
        Sterne

(2) William Makepeace Thackeray, *Vanity Fair*. (Orig. 1848)

- -

HAWORTH, NOVEMBER 1904 (BP and WW)--*Guardian*, Dec. 21, 1904, p. 2159

Important Allusions:

(1) Charlotte Brontë, Anne Brontë, Emily Brontë

(2) Elizabeth Gaskell, *The Life of Charlotte Brontë*. (See "Mrs. Gaskell.")

Passing Allusion:

Thomas Carlyle

- -

HENRY JAMES'S GHOST STORIES (I)--*TLS,* Dec. 22, 1921, pp. 849-50; first collected in *G.R.*   Reading notes #26

Supportive Sources:

Various James works:

(1) "The Great Good Place." In James, *The Soft Side*. Methuen, 1900.

This is indicated by the reading notes.+

(2) "The Friends of the Friends." As "The Way It Came," in James, *Embarrassments*. W. Heinemann, 1896.

This is indicated by the reading notes+ and is listed in Holleyman Addendum.

(3) "Owen Wingrave." (Orig. 1892) In James, *Novels and Tales*. "New York Edition." 24 vol. Macmillan, 1908-09. Vol. XVII.

This is indicated by the reading notes.+

(4) "Sir Edmund Orme." (Orig. 1891) In *ibid*.

This is indicated by the reading notes.+

(5) *The Turn of the Screw*. Heinemann, 1898.

This is indicated by the reading notes.+

Important Allusions:

(1) "preface to the volume containing *Altar of the Dead* [orig. 1895]"

I.e., Vol. XVII of "New York Edition" (see above)

(2) "what did Henry James say of *The Great Good Place*?"

In preface to Vol. XVI of "New York Edition" (see above)

(3) Ann Radcliffe

(4) Henry James, *The Wings of the Dove*. (Orig. 1902)

This is listed in the reading notes.

- -

HERMAN MELVILLE (BP)--*TLS,* Aug. 7, 1919, p. 423   Reading notes B2L

Supportive Sources:

(1) Herman Melville, *Typee,* edited by W.P. Trent. Society for Promoting Christian Knowledge, 1903. (Orig. 1846)

(2) "his next book"

Herman Melville, *Omoo*. Everyman's Ed. Dent, 1908. (Orig. 1847)

Both are indicated by the reading notes.+

Important Allusions:

(1) "as Stevenson said" (p. 81)

Robert Louis Stevenson to Charles Baxter, Sept. 6, 1888; repr. in *The Letters of ... Stevenson,* edited by Sidney Colvin. (Orig. 1899) Prob. ed.: 4th ed. 2 vol. Methuen, 1901.

This is listed in Holleyman Addendum.

(2) [Lord Pembroke (George Robert Charles Herbert) and G.H. Kingsley], *South Sea Bubbles. By the Earl and the Doctor*. Richard Bentley, 1872.

This is indicated by the reading notes.

Quote, top of p. 83, is from here.

Passing Allusions:

(1) Miscellaneous travelling writers: Rupert Brooke, John Herman Merivale, George John Whyte-Melville

(2) Harriet Beecher Stowe, *Uncle Tom's Cabin*. (Orig. 1851)

- -

THE HISTORIAN AND "THE GIBBON" (I)--*TLS*, Apr. 24, 1937,
                               pp. 297-98; first col-
                                lected in *D.M.*
                                Reading notes #6

Inferred Source
(mentioned in first paragraph):

> "the *Decline and Fall*"

> Edward Gibbon, *The History of the Decline and Fall
> of the Roman Empire.* (Orig. 1776-88) 12 vol.

> 2 poss. eds., as indicated by the reading notes:

> (1) Cadell and Davies, 1807.+ OR:

> (2) T. Cadell, 1811.

> Quotes, pp.117-top of 120, and quote, p. 123, are
> from here.

Supportive Sources:

> (1) "Professor Bury reminds us" (p. 120)

>> Edward Gibbon, *Autobiography,* edited by Lord
>> Sheffield (John Holroyd), w/introduction by
>> J[ohn] B[agnell] Bury. World's Classics ser.
>> Oxford U. Pr., 1907.

>> This is indicated by the reading notes.+

>> First quote, p. 115; quotes, p. 116; and quote,
>> top of p. 121, are also from here.

> (2) "in [Gibbon's] letters"

>> *Private Letters of Edward Gibbon,* edited by R.E.
>> Prothero. 2 vol. John Murray, 1896.

>> This is indicated by the reading notes.

>> (a) First quote, p. 122

>>> Edward Gibbon to Dorothea Gibbon, May 3, 1786

>> (b) "Lord Sheffield bursts out"

>>> John Baker Holroyd, Lord Sheffield, to E.
>>> Gibbon, May 14, 1793

(c) "the old stepmother ... takes up her pen"

Dorothea Gibbon to Edward Gibbon, Aug. 29, 1793

(3) 2nd and 5th quotes, p. 122

Cannot locate

Important Allusions:

(1) "Hannah More exclaimed"

More, diary, Jan. 19, 1774

Cannot locate

(2) "the autobiography, or rather the six autobiographies"

E.g., *The Autobiographies of Edward Gibbon*, edited by John Murray. J. Murray, 1896.

This is indicated by the reading notes as *"The Six Autobiographies."*

[Cf. (1) under "Supportive Sources," above.]

Passing Allusions:

(1) Miscellaneous writers:

(a) Mentioned by Gibbon in *Autobiography*: George Buffon, Sir Walter Raleigh

(b) Thomas Carlyle, Gustave Flaubert, Oliver Goldsmith, Thomas Babington Macaulay, Sir Walter Scott

(2) Various works by Xenophon (c. 431–c. 357 B.C.; mentioned by Gibbon in ... *Decline and Fall*)

(a) "the Cyropaedia" (a political romance about Cyrus the Great)

(b) "the Anabasis" (a history of the retreat from Babylonia led by Cyrus the Younger)

- -

HONEST FICTION (CW)--*TLS*, Oct. 10, 1918, p. 481

Obvious Source
(stated in *TLS* with essay and in headnote):

Frank Swinnerton, *Shops and Houses*. Methuen, 1918.

- -

HORACE WALPOLE (III)--*TLS,* July 31, 1919, p. 411; first
collected in *G.R.*   Reading notes
B2L

Obvious Source
(stated in *TLS* with review and in footnote):

*Supplement to the Letters of Horace Walpole, Fourth
Earl of Orford,* arranged and edited by Paget Tonybee.
2 vol.   Oxford: Clarendon, 1918.

This is listed in the reading notes.

Specific letters quoted from:

(1) "[letter] with which the book opens"

   To Lady Catherine Walpole, [1725]

(2) "At the age of twenty-three" (p. 106)

   To Horace Mann, Apr. 16, 1740

(3) "he could devote several pages" (p. 107)

   To C.O. [*sic*], Sept. 17, 1757

(4) "His eagerness to know" (p. 107)

   To William Fermor, Sept. 16, 1784

(5) First quote, p. 108

   To Madame (Marquise de) Marie Anne du Deffand,
   [Oct. 10, 1766]

(6) 2nd and 3rd quotes, p. 108

   From Madame du Deffand

   (a) Oct. 19, 1766

   (b) Nov. 2, 1773

    (7) First quote, p. 109

        To Madame du Deffand, [July 1768]

    (8) 2nd-7th quotes, p. 109

        To Robert Jephson

        (a) First 4 quotes

            [Feb. 1775, Letter 1608***]; "energie"
            should read "energic"

        (b) Last 2 quotes

            [Feb. 1775, Letter #1608**]

    (9) "a little confession" (p. 109)

        To Madame du Deffand, [March 13, 1767]

Supportive Sources:

    (1) Walpole "pronounce[s] his sentence" (p. 107)

        To John Nichols, Oct. 31, 1781; repr. in Walpole,
        Letters, selected and edited by C.B. Lucas. G.B.
        Newnes, [1904].

        This is listed in Holleyman Addendum.

    (2) Austin Dobson, *Horace Walpole.* (Orig. 1890)
        Osgood, McIlvaine, 1893.

        This is indicated by the reading notes.†

        4th and 5th quotes, p. 108, are from here:

        (a) *Re* Thomas Gray

            To Rev. William Mason, March 2, 1773; repr.
            in *The Correspondence of H.W. [sic] ... and
            the Rev. W. Mason,* edited w/notes by J. Mit-
            ford. 2 vol. London: n.p., 1851.

        (b) Walpole, *Anecdotes of Painting.* (Orig. 1762-
            [80])

    (3) 6th quote, p. 108 (quoted also by Paget Toynbee)

        Walpole, "note-book," n.d. given; there should
        be ellipses between "in" and "wax"

Important Allusion:

    Horace Walpole, *The Castle of Otranto.* (Orig. 1764)

Passing Allusions (mentioned by Walpole):

   (1) Horace Walpole, *The Mysterious Mother*. (Orig. 1768)

   (2) Miscellaneous French writers: Pierre Corneille, Jean Racine, Francois Arouet de Voltaire

   (3) "the phrase 'a bare bodkin'" (p. 109)

       William Shakespeare, *Hamlet*: III:i:76   (Orig. 1603)

   (4) William Shakespeare, *Henry IV, Part Two*. (Orig. 1600)

- -

HOURS IN A LIBRARY (II)--*TLS,* Nov. 30, 1916, pp. 565-66; repr. as pamphlet by Harcourt, Brace, 1958; first collected in *G.R.*

Important Allusions:

   (1) George Meredith, *Rhoda Fleming*. (Orig. 1865)

   (2) George Meredith, *The Shaving of Shagpat*. (Orig. 1855)

   (3) Henry Fielding, *The History of Tom Jones*. (Orig. 1749)

   (4) "*The [sic] Laodicean*"

       Thomas Hardy, *A Laodicean*. (Orig. 1881)

   (5) John Dewey, *Psychology*. (Orig. 1887)

   (6) The Book of Job. (Orig. 6th cent.[?] B.C)

   (7) William Webbe, *A Discourse of English Poetrie*. (Orig. 1586)

   (8) John Webster, *The Duchess of Malfi*. (Orig. 1623)

   (9) Cyril Tourneur, *The Revenger's Tragedy*. (Orig. 1607)

 (10) Miscellaneous writers read by "typical" 20-year-old: Jane Austen, Robert Browning, William Con-

greve, Euripides, Henrik Ibsen, Thomas Love Peacock, George Bernard Shaw, Percy Bysshe Shelley,
Edmund Spenser

(11) "Voltaire in eighty-nine volumes octavo"[*sic*]

Prob. ed.: [Francois Marie Arouet de Voltaire],
Oeuvres complètes de Voltaire, edited by P.A.
Caron de Beaumarchais, *et al.* 70 vol. Kehl:
Imprimerie de la Société Littéraire Typographique,
1785-89. (Printed in Baskerville type.)

This edition is listed in Holleyman; it belonged
to Leonard Woolf, who comments in *Sowing* (1960):
"I got ready everything which I was to take with
me to Ceylon, which included ninety [*sic*] large
volumes of the beautiful eighteenth-century edition of Voltaire printed in the Baskerville type
and a wire-haired fox-terrier." (*Sowing* covers
the years 1880 to 1904.)

(12) John Milton, *Comus.* (Orig. publ. 1637)

(13) John Milton, *Lycidas.* (Orig. 1638)

(14) Sir Thomas Browne, *Hydriotaphia, Urne-Burial*[1].
(Orig. 1658)

(15) William Shakespeare, *Antony and Cleopatra.* (Orig.
publ. 1623)

Passing Allusions:

Miscellaneous writers: Thomas Carlyle, Henry James,
Alexander Pope, Jean Racine, John Ruskin, Alfred Lord
Tennyson

- -

HOW IT STRIKES A CONTEMPORARY (II)--*TLS,* Apr. 5, 1923, pp.
221-22; first col-
lected in *C.R. I* (w/var.
Reading notes #19 and
B2d

Supportive Source:

"wrote Matthew Arnold"

Arnold, "The Study of Poetry," *The English Poets,*
Vol. I, edited by Thomas Humphry Ward. Oxford: University Pr., 1880.

This is listed in the reading notes (B2d).

Important Allusions:

- (1) Sir Walter Scott, *Waverley*. (Orig. 1814)

- (2) William Wordsworth, *The Excursion*. (Orig. 1814)

- (3) Samuel Taylor Coleridge, *Kubla Khan*. (Orig. publ. 1816)

- (4) George Gordon, Lord Byron, *Don Juan*. (Orig. 1819, 1821, 1823-24)

- (5) Jane Austen, *Pride and Prejudice*. (Orig. 1813)

- (6) John Keats, *Hyperion*. (Orig. 1819)

- (7) Percy Bysshe Shelley, *Prometheus Unbound*. (Orig. 1820)

- (8) W.H. Hudson, *Far Away and Long Ago*. Dent, 1918.

- (9) James Joyce, *Ulysses*. Egoist Pr., 1922.

- (10) "the recent publication of *The Watsons*"

  Jane Austen, *The Watsons,* w/introduction by A.B. Walkley. (Orig. publ. 1871) Leonard Parsons, 1923.

Passing Allusions:

- (1) Miscellaneous writers: Max Beerbohm, Joseph Conrad, W.H. Davies, Walter De la Mare, John Dryden, Gustave Flaubert, Thomas Hardy, William Hazlitt, Samuel Johnson, D.H. Lawrence, John Milton, Stephen Phillips, W.B. Yeats

- (2) Mrs. Humphry Ward [*née* Mary Augusta Arnold], *Robert Elsmere*. (Orig. 1888)

- (3) "these two quotations" (p. 155n)

  - (a) *Re* review of Rose Macaulay, *Told by an Idiot* (W. Collins, [1923]): Sylvia Lynd, *The Daily News,* Nov. 1,+ 1923.

  - (b) *Re* review of Thomas Stearns Eliot, *The Waste Land* (Richmond, Surrey: L. and A. Woolf, 1923): C.P. [*sic*], *The Manchester Guardian,* Oct. 31, 1923.

  These are indicated by the reading notes (#19).

(4) Mentioned by [Sylvia Lynd] (see above)

    (a) William Shakespeare, *The Tempest*. (Orig. publ. 1623)

    (b) Jonathan Swift, *Gulliver's Travels*. (Orig. 1726)

- -

HOW SHOULD ONE READ A BOOK? (II)--*Yale Review*, Oct. 1926, pp. 32-44; first collected in *C.R. II* (w/var.)

Important Allusions:

(1) Daniel Defoe, *The Life and Adventures of Robinson Crusoe*. (Orig. 1719)

(2) "Tate Wilkinson remembering ... Captain Jones"

Tate Wilkinson, *Memoirs of His Own Life*.

(See "Jones and Wilkinson.")

(3) "Arthur Wellesley [Wellington]"

Letters of the Duke of Wellington to Miss J. [sic], 1834-1851 ... with Extracts from the Diary of the Latter, edited by Christine Terhune Herrick. Unwin, 1924.

This is listed in Holleyman; it belonged to Leonard Woolf.

(4) "Maria Allen"

(See "Fanny Burney's Half-Sister.")

(5) "the Bunburys"

    (a) *Memoir and Literary Remains of Lt.-Gen. Sir Henry Edward Bunbury (1778-1860),* edited by Sir Charles Bunbury. Spottiswoode, 1868.

    (b) *Life, Letters and Journals of Sir Charles J.F. Bunbury, Bart,* edited by Frances Joanne Bunbury. 3 vol. London: n.p., 1894. (Also abbreviated edition, edited by Mrs. Henry Lyall. 2 vol. John Murray, 1906.

Passing Allusions:

(1) William Shakespeare, *Hamlet*. (Orig. 1603)

(2) William Shakespeare, *King Lear*. (Orig. 1608)

(3) Miscellaneous writers: Denis Diderot, John Donne, John Dryden, Oliver Goldsmith, Samuel Johnson, George Meredith, Thomas Love Peacock, Alexander Pope, Sir Walter Scott, Jonathan Swift, William Makepeace Thackeray, Anthony Trollope, Francois Marie Arouet de Voltaire, Horace Walpole, Lady Lucy Bedford

(4) Philip Sidney, *The Countess of Pembroke's Arcadia*. (Orig. 1590)

(5) "Anne Clifford"

   (See "Donne After Three Centuries."   Lady Anne's dates were 1590-1676.)

(6) "Gabriel Harvey ... arguing ... with [Edmund] Spenser"

   (See "The Strange Elizabethans.")

(7) "the Temples and the Swifts"

   (See "Dorothy Osborne's *Letters*.")

(8) "the Harleys"

   Letters of the Lady Brilliana Harley, edited by T.T. Lewis. Camden Society, 1854. (Lady Brilliana's dates were 1600[?]-43.)

(9) "the St. Johns"

   Early History of the St. John Family. Mitre, [1931].

(10) Quotes, pp. 6-8

   (a) P. 6

      16th-century lyric. Anonymous.

   (b) P. 7

      (i) Cannot locate

      (ii) John Ford, *The Lover's Melancholy*: IV:iii:57-64. (Orig. 1629) Poss. ed.: see "Notes on an Elizabethan Play."

    (iii) William Wordsworth, *The Prelude*. (Or-
          ig. 1850)

     (iv) Samuel Taylor Coleridge, *Rime of the
          Ancient Mariner*. (Orig. 1798)

  (c) P. 9

      Cannot locate

(11) Jane Austen, *Emma*. (Orig. 1816)

(12) Thomas Hardy, *The Return of the Native*. (Orig.
     1878)

(13) Jean Racine, *Phèdre*. (Orig. 1677)

(14) Aeschylus, *Agamemnon*. (Orig. 4th cent. B.C.)

- -

THE HUMANE ART (I)--*New Statesman and Nation,* June 8, 1940,
                p. 726; first collected in *D.M.*

Obvious Source
(stated in *New Statesman and Nation* with essay and mentioned in first paragraph):

  R.W. Ketton-Cremer, *Horace Walpole*. Duckworth, 1940.

Supportive Sources (mentioned by Ketton-Cremer:

  (1) "the sixteen volumes of the Paget Toynbee *[sic]*
      edition of Walpole's letters"

      *The Letters of Horace Walpole, Fourth Earl of Or-
      ford*, edited by Mrs. Paget Toynbee. 16 vol.
      Oxford: Clarendon, 1903-05.

      (See also "Horace Walpole.")

  (2) "[Walpole] wrote serenely" (quoted also by Ketton-
      Cremer);there should be ellipses before "place-
      man"

      Walpole, "Account of My Conduct ..." (1782),
      in *The Works of Horatio Walpole, Earl of Orford*,
      edited by [Mary Berry]. 5 vol. London: n.p.,
      1798.

  (3) "[Walpole was] trounced by Lord Macaulay"

Thomas Babington Macaulay, "Horace Walpole," orig. in *Edinburgh Review,* October 1833; repr. in *Critical and Historical Essays.* (Orig. 1843)
Poss. ed.: see "Addison."

Important Allusions:

(1) "[Walpole's] correspondence with Cole ... in Mr. Lewis's edition" (mentioned by Ketton-Cremer)

(See "Two Antiquaries.")

(2) Marie de Sévigné, *Lettres de Madame de Sévigné,* edited by J.L.N. Monmerque, rev. and enl. by E. Sommer.

(See "Madame de Sévigné.")

(3) "Open [Walpole's letters] at random"

The Letters ... , edited by Mrs. Paget Tonybee (see above)

Quotes, middle of p. 103 and middle of p. 105, are from here:

(a) To George Montagu, Apr. 15, 1768 (there should be ellipses before "the brave") and Sept. 17, 1869

(b) To Sir Horace Mann, Aug. 13, 1768

(4) "Macaulay, writing to his sister"

George O. Trevelyan, *The Life and Letters of Lord Macaulay.* (Orig. 1876)

(3) "Tennyson" (quote, p. 103)

Cannot locate

(4) "Keats['] ... talk about Fanny"

E.g., as listed in Holleyman and Addendum:

(a) John Keats, *Letters of* ... , edited by Sidney Colvin.

(See "Walter Raleigh.")

(b) John Keats, *Letters of* ... , edited by Maurice Buxton Forman. 2nd ed., rev. Oxford U. Pr., 1935. (Orig. 1931)

(5) "[letters of] Elizabeth and Robert Browning"

(E.g., see "*Aurora Leigh.*")

(6) "notebooks, like M. Gide's"

E.g., André Gide, *Pages de Journal (1929-1932).*
Paris: Gallimard, 1934.

This is listed in Holleyman Addendum.

Passing Allusion:

Thomas Gray (mentioned by Walpole)

- -

"I AM CHRISTINA ROSSETTI" (IV and WW)--*Nation and Athenae-
                                      um,* Dec. 6, 1930,
                                      pp. 322-24; repr.
                                      in *New York Herald
                                      Tribune Books*
                                      (w/var.), Dec. 14,
                                      1930, pp. 1, 6;
                                      first collected in
                                      C.R. II (w/var.)
                                      Reading notes #22

Obvious Source
(stated in *Nation and Athenaeum* with essay and mentioned
in first paragraph):

Mary F. Sandars, *The Life of Christina Rossetti.* Hutchinson, 1930.

This is listed in the reading notes.

Stated Co-Source
(stated in *Nation and Athenaeum* with essay, but published
after essay written--see copy of book at Washington State
University, with enclosed letter from *Nation and Athenaeum* editor):

Edith Birkhead, *Christina Rossetti and Her Poetry.*
G.G. Harrap, 1930.

Supportive Sources:

(1) "Swinburne exclaimed"

Algernon Charles Swinburne to William Michael
Rossetti, Jan. 25, 1904; repr. in *The Letters of
Algernon Charles Swinburne,* edited by Thomas Hake
and Arthur Compton Rickett. Murray, 1918.

Woolf reviewed this for *TLS,* March 21, 1918, p.
139.

(2) Swinburne "went on to say"

Swinburne, "Matthew Arnold's New Poems," in *Es-says and Studies.* (Orig. 1875)

By "her great new-year hymn," Swinburne probably meant "Old and New Year Ditties," especially the distinguished 3rd part, "Passing Away." (Orig. 1860)

(3) "Professor Saintsbury ... reports" (quoted by Sandars)

George Saintsbury, *A History of English Prosody.* (Orig. 1906)

(4) "Sir Walter Raleigh" (quoted by Sandars)

In a letter to his sister Alice, Jan. 11, 1892; repr. in his *Letters,* Vol. I.

(See "Walter Raleigh.")

(5) Specific Rossetti poems quoted from:

(a) P. 58: "Summer" (1845); "From House to Home" (1858); *ibid.*

(b) P. 59: "Looking Forward" (1849); "Song" (1848); "A Birthday" (1857)

According to Holleyman Addendum, the Woolfs owned Christina Rossetti, *Poetical Works,* w/notes and memoir by William Michael Rossetti. Macmillan, 1906. (Orig. 1904) Page numbers in the reading notes fit this edition.

Important Allusion (mentioned by Saintsbury):

Christina Rossetti, *Goblin Market.* (Orig. 1862)

Passing Allusions:

(1) Mentioned by C. Rossetti, reported by Sandars: "the works of Jean Ingelow ... went into eight editions"

Jean Ingelow, *Poems,* reached 23 "editions" between 1863 and 1880.

(2) Miscellaneous English poets (mentioned by Saintsbury): Matthew Arnold, Geoffrey Chaucer, Frank Sayers, John Skelton, Edmund Spenser

- -

"IMPASSIONED PROSE" (I)--*TLS,* Sept. 16, 1926, pp. 601-02;
                        first collected in *G.R.*
                        Reading notes #15 and B2e

Inferred Source:

"these sixteen volumes"

(1) Thomas DeQuincey, *The Works of ...* 2nd ed., rev.
and enl. 15 vol. Edinburgh: Adam and Charles
Black, 1862-63.

Quotes, top of p. 168, are from Preface to Vol.
I.

(2) Thomas DeQuincey, *The Posthumous Works of ...*
Vol. I [only]: *Suspiria de Profundis and Other
Essays,* edited by Alexander H. Japp. William
Heinemann, 1891.

2nd quote, p. 167, is from here; "if" should
come between "as" and "on" in 2nd line

Both items are listed in Holleyman; they belonged to
Leslie Stephen.

Supportive Sources:

(1) Repr. in DeQuincey, *Works.* Prob. ed,: see above.

These are listed in the reading notes (B2e).

(a) "The Spanish Military Nun"; orig., as "The
Nautico-Military Nun of Spain," in *Tait's
Edinburgh Magazine,* 1847.

Last quote, p. 168, is from here.

(b) *Autobiographic Sketches, 1790-1833;* orig.,
as "Sketches of Men and Manners from the
Autobiography of an English Opium Eater," in
Tait's Edinburgh Magazine, 1834-40, *passim.*

[Cf. "DeQuincey's Autobiography."]

First quote, p. 165 ("his" should be in
brackets), first quote, p. 167, and quote, p.
170, are from here.

(c) "Levana and Our Ladies of Sorrow"; orig. in
Blackwood's Magazine, 1845.

(2) 2nd quote, p. 169:

DeQuincey to James Hogg, Sept. 21, 1850; repr. in
Alexander H. Japp, *Thomas DeQuincey.* (Orig.
1877) Prob. ed.: Rev. ed. Hogg, 1890.

This is listed in Holleyman; it belonged to
Leslie Stephen.

Important Allusions:

(1) Second quote, p. 165, and quote, middle of p.
169

Cannot locate

(2) "scenes like that of the laurelled coach"

DeQuincey, "The English Mail-Coach"; orig. in
Blackwood's Magazine, 1849; repr. in *Works*
(see above). Vol. IV.

This is indicated by the reading notes+ (#15).

(3) "stories like that of the phantom woodcutter"

In *Autobiographic Sketches* (see above)

(4) "Mr. Binyon wrote the other day"

Laurence Binyon, *Tradition and Reaction in Modern Poetry.* The English Association, 1926.

This is listed in Holleyman.

(5) DeQuincey, *Confessions of an English Opium Eater.*
(Orig. 1822) Prob. ed.: Edited by Richard
Garnett. Kegan Paul, Trench, 1885.

This is indicated by the reading notes for "De-
Quincey's Autobiography"+ (B2p) and is listed in
Holleyman; it belonged to Leslie Stephen.

Passing Allusions:

Miscellaneous British writers: Sir Thomas Browne,
Robert Browning, Emily Brontë, Samuel Butler, Thomas
Carlyle, Charles Lamb (mentioned by DeQuincey, Wal-
ter Savage Landor, Thomas Love Peacock, John Ruskin

- -

IN A LIBRARY (CW)--*TLS,* Nov. 23, 1916, p. 559

Obvious Source
(stated in *TLS* with essay and in headnote):

William Henry Hudson,* *A Quiet Corner in a Library.*
G.G. Harrap, [1916].

Important Allusions (mentioned by Hudson):

(1) Henry Carey, "Sally in Our Alley." (Orig. c.
1715)

(2) George Lillo, *The London Merchant*.   (Orig. 1731)

Passing Allusions:

(1) Quote, middle of p. 22:

Thomas Nashe, "Adieu! Farewell Earth's Bliss!" in *Summer's Last Will and Testament*.   (Orig. 1600)

(2) Mentioned by Hudson: Henrik Ibsen

* Of Cornell University, this is not the W.H. Hudson who wrote, e.g., *Far Away and Long Ago*.

- -

INDISCRETIONS (WW)--*Vogue* (London), late Nov. 1924, pp. 47, 88

Important Allusions:

(1) Miscellaneous women writers: Jane Austen, Anne Brontë, Charlotte Brontë, Emily Brontë, George Eliot, Elizabeth Gaskell, Marie de Sévigné, Hester Thrale

(2) Miscellaneous men writers: John Donne, Samuel Johnson, John Keats, John Milton, Walter Scott, William Shakespeare

(3) George Gordon, Lord Byron, *Don Juan*.   (Orig. 1819-24)

(4) George Gordon, Lord Byron, *Letters and Journals of*.   (Orig. 1830)

Passing Allusions:

Miscellaneous writers: Matthew Arnold, Sir Thomas Browne, Maria Edgeworth, Ralph Waldo Emerson, Walter Savage Landor, Harriet Martineau, Andrew Marvell, John Ruskin, Sappho, Herbert Spencer, Alfred Lord Tennyson, William Wordsworth

- -

THE INTELLECTUAL IMAGINATION (BP)--*TLS*, Dec. 11, 1919, p. 739

Obvious Source
(stated in *TLS* with essay and in footnote):

> Walter de la Mare, *Rupert Brooke and the Intellectual Imagination*. Sidgwick and Jackson, 1919.

Important Allusion:

> Rupert Brooke, "The Fish." (Orig. 1911)

Passing Allusions:

> (1) Miscellaneous English poets (mentioned by de la Mare): William Blake, George Meredith, Percy Bysshe Shelley
>
> (2) "[John] Donne himself, as Mr. Pearsall Smith has ... shown us"
>
> > *A Treasury of English Prose,* edited by Logan Pearsall Smith. Espec. pp. 42-62.
>
> > (See "English Prose.")
>
> (3) John Dryden

- -

THE INWARD LIGHT (CW)--*TLS,* Feb. 27, 1908, p. 68

Obvious Source
(stated in *TLS* with essay and in headnote):

> H[arold] Fielding Hall, *The Inward Light*. Macmillan, 1908.

- -

JACK MYTTON (IV)--*Vogue* (London), early March 1926, pp.
                 61, 85; first collected in *C.R. II*
             (w/var.)   Reading notes B3a

Obvious Source
(stated in *Vogue* with essay and mentioned in second paragraph):

> "The Life of Jack Mytton"; "Nimrod ... make[s] no mean reading"

Memoirs of the Life of John Mytton Esq. by Nimrod [pseud. of Charles James Apperley].   E. Arnold, 1925. (Orig. 1837)

This is listed in the reading notes.

Important Allusions:

(1) "the English sporting writers [such as] Beckford"

E.g., Peter Beckford, *Thoughts on Hunting,* w/introduction by Charles Richardson.   Chapman and Dodd, [1923].   (Orig. 1781)

This is listed in Holleyman Addendum.

(2) Miscellaneous English "sporting writers": Percy B. St. John, Robert Smith Surtees

Passing Allusions:

(1) William Shakespeare

(2) Mentioned by Apperley:

(a) "Sophocles--'the beautiful passage ... '"

Sophocles, *Oedipus Tyrannus*.   (Orig. c. 425 B.C.)

(b) *The Greek Anthology*.   (Orig. 6th cent. B.C.- 6th cent. A.D.; combination of anthology col- lected by Maximum Planudes [c. 1255-1305] and the so-called "Palatine Anthology" [10th cent. A.D.]; numerous editions and transla- tions)

- -

JAMES WOODFORDE (III)--*New Republic,* Aug. 20, 1927, pp. 330-32; repr. in *Nation and Athe- naeum* (w/var.), Aug. 20, 1927, pp. 661-63; first collected in *C.R. II* (w/var.)*   Reading notes #s15, 19, and B2e, B2p

Obvious Source (stated in *New Republic* with essay):

James Woodforde, *The Diary of a Country Parson,* edit- ed by John Beresford. 5 vol. Oxford U. Pr., 1927- 31. Vol. III.

The combined reading notes and Holleyman show that
Woolf owned all 5 volumes;   when reprinted
in *C.R. II* (1932), the essay was revised and extended.

*
Apparently by mistake, Leonard Woolf included the *New
Republic* version (called "Life Itself") in *C.D.B.*, 1950.

- -

JANE AUSTEN (I)--date unknown[*]; first published in *C.R. I*

Obvious Source
(stated in *Nation and Athenaeum* with essay "Jane Austen
at Sixty" [Dec. 15, 1923, pp. 433-34], of which this is
an extension):

"*The Works of Jane Austen*"

Prob. ed.: *The Novels of Jane Austen,* edited by R.W.
Chapman. 5 vol. Oxford: Clarendon, 1923.

Supportive Sources:

(1) "says little Philadelphia Austen" [*sic*]

Philadelphia Walter to her brother James, July
23, 1788; repr. in William and Richard A. Austen-
Leigh, *Jane Austen: Her Life and Letters.* Smith,
Elder, 1913.

Woolf reviewed this for *TLS,* May 8, 1913, pp.
189-90.

(2) "Mrs. Mitford ... Miss Mitford" (quoted in *Jane
Austen: Her Life and Letters, ibid.*)

Mary Russell Mitford to Sir William Elford, Apr.
13, 1815; repr. in *The Life of Mary Russell Mitford in a Selection from Her Letters,* edited by
A.G. L'Estrange. 3 vol. Richard Bentley, 1870.

(3) Included in Austen, *Novels* (see above)

(a) *Pride and Prejudice.* (Orig. 1813)

(b) *Love and Freindship [sic].* (Orig. publ.
1922)

Woolf reviewed this for *New Statesman,* July
15, 1922, pp. 419-20. (See "Jane Austen
Practising.")

(c) *The Watsons*.   (Orig. publ. 1871)

(d) *Mansfield Park*.   (Orig. 1814)

Not mentioned by Woolf; but quotes, bottom of p. 151, are from here.

(e) *Persuasion*.   (Orig. 1818)

(4) "Dr. [William] Whewell ... insist[ed]"

Quoted in James Austen-Leigh (see below)

(5) "wrote Mr. Austen Leigh" (p. 153)

James Austen-Leigh, *A Memoir of Jane Austen*. (Orig. 1870)

Quotes, bottom of p. 144, top of p. 151, and p. 154, are also from here.

Passing Allusions:

(1) William Shakespeare, *Macbeth*.   (Orig. publ. 1623)

(2) Miscellaneous novelists: Emily Brontë, Henry James, Marcel Proust

(3) Various Austen characters not specifically attributed by Woolf: *Pride and Prejudice*--Mr. Collins, Mrs. Bennet; *Persuasion*--Sir Walter Elliott [*sic*; i.e., Eliot], Admiral Croft; *Mansfield Park*--Dr. Grant, Mary Crawford

* Woolf's essay "Jane Austen," *TLS,* May 8, 1913, pp. 189-90, acted as basis for this essay, along with "Jane Austen at Sixty" (see above); both are uncollected.

- -

JANE AUSTEN AND THE GEESE (BP)--*TLS,* Oct. 28, 1920, p. 699

Obvious Source
(stated in *TLS* with essay and in footnote):

Mary Augusta Austen-Leigh, *Personal Aspects of Jane Austen*.   John Murray, 1920.

Important Allusions (mentioned by M.A. Austen-Leigh):

(1) Jane Austen's "own statement" (p. 135)

Jane Austen to Anna Austen, [Sept. 28, 1814];
repr. in *Jane Austen: Life and Letters,* edited
by W. and R.A. Austen-Leigh

(See "Jane Austen.")

(2) "The testimony of Archbishop Whately"

Richard Whately, *"Northanger Abbey* and *Persuasion," Quarterly Review,* 24 (Jan. 1821), 352-76.

(3) Oliver Goldsmith, *The History of England.* (Orig.
1771)

Passing Allusions:

(1) Miscellaneous British writers: Lord Byron, Frederick Marryat, George Moore, Sir Walter Scott

(2) Mentioned by Jane Austen (see [1] under "Important Allusions"):

William Sherlock, *Sermons.* (Orig. 1719)

- -

JANE AUSTEN PRACTISING (WW)--*New Statesman,* July 15, 1922,
                        pp. 419-20 Reading notes B2q
Obvious Source
(mentioned in *New Statesman* with essay and in headnote):

Jane Austen, *Love and Freindship [sic],* w/preface by
G.K. Chesterton. Chatto and Windus, 1922.

This is listed in the reading notes.

Important Allusions:

(1) "Macaulay compared [Austen] with Shakespeare"

Thomas Babington Macaulay, "Diary and Letters of
Madame D'Arblay," *Edinburgh Review,* 76 (Jan. 1843),
550-70, espec. pp. 561-62; repr. in *Critical and
Historical Essays.* (Orig. 1843) Poss. ed.: see
"Addison."

(2) Jane Austen, *Mansfield Park.* (Orig. 1814)

Passing Allusions:

(1) Miscellaneous English women novelists: the Brontës, Ann Radcliffe

(2) Mentioned by Austen: William Shakespeare, *Macbeth.* (Orig. publ. 1623)

(3) Jane Austen, *Pride and Prejudice*. (Orig. 1813)

(4) Jane Austen, *Emma*. (Orig. 1816)

= =

JANE EYRE AND *WUTHERING HEIGHTS* (I and WW)--date unknown;[*]
first published
in *C.R.I*

Obvious Sources:

(1) Charlotte Brontë, *Jane Eyre*. (Orig. 1847)

(2) Emily Brontë, *Wuthering Heights*. (Orig. 1847)

Important Allusions:

(1) Miscellaneous novelists: Jane Austen, Leo Tolstoy

(2) Thomas Hardy, *Jude the Obscure*. (Orig. 1895)

(3) Quote, p. 187

Cannot locate

(4) Charlotte Brontë, *Villette*. (Orig. 1853)

Passing Allusions:

Miscellaneous English writers: Alfred Lord Tennyson, Dorothy Wordsworth

[*] This is an extension of "Charlotte Brontë," *TLS*, Apr. 13, 1916, pp. 169-70.

- -

JAVA HEAD (CW)--*TLS*, May 29, 1919, p. 293

Obvious Source:

Joseph Hergesheimer, *Java Head*. William Heinemann, 1919.

Important Allusions:

(1) Joseph Hergesheimer, *The Three Black Pennys*.

(See "The Three Black Pennys.")

(2) Joseph Conrad

- -

JOHN DELANE (BP)--*Cornhill Mag.*, 1908, pp. 765-70; repr.
                   in *Living Age,* July 18, 1908, pp. 139-
                   42

Obvious Source
(stated in footnote):

   "*The Life and Letters of John Thadeus Delane*"

   I.e., Arthur Irwin Dasent, *John Thadeus Delane ... :
   His Life and Correspondence.* 2 vol. John Murray,
   1908.

Passing Allusion:

   Nathaniel Hawthorne

- -

JONES AND WILKINSON (III)--*Bermondsey Book,* June 1926, pp.
                           48-53; first collected in *D.M.*
                           Reading notes #18

Obvious Source
(stated in *Bermondsey Book* with essay and in footnote):

   Tate Wilkinson, *Memoirs of His Own Life.* 4 vol.
   York: n.p., 1790.

   As shown by Woolf's reading notes, the account of
   Jones and Wilkinson is from Vol. I.

Passing Allusion:

   Juliet

- -

JOSEPH CONRAD (I)--*TLS,* Aug. 14, 1924, pp. 493-94; first
                   collected in *C.R. I*   Reading notes
                   B2o

Supportive Sources:

Works by Joseph Conrad:

(1) *Nostromo.* (Orig. 1904) Poss. ed.: Dent, 1918.

Woolf reviewed this for *TLS,* March 14, 1918, p. 126.

Quote, top of p. 306, is from "Author's Note."

(2) *Lord Jim.* (Orig. 1900) Poss. ed.: Dent, 1917.

Woolf reviewed this for *TLS,* July 26, 1917, p. 355.

Quote, middle of p. 305, is from here.

(3) *Typhoon.* (Orig. 1902) Poss. ed.: J.M. Dent, 1923.

(See "Mr. Conrad: A Conversation.")

(4) *The Nigger of the "Narcissus."* (Orig. 1897) W. Heinemann, 1910.

This is indicated by the reading notes+ and is listed in Holleyman.

Quote, top of p. 304, is from here.

(5) *Youth.* (Orig. 1902) Poss. ed.: Dent, 1917.

Woolf reviewed this for *TLS,* Sept. 20, 1917, p. 451.

Quote, bottom of p. 304, is from "Author's Note."

(6) "Conrad wrote" (bottom of p. 305)

Conrad, "Books," *Speaker,* 12 (1905), 369-70; repr. in *Notes on Life and Letters.* Prob. ed.: J.M. Dent, 1921.

Woolf reviewed this for *TLS,* March 3, 1921, p. 141. It is listed in Holleyman.

(7) *Chance.* (Orig. 1913) Poss. ed.: Methuen, 1914.

This is listed in Holleyman.

(8) *The Arrow of Gold.* Poss. ed.: T.F. Unwin, 1919.

This is listed in Holleyman.

(9) Quote, middle of p. 307 ("this world ... is based upon")

Some Reminiscences. Eveleigh Nash, 1912.

This is indicated by the reading notes+ and is listed in Holleyman Addendum.

Important Allusions:

(1) Miscellaneous novelists: James Fenimore Cooper, Charles Dickens, G.A. Henty, Frederick Marryat, Sir Walter Scott

(2) Various Conrad characters: Charles Marlow (*Lord Jim, Chance, Youth, Heart of Darkness* [1902]); Old Singleton (*The Nigger of the "Narcissus"*); Captain Whalley (*The End of the Tether* [1902])

Passing Allusion:

"Conrad wrote a very fine essay upon [Henry James]"

"Henry James," *North American Review,* 180 (1905), 102-08; repr. in *Notes on Life and Letters* (see above)

- -

JOURNEYS IN SPAIN (CW)--*TLS,* May 26, 1905, p. 167

Obvious Sources
(stated in *TLS* with essay and in headnote):

(1) Ro[w]land Thirlmere [pseud. of John Walker], *Letters from Catalonia.* 2 vol. Hutchinson, 1905.

(2) W. Somerset Maugham, *The Land of the Blessed Virgin.* William Heinemann, 1905.

Important Allusions:

(1) Laurence Sterne, *A Sentimental Journey Through France and Italy.* (Orig. 1768)

(2) George Borrow, *The Bible in Spain.* (Orig. 1843)

(3) Various travel writers: Lord Dufferin [and Ava] (Frederick Temple Hamilton Blackwood), Henry James, Alexander Kinglake

- -

LADY DOROTHY NEVILL (IV)--*Athenaeum,* Dec. 12, 1919, pp.
                              1331-32; first collected in
                              C.R.I

Obvious Source
(stated in *Athenaeum* with essay):

   Ralph Nevill, *The Life and Letters of Lady Dorothy
   Nevill.* Methuen, 1919.

Important Allusions:

   (1) Miscellaneous English writers (mentioned by Lady
       Dorothy): Charles Darwin, Thomas Hardy, Horace
       Walpole

   (2) Specific letters quoted from *Life and Letters:*

       (a) P. 113:

           Horatio Walpole, 3rd Earl of Orford, to Pres-
           ident, Norwich Bible Society, 1824(?)

       (b) 3rd quote, p. 115:

           Lady Dorothy to Elizabeth Haldane, n.d. giv-
           en (1912?); there should be ellipses after
           "etc."

       (c) Middle of p. 115:

           Joseph Chamberlain to Lady Dorothy, Aug. 19,
           1892

Passing Allusions:

   Miscellaneous writers: Jacques Bossuet (mentioned by
   Lady Dorothy), William Shakespeare

- -

LADY HESTER STANHOPE (BP)--*TLS,* Jan. 20, 1910, p. 20

Obvious Source
(stated in *TLS* with essay and in footnote):

   Mrs. Charles [Julia Anne] Roundell, *Lady Hester Stanhope.* John Murray, 1909.

Supportive Sources (mentioned by Roundell):

   (1) Charles Meryon, editor:

(a) *Memoirs of Lady Hester Stanhope.* 3 vol. London: n.p., 1845.

(b) *Travels of Lady Hester Stanhope.* 3 vol. London: n.p., 1846.

(2) "a French lady describes [Lady Hester]" (quoted also by Roundell)

Marie Louise Josephine de Gontaut-Biron, Duchesse de Gontaut, *Mémoires de ...* (Orig. publ. 1891)

Important Allusion:

"The writers in the Dictionary of National Biography"

(For *DNB,* see "White's Selborne." Thomas Seccombe wrote the sketch of Lady Stanhope.)

- -

LADY STRACHEY (BP)--*Nation and Athenaeum,* Dec. 22, 1928, pp. 441-42

Supportive Source:

"In her old age [Lady Jane Maria Strachey] wrote down a few memories"

Lady Strachey, "Some Recollections of a Long Life" (in MS). Selections were published in *Nation and Athenaeum,* Jan. 5-Aug. 30, 1924, *passim.**

Important Allusions (mentioned by Lady Strachey):

(1) Miscellaneous English writers: Thomas Huxley, George Lewes, Alfred Lord Tennyson

(2) Quote, p. 209, *re* Robert Browning

Paraphrase of:

"Ah, did you once see Shelley plain, And did he stop and speak to you ... ?" (from Browning, "Memorabilia." [Orig. 1855])

(3) George Eliot, *Middlemarch.* (Orig. 1872-73)

Passing Allusions:

(1) Miscellaneous English writers: Thomas Beddoes, William Shakespeare. T.E. Lawrence (mentioned by Lady Strachey)

(2) John Milton, *Lycidas*. (Orig. 1638)

* I am grateful to Michael Holroyd for a personal note to this effect. Elizabeth French Boyd, *Bloomsbury Heritage* (N.Y.: Taplinger, 1976), p. 132, identifies the MS as a "172-page typescript," of which *Nation and Athenaeum* published "about one-fourth ... in four installments."

- -

LAETITIA PILKINGTON (IV)--*Nation and Athenaeum,* June 30, 1923, pp. 424-25; first collected in *C.R.I* (w/var.)

Stated Source
(as mentioned in first paragraph):

> "Memoirs of Mrs. Pilkington, three vols. bound in one, printed by Peter Hoey in Dublin, MDCCLXXVI"

> No 1776 edition is listed in the British Museum Catalogue, the London Library Catalogue, nor the National Union Catalogue. According to the former, *Memoirs of Mrs. L. Pilkington ... Written by Herself,* 3 vol., was printed in Dublin and reprinted in London (by R. Griffiths), 1748-54. There were later editions, one of which may have been the one described by Woolf.

Important Allusion (mentioned by Pilkington):

> Jonathan Swift

Passing Allusions:

> (1) Moll Flanders

> (2) Miscellaneous writers:

>> (a) Jane Austen, Maria Edgeworth, Mary Russell Mitford, Lady Anne Thackeray Ritchie, Mme. Marie de Sévigné

>> (b) Mentioned by Pilkington: Colley Cibber, Alexander Pope, Samuel Richardson, William Shakespeare

> (3) Mentioned by Pilkington:

>> Samuel Butler, *Hudibras*. (Orig. 1662, 1663)

- -

THE LEANING TOWER (II)--*Folios of New Writing,* Autumn 1940, pp. 11-33; first collected in *M.*
Supportive Sources:

(1) "Desmond MacCarthy's answer ... in the *Sunday Times*"

MacCarthy, "Lytton Strachey and the Art of Biography," *The Sunday Times,* Nov. 5, 1933

(2) "Mr. Auden ... says" (p. 170)

W.H. Auden, "XXIV. (To Christopher Isherwood)," in Auden, *Look, Stranger!* Faber and Faber, 1936.

Ll. 27-29: "Half-boys, we spoke of books and praised/The acid and austere, behind us only/The stuccoed suburb and expensive school."

(3) Louis MacNeice, *Autumn Journal.* Faber and Faber, 1939.

(4) "Listen to Mr. Day Lewis"; there should be ellipses between "friends" and "appeal[s]"

Cecil Day Lewis, *A Hope for Poetry.* Oxford: Basil Blackwell, 1934.

"'Mr. Spender'" (quoted by Day Lewis): Stephen Spender, "After they have tired"; orig. in Spender, *Poems.* Faber and Faber, 1933.

(Should read:
....
Where light equal, like the shine from snow,
                        stripes all faces.
....
.... building, could ever hide
The palpable [etc.])

(5) "Listen now to Wordsworth"

William Wordsworth, "Song at the Feast of Brougham Castle." (Orig. 1807)

(First line should read: "Love had he found in huts where poor men lie.")

(6) "[Robert Louis] Stevenson wrote"

Stevenson said, rather than wrote, this to his stepson, Lloyd Osbourne, according to the latter's *An Intimate Portrait of RLS [sic].* N.Y.: Charles Scribner's, 1924. P. 433.

(7) "One of these parents wrote to the *New Statesman*"

Molly Fordham, "The Public School Problem," *New Statesman,* Apr. 13, 1940, p. 496.

Important Allusions:

"Wordsworth's famous saying"

In Preface to 1800 edition of William Wordsworth and Samuel Taylor Coleridge, *Lyrical Ballads*. (Orig. 1798)

Passing Allusions:

(1) Miscellaneous writers:

   (a) Aeschylus, Matthew Arnold, Jane Austen, Hilaire Belloc, James Boswell, the Brontës, the Brownings, Lord Byron, Thomas Carlyle, Geoffrey Chaucer, Dante Alighieri, Charles Dickens, John Dryden, George Eliot, Thomas Stearns Eliot, James Elroy Flecker, Thomas Hardy, Aldous Huxley, Henry James, John Keats, David Herbert Lawrence, W. Somerset Maugham, John Middleton Murry, Wilfrid Owen, Alexander Pope, John Ruskin, Sir Walter Scott, William Shakespeare, Percy Bysshe Shelley, Osbert and Sacheverell Sitwell, Lytton Strachey, Jonathan Swift, Alfred Lord Tennyson, Leo Tolstoy, G.M. Trevelyan, Anthony Trollope, Virgil, Francois Marie Arouet de Voltaire, Hugh Walpole, William Butler Yeats, Sigmund Freud, Christopher Isherwood, Karl Marx
   (b) Mentioned by Stevenson (see above): Honoré de Balzac, Gustave Flaubert

(2) William Makepeace Thackeray, *Vanity Fair*. (Orig. 1848)

(3) Various characters: Dickens, *Martin Chuzzlewit* (1844)--Pecksniff; Thackeray, *Vanity Fair*--Becky Sharp; Austen, *Emma* (1816)--Mr. Woodhouse

(4) "Rupert Brooke's poems"

(See, e.g., "Rupert Brooke.")

(5) E.M. Forster, *A Room with a View*. (Orig. 1908)

(6) "G[ilbert] K[eith] Chesterton's essays"

62 books of belles lettres by Chesterton were published between 1901 and his death in 1934.

- -

LESLIE STEPHEN (IV)--*The Times*, Nov. 28, 1932, pp. 15-16;
                          repr. in *Atlantic Monthly,* March
                          1950, pp. 39-41; first collected in
                          C.D.B.

Supportive Sources:

  (1) "Meredith saw him"

      George Meredith, *The Egoist* (orig. 1879), where
      Leslie Stephen is pictured as "Vernon Whitford"

  (2) "Thomas Hardy ... thought of [Stephen]"

      Hardy, "The Schreckhorn." (Orig. 1897)

  (3) "Meredith's tribute"

      George Meredith to Vanessa Stephen, Feb. 23,
      1904; repr. in Meredith, *Letters* ...

      (See "George Eliot.")

  (4) "Lowell ... called him ... "

      James Russell Lowell, "On a Certain Condescen-
      sion in Foreigners," in *My Study Windows.* (Orig.
      1871)

      (See "Oliver Wendell Holmes.")

Important Allusions:

  Works by Leslie Stephen:

  (1) *History of English Thought in the Eighteenth
      Century.* (Orig. 1876)

  (2) *The Science of Ethics.* (Orig. 1882)

  (3) *The Playground of Europe.* (Orig. 1871)

Passing Allusions:

  Miscellaneous English writers: John Milton, Lady
  Anne Ritchie, William Wordsworth

- -

A LETTER TO A YOUNG POET (II)--*Yale Review,* June 1932,
                             pp. 696-710; repr. as pam-
                             phlet (w/var.) by Hogarth,
                             1932; first collected in
                             D.M. (text in *D.M.* and
                             C.E. from pamphlet)

Supportive Sources:

(1) "one of the thin books of modern verse ... on your table"; "the poet is making his muse face facts"

W.H. Auden, "Which of you," in *Poems*. Faber and Faber, 1930.

(2) "I open at random and read ... [in] another of the books"

John Lehmann, "To Penetrate that room," in *A Garden Revisited*. Hogarth, 1931.

(Lehmann is the "you" of the Letter--the "young poet." See, e.g., Lehmann, *Thrown to the Woolfs.* N.Y.: Holt, Rinehart and Winston, 1978. Pp. 29-31.)

(3) "And then this" [a]

Cecil Day Lewis, "There is a dark room," in *From Feathers to Iron*. Hogarth, 1931.

(4) "And then this" [b]

Stephen Spender, "Never being," in *Twenty Poems*. Basil Blackwood, 1930.

This is listed in Holleyman.

Passing Allusions:

(1) Miscellaneous writers: Robert Browning, Geoffrey Chaucer, George Crabbe, John Donne, John Dryden, Thomas Gray, Gerard Manley Hopkins, John Keats, Pliny, Alexander Pope, Sappho, Mme. Marie de Sévigné, William Shakespeare, Percy Bysshe Shelley, Alfred Lord Tennyson, Horace Walpole, William Wordsworth, W.B. Yeats

(2) Various Shakespeare characters: Cleopatra, Falstaff, Hamlet

(3) George Gordon, Lord Byron, *Don Juan*. (Orig. 1819, 1824)

- -

THE LETTERS OF HENRY JAMES (I)--*TLS,* Apr. 8, 1920, pp. 217-
                              18; first collected in
                              D.M.   Reading notes
                              B2k

Obvious Source
(stated in *TLS* with essay and in footnote):

> *The Letters of Henry James,* edited by Percy Lubbock.
> 2 vol. Macmillan, 1920.

This is listed in the reading notes.

Supportive Sources:

    (1) Specific letters quoted from:

        (a) Bottom of p. 277

            To Alice James, Sept. 15, 1878

        (b) Middle of p. 278

            To William James, March 29, 1877

        (c) Bottom of p. 278

            To same, Nov. 14, 1878

        (d) Top of p. 279

            To Grace Norton, Oct. 17, [1882]

        (e) Middle of p. 279

            To William Dean Howells, Jan. 31, [1880]

        (f) 3rd quote, p. 279 (*re* Italy)

            To Grace Norton, Dec. 15, [1877]; "the" should
            read "that"

        (g) 4th quote, p. 279 (*re* Paris)

            To Howells, May 28, [1876]

        (h) 5th quote, p. 279 (*re* London)

            To Charles Eliot Norton, Nov. 13, 1880; "at-
            tracted" should read "attached"

        (i) Middle of p. 280

            To same, Jan. 16, 1871; the two sentences
            are not consecutive in the original

        (j) Middle of p. 281

            To Howells, Jan. 2, 1888

(k) 2nd quote, p. 281

    Ibid.; there should be ellipses between "than" and "ever"

(l) 3rd quote, p. 281

    Ibid.; there should be ellipses before "singular"

(m) Last 3 quotes, p. 281 (*re Guy Domville* [1894])

    (i) To William James, Jan. 9, 1895

    (ii) To same, Feb. 2, 1895

    (iii) *Ibid.*

(n) Top of p. 282

    To Howells, Jan. 22, 1895; "and" in line 2 should read "or"

(o) Bottom of p. 282 (*re* Henrik Ibsen)

    To Julian R. Sturgis, n.d. [1893]

(p) Pp. 282-83 (*re* Hardy, *Tess of the d'Urbervilles* [1891])

    To Robert Louis Stevenson, Feb. 17, 1893

(q) P. 283 (*re* George Meredith)

    To Edmund Gosse, Oct. 13 and 15, 1912

(r) P. 283 (*re* Leo Tolstoy and Fyodor Dostoevsky)

    To Hugh Walpole, May 19, 1912

(s) P. 284: "two passages--one upon conduct, the other upon ... a leather dressing-case"

    (i) To Arthur Christopher Benson, Dec. 28, 1896; the second "that" should be omitted

    (ii) To Walter V.R. Berry, Feb. 8, 1912

(t) P. 285 (*re* Lamb House)

    To W.E. Norris, Sept. 17, 1903

(u) "his own injunction" (p. 285)

    To Grace Norton, July 28, [1883]

(v) 3rd quote, p. 285

   To Hugh Walpole, Aug. 21, 1913

(w) 4th quote, p. 285

   To Henry Adams, March 21, 1914

(x) 5th quote, p. 285

   To Edmund Gosse, [Dec. 13, 1904]; "take it" should read "have taken it out all"

(2) "Henry James speaks aloud to himself" (p. 285)

   Quoted in Introduction, by Lubbock, who attributes it to "certain pencilled pages" in MS; [later printed in *The Notebooks of Henry James,* edited by F.O. Matthiessen and Kenneth Murdock (1947): Jan. 4, 1910 entry].

Important Allusions (mentioned by James):

Various works by James:

(1) *The Bostonians.* (Orig. 1886)

(2) *The Princess Casamassima.* (Orig. 1886)

Passing Allusion (mentioned by James):

Alfred Lord Tennyson

- -

LEWIS CARROLL (I)--*New Statesman and Nation,* Dec. 9, 1939, p. 829; first collected in *M.*   Reading notes B2f

Obvious Source
(stated in *New Statesman and Nation* with essay and mentioned in first paragraph):

   The Complete Works of Lewis Carroll, w/introduction by Alexander Woolcott. London: Nonesuch; N.Y.: Random House, 1939.

Supportive Source:

   "we turn to the Life"; "his nephew ... hints"

Stuart Dodgson Collingwood, *The Life and Letters of Lewis Carroll* ... T. Fisher Unwin, 1898.

Important Allusions:

Specific works by Carroll:

(1) *Alice in Wonderland.* (Orig. 1865, under title *Alice's Adventures in Wonderland*)

(2) 2nd quote, p. 255:

The Hunting of the Snark. (Orig. 1865)

Passing Allusion (mentioned by Carroll):

William Shakespeare

- -

LIFE AND THE NOVELIST (II)--*New York Herald Tribune Books,* Nov. 7, 1926, pp. 1, 6; first collected in *G.R.*

Obvious Source
(stated in *New York Herald Tribune Books* with essay and mentioned in fourth paragraph):

G.B. Stern, *A Deputy Was King.* Chapman and Hall, 1926.

Important Allusion:

G.B. Stern, *The Matriarch.* N.Y.: A.A. Knopf, 1925. (English title: *Tents of Israel.* [1924])

Passing Allusions:

Miscellaneous writers: Joseph Addison, John Donne, Fyodor Dostoevsky, Gustave Flaubert, Marcel Proust

- -

LITERARY GEOGRAPHY (BP)--*TLS,* March 10, 1905, p. 81

Obvious Sources
(stated in *TLS* with essay and in footnote):

(1) Lewis Melville [pseud. of Lewis S. Benjamin], *The Thackeray Country.* Adam and Charles Black, 1905.

(2) Frederic George Kitton, *The Dickens Country*.
Adam and Charles Black, 1905.

Important Allusions:

(1) Miscellaneous local-color writers: Emily Brontë,
Thomas Hardy, George Meredith, Sir Walter Scott

(2) Novels by William Makepeace Thackeray (mentioned
by Melville):

(a) *Vanity Fair*. (Orig. 1848)

(b) *The History of Pendennis*. (Orig. 1849-50)

(c) *The Newcomes*. (Orig. 1854-55)

(3) Mentioned by Kitton:

Charles Dickens, *David Copperfield*. (Orig. 1850)

- -

LOCKHART'S CRITICISM (I)--*TLS*, Apr. 23, 1931, p. 323;
repr. in *New Republic* (w/var.),
July 15, 1931, pp. 227-29;
first collected in *M*. (text in
M. and *C.E.* from *TLS*)

Obvious Source
(stated in *TLS* with essay and in footnote):

John G. Lockhart, *Lockhart's Literary Criticism*,
w/introduction by M. Clive Hildyard. Basil Blackwell, 1931.

Supportive Source:

"Sir Walter complained"

Sir Walter Scott to Lockhart, Oct. 15, 1825; repr.
in *Familiar Letters of Sir Walter Scott*, [edited by
David Douglas]. 2 vol. Edinburgh: D. Douglas; Boston: Houghton Mifflin, 1894. Vol. II.

Important Allusions (included by Hildyard):

(1) "[Lockhart] said" (p. 181)

Rev. of Col. William Mure of Caldwell, *History
of the Language and Literature of Greece*, Vol.
I, in *Quarterly Review*, 87 (Sept. 1850), 443.

(2) Miscellaneous writers reviewed by Lockhart: William Beckford, George Borrow, Samuel Taylor Coleridge, William Godwin, Theodore Hook, Leigh Hunt, John Keats, Thomas Babington Macaulay, Alfred Lord Tennyson, George Crabbe

(3) "[Lockhart] placed *Jane Eyre*"

Charlotte Brontë, *Jane Eyre* (orig. 1847): analyzed by Lockhart in letter to his daughter, Charlotte Hope-Scott, Dec. 1847

(4) "[Lockhart] predicted a long life for *Zohrab the Hostage*"

Rev. of James Justinian Morier, *Zohrab the Hostage, Quarterly Review,* 48 (Dec. 1832), 381.

(5) "as [Lockhart] perceived" (p. 184; *re* Francis Jeffrey and William Gifford)

[Lockhart], "Remarks on the Periodical Criticism of England--in a Letter to a Friend," *Blackwood,* 2 (March 1818), 670.

(6) Last quote, p. 184 (*re* Percy Bysshe Shelley)

Lockhart, "Translations of Goethe's Faust," [incl. rev. of Shelley, *Posthumous Poems* (orig. 1824)], *Quarterly Review,* 34 (June 1826), 136.

- -

LORD CHESTERFIELD'S LETTERS TO HIS SON (III)--*TLS,* March 8, 1928, p. 167; repr. in *New Republic* (w/var.), March 21, 1928, pp. 160-61; first collected in *C.R. II* (w/var.) Reading notes #14 and B2n, B2p

Stated Source
(stated in *TLS* with essay and mentioned in sixth paragraph):

"*The Characters of Lord Chesterfield,* edited by Charles Whibley"

Philip Dormer Stanhope, *Lord Chesterfield's Characters.* Peter Davies, 1927. (Orig. 1777-78)

This is listed in the reading notes (B2p and #14).

Obvious Source
(stated in title and mentioned in first paragraph):

"Lord Mahon edited the letters of Lord Chesterfield"

Letters of P.D. Stanhope, Earl of Chesterfield, edited by Lord Mahon [Philip Henry Stanhope]. 5 vol. Lippincott, 1892. (Orig. 1845-53) Vols. I and II contain the letters to his son, orig. publ. 1774.

This is indicated by the reading notes+ (B2n and #14).

Important Allusion:

Alexander Pope, *The Rape of the Lock.* (Orig. 1714)

Passing Allusions:

Miscellaneous writers (mentioned by Chesterfield): Joseph Addison, George Berkeley, Jean de La Bruyère

- -

MADAME DE SÉVIGNÉ (III)--1939(?);* first published in *D.M.*
                        Reading notes #16 and B2b, B2c,
                        B3e

Inferred Source:

"the fourteen volumes of her letters"

Marie de Sévigné, *Lettres de Madame de Sévigné, de sa Famille et de ses Amis,* edited by L.J.N. Monmerque, rev. and enl. by E. Sommer. New ed.+ 14 vol. Paris: Hachette,+ 1862-66. (Mme. Sévigné's dates were 1628-96.)

This is indicated by the combined reading notes. It is listed in Holleyman as containing 15 vol. and an "Album," which the British Museum Catalogue identifies as 2 vol.: *Iconographie des Lettres de Mme de*

Sévigné. Collection de 137 portraits. 1868.

Passing Allusions:

Miscellaneous writers:

(1) Thomas Gray, Horace Walpole

(2) Mentioned by de Sévigné: Josephus, Marie Madeleine de La Fayette, Michel de Montaigne, Blaise Pascal, Rabelais, Jean Racine, Francois de la Rochefoucauld

* Quentin Bell, *Virginia Woolf,* II, 210n, gives the date of this essay as "almost certainly" around June 1939.

- -

THE MAN AT THE GATE (III)--*New Statesman and Nation,* Oct. 19, 1940, p. 382; first collected in *D.M.*   Reading notes #24 and B5b

Obvious Source
(stated in *New Statesman and Nation* with essay and in footnote):

Coleridge the Talker, edited by Richard W. Armour and Raymond F. Howes. Oxford U. Pr., 1940.

This is indicated by the reading notes+ (#24).

3rd quote, p. 219, is from here; "excremental" should read "excrementitious"

Supportive Source:

"the volumes of Coleridge's letters"

E.g., Samuel Taylor Coleridge, *Unpublished Letters,* edited by Earl Leslie Griggs. 2 vol.

(See "Sara Coleridge.")

Specific letters quoted from:

(1) 2nd quote, p. 217

To Joseph Cottle, Apr. 26, 1814

(2) Quotes, p. 218

    (a) To George Coleridge, [Oct., 1809]

    (b) To Dr. R. Brabant, [March 1816]; "Charges" should read "charge"

    (c) To Matilda Betham, Apr. 4, 1808

    (d) To Thomas Allsop, Oct. 8, 1819

(3) Quotes, p. 219

    (a) Cannot locate

    (b) *Re* Hazlitt

        (See "William Hazlitt.")

    (c) *Re* Hartley Coleridge

        To Derwent Coleridge, [May 16, 1821]; "Bourton" should read "Burton"

(4) Quotes, p. 220

    (a) *Ibid.*

    (b) To William Sotheby, [Apr. 28, 1808]; "attention" should be preceded by "the"

Important Allusions:

(1) "Coleridge as DeQuincey saw him"; "which" should be in brackets

    Thomas DeQuincey, "Samuel Taylor Coleridge," *Recollections of the Lakes and the Lake Poets.* (Orig. 1839-40) In DeQuincey, *Works.*

    (See "Impassioned Prose.")

(2) "Crabb Robinson remarks" (quoted in *Coleridge the Talker*)

    Henry Crabb Robinson, *On Books and Their Writers,* edited by Edith J. Morley. J.M. Dent, 1938.

Passing Allusions:

(1) Miscellaneous writers:

    (a) Charles Dickens, Henry James, Marcel Proust, Percy Bysshe Shelley, William Wordsworth

  (b) Mentioned by Coleridge: Dr. Erasmus Darwin,
    John Keats, John Milton

 (2) Various Dickens characters: *David Copperfield*
   (1850)--Micawber; *Martin Chuzzlewit* (1844)--Peck-
   sniff

- -

A MAN WITH A VIEW (CW)--*TLS,* July 20, 1916, p. 343

Obvious Source
(mentioned in *TLS* with essay and in headnote):

 John F[rederick] Harris, *Samuel Butler, Author of
 Erewhon: The Man and His Work.* Grant Richards, 1916.

Supportive Source:

 Samuel Butler, *Note-books: ... Selections,* edited by
 H.F. Jones. (Orig. 1912) Prob. ed.: 3rd ed. A.C.
 Fifield, 1915.

 This is listed in Holleyman.

Important Allusions:

 (1) Gilbert Cannan, *Samuel Butler: A Critical Study.*
   Martin Secker, 1915.

 (2) Mentioned by Butler in *Note-books* (see above):

   (a) *Re* Walter Pater (p. 29)

   (b) *Re* Matthew Arnold (p. 29); "which was" should
    be in brackets

   (c) *Re* George Eliot (p. 30; quoted by Harris)

 (3) "Tennyson declaiming" (mentioned by Harris)

   Edmund Gosse, *Portraits and Sketches.* (Orig.
   1912)

 (4) 3 quotes, middle of p. 30

   Butler, *Note-books.*

 (5) Miscellaneous writers Butler "worshipped": Homer,
   William Shakespeare

 (6) Mentioned by Harris:

(a) Butler, *The Authoress of* The Odyssey. (Orig. 1897)

(b) Butler, *The Way of All Flesh*. (Orig. 1903)

(7) "[Butler's] account of buying new-laid eggs"

In *Note-books*.

(8) "[Butler's] story of 'The Aunt, the Nieces, and the Dog'"

Orig. in *Universal Review,* May 1889; repr. in Butler, *Essays on Life, Art and Science,* edited by R.A. Streatfeild. (Orig. 1904)

(9) "the anecdote of the old lady and her parrot in [Butler, *A Lecture on*] *the Humour of Homer."* Cambridge: University Pr., 1892.

Passing Allusions:

Miscellaneous English writers: Edward FitzGerald (mentioned by Harris), Samuel Johnson

- -

MARIA EDGEWORTH AND HER CIRCLE (BP)--*TLS,* Dec. 9, 1909, p. 482
Obvious Source
(stated in *TLS* with essay and in footnote):

Constance Hill, *Maria Edgeworth and Her Circle.* John Lane, 1909.

Important Allusions (mentioned by Hill):

(1) "Lord Byron's ... verdict" (p. 131)

George Gordon, Lord Byron, Journal, Jan. 19, 1821; in Byron, *Letters and Journals.*

(See "Sheridan.")

(2) Maria Edgeworth on Byron (p. 131)

Maria Edgeworth to Sophy Ruxton, May 16, 1813; repr. in, e.g., *Life and Letters of Maria Edgeworth,* edited by A[ugustus] J.C. Hare. 2 vol. E. Arnold, 1894. (See also [4] and [5] below.)

(3) *Re* Joanna Baillie (2 quotes, p. 132)

    (a) Lucy Akin, "Recollections of Joanna Baillie,"
in Akin, *Memoirs, Miscellanies and Letters,*
edited by Philip H. Le Breton. Longman,
Green, 1864.

    (b) Quoted by Anna Letitia Le Breton, *Memories
of Seventy Years,* edited by Mary Amma Martin.
Griffith and Farran, 1883.

(4) *Re* Lady Breadalbane [*sic;* i.e., Bredalbane]
(pp. 132-33)

Maria Edgeworth to Margaret Ruxton, Apr. 28,
1819.

(5) *Re* Mr. Standish (p. 133)

Same to same, Jan. 20, 1819.

Passing Allusions:

(1) Mrs. Humphry Ward (*née* Mary Augusta Arnold)

(2) Mentioned by Hill:

    (a) Miscellaneous writers: Mme. d'Arblay (Fanny
Burney), Mme. de Staël (Baroness Anne Luise
Germaine Necker de Staël), Samuel Rogers

    (b) Various works:

        (i) Joanna Baillie, *A Series of Plays ...
to Delineate the Stronger Passions of
the Mind.* 3 vol. (Orig. 1798-1812)

        (ii) Joanna Baillie, "The Outlaw's Song,"
in *Orra.* (Orig. 1812)

           This was "admired by Scott": Sir Walt-
er Scott to Joanna Baillie, [1812].

       (iii) Anna L. Barbauld, *Eighteen Hundred and
Eleven.* J. Johnson, 1812.

- -

MARY WOLLSTONECRAFT (III and WW)--*Nation and Athenaeum,*
                            Oct. 5, 1929, pp. 13-
                            15; repr. in *New York
                            Herald Tribune Books*
                            (w/var.), Oct. 20, 1929,
                            pp. 1, 6; first collect-
                            ed in *C.R.II* (w/var.)
                            Reading notes #9

Inferred Source:

"Godwin ... the memoir of his wife"

William Godwin, *Memoirs of Mary Wollstonecraft,* edited by W. Clark Durant. Constable, 1927. (Orig. 1798)

This is listed in Holleyman and is indicated by the reading notes.

Supportive Sources:

(1) "the staple of her doctrine ... [and] her highest boast" (pp. 194-95); "readily" should read "resolutely"

Mary Wollstonecraft to Joseph Johnson, Sept. 13, [1789]; repr. in *Memoirs* (see above)

(2) "Imlay, ... to whom the letter was addressed"

Mary Wollstonecraft to Gilbert Imlay, [Jan. 1-2, 1794]; repr. in Wollstonecraft, *Letters to Imlay,* edited by Charles Kegan Paul. Kegan Paul,+ 1878.

This is listed in the reading notes.

(3) "[Mary] cried out" (p. 199)

Mary Wollstonecraft, *Letters Written During a Short Residence in Sweden, Norway, and Denmark.* Joseph Johnson, 1796.

This is indicated by the reading notes.+

Important Allusions:

(1) "*Reply to Burke*"

Mary Wollstonecraft, *A Vindication of the Rights of Men, in a Letter to ... E[dmund] Burke.* (Orig. 1790)

(2) Mary Wollstonecraft, *A Vindication of the Rights of Women,* w/introduction by Mrs. Henry Fawcett. Unwin, 1891. (Orig. 1792)

This is indicated by the reading notes.+

(3) "the letter ended" (p. 195)

Mary Wollstonecraft to Joseph Johnson, Dec. 26, 1792; repr. in *Memoirs* (see above)

(4) "Southey thought"

> Robert Southey to J[oseph] Cottle, March 13, 1797.

> Quoted in Charles Kegan Paul, *William Godwin, His Friends and Contemporaries.* 2 vol. King,+ 1796.

> This is listed in Holleyman and in the reading notes; it belonged to Leslie Stephen.

(5) "wrote Madame Schweizer [*sic*]"

> Durant above quotes Madeleine Schweitzer's journal in his supplement to *Memoirs*. He spells the Baron's name Wa̲lzogen.

(6) "[Godwin] had written" (first 2 quotes, p. 198; quoted also in Paul, *William Godwin* [see above])

> Godwin, *An Enquiry Concerning Political Justice.* 3 vol. London: n.p., 1793.

Passing Allusions:

(1) Miscellaneous writers: Jane Austen, Joel Barlow (mentioned by Godwin), Charles Lamb

(2) "Wordsworth ... saw" (p. 193)

> William Wordsworth, *The Prelude.* Moxon, 1850.

> This is indicated by the reading notes+ and is listed in Holleyman; it belonged to Leonard.

- -

THE MEMOIRS OF SARAH BERNHARDT (BP)--*Cornhill Mag.,* 1908, pp. 190-96

Inferred Source:

> Sarah Bernhardt, *My Double Life.* William Heinemann, 1907.

- -

MEN AND WOMEN (BP and WW)--*TLS,* March 18, 1920

Obvious Source
(stated in *TLS* with essay and in footnote):

Léonie Villard, *La Femme Anglaise au XIXème Siècle
et Son Evolution d'Après le Roman Anglais Contempor-
aine.* Paris: n.p., 1920.

Important Allusions:

Various characters in English drama and fiction:
Hardy, *Far from the Madding Crowd* (1874)--Bathsheba
Everdene; Samuel Richardson, *Clarissa Harlowe* (1747-
48)--Clarissa; Shakespeare, *King Lear* (publ. 1608)--
Cordelia; Meredith, *Diana of the Crossways* (1885)--
Diana; Dickens, *David Copperfield* (1850)--Dora;
Thackeray, *Pendennis* (1849-50)--Helen Pendennis; Bor-
row, *Lavengro* (1851) and *The Romany Rye* (1858)--Isopel
Berners; C. Brontë, *Jane Eyre* (1847)--Jane Eyre,
Rochester; Shakespeare, *Macbeth* (publ. 1623)--Lady
Macbeth; Shakespeare, *Hamlet* (publ. 1603)--Ophelia

- -

MISS MITFORD (IV)--*TLS,* May 6, 1920, p. 283; repr. in *Daily
Herald* (w/var.), May 26, 1920, p. 7; and
Athenaeum (w/var.), May 28, 1920, pp.
695-99;* first collected in *C.R. I*
(w/var.)

Obvious Source
(stated in *TLS* with essay and mentioned in first paragraph):

Constance Hill, *Mary Russell Mitford and Her Sur-
roundings.* John Lane, 1920.

Supportive Source:

Mitford, *Recollections of a Literary Life.* 3 vol.
Richard Bentley, 1852.

Specific quotes from (quoted by Hill):

(1) "Miss Mitford writes" (p. 101); "house" should
read "home" [misquoted by Hill]

(2) Quote, top of p. 103; "that of" should be in
brackets

(3) "Miss Mitford herself spoke out" (p. 106); there
should be ellipses before "grief" and "there"

Important Allusions:

(1) William Wordsworth and Samuel Taylor Coleridge,
Lyrical Ballads. (Orig. 1798)

(2) Mentioned by Hill: Mitford, *Our Village.* (Orig.
1824)

Passing Allusions:

    (1) Miscellaneous writers:

        (a) the Brontës, Elizabeth Browning, Fanny Burney, Geoffrey Chaucer, Maria Edgeworth, George Eliot, Harriet Martineau, Coventry Patmore, Alexander Pope, George Sand, Sappho

        (b) Mentioned by Hill: Jane Austen, Mary Martha Sherwood

    (2) "Mr. Crissy" (p. 105; mentioned by Hill):

        J. Crissy published Mitford's first "collected works," *The Works of M.R. [sic] Mitford, Prose and Verse.* Philadelphia: n.p., 1840.

    (3) "*Adam's Geography*" (mentioned by Hill)

        Alexander Adam, *A Summary of Geography and History Both Ancient and Modern.* (Orig. 1794)

* First 4 paragraphs of final essay are based on the *Athenaeum* article; the remainder, on the *TLS* version.

- -

MISS ORMEROD (not in *C.E.*)--*Dial,* Dec. 1924, pp. 466-74; collected in *C.R.I* (Amer. ed. only)

  Obvious Source
(stated in *Dial* with essay and in footnote):

    "*The Life of Eleanor Ormerod,* by Robert Wallace Murray" [*sic*]

    Eleanor Ormerod, LL. D., Economic Entomologist, Autobiography and Correspondence, edited by Robert Wallace. John Murray, 1904.

- -

THE MODERN ESSAY (II)--*TLS,* Nov. 30, 1922, pp. 769-70; first collected in *C.R.I* (w/var.) Reading notes B2q

Obvious Source
(stated in *TLS* with essay and in footnote):

> *Modern English Essays, 1870-1920,* edited by Ernest
> Rhys. 5 vol. J.M. Dent, 1922.

This is listed in the reading notes.

Specific essays mentioned:

(1) "about God and Spinoza"

Matthew Arnold, "A Word About Spinoza" (Vol. I)

(2) "about turtles and Cheapside"

Samuel Butler, "Ramblings in Cheapside" (Vol. II)

(3) Mark Pattison, "Montaigne" (Vol. I)

(4) "Mr. Hutton"

R.H. Hutton, "Autobiography" (Vol. I; quoted
from)

(5) Walter Pater, "Notes on Leonardo da Vinci" (Vol.
I; quoted from)

(6) Robert Louis Stevenson, "Walking Tours" (Vol. II;
quoted from)

(7) "In volume iii we find Mr. Birrell"

Augustine Birrell, "The Essays of Elia"

(8) "Mr. Birrell on Carlyle"

Augustine Birrell, "Carlyle" (Vol. II)

(9) Max Beerbohm, "A Cloud of Pinafores" (Vol. III)

(10) Leslie Stephen, "A Cynic's Apology" (Vol. II)

(11) "Henley ... [is] ... impressive"

W.E. Henley, "William Hazlitt" (Vol. III)

(12) Hilaire Belloc, "On an Unknown Country" (Vol. IV;
quoted from)

(13) Joseph Conrad, "Tales of the Sea" (Vol. IV)
(described as "a gentleman of Polish extraction"
[p. 44])

(14) W.H. Hudson, "The Samphire Gatherer" (Vol. V)

(15) E.V. Lucas, "A Philosopher That Failed" (Vol. IV)

(16) Robert Lynd, "Hawthorne" (Vol. V)   ˙

(17) J.C. Squire, "A Dead Man" (Vol. V; quoted, middle of p. 50, without identification)

(18) R. Clutton-Brock, "The Magic Flute" (Vol. V)

(19) Vernon Lee [pseud. of Violent Paget], "Genius Locus" (Vol. III)

Important Allusions:

(1) Miscellaneous British essayists: Joseph Addison, Sir Thomas Browne, James Anthony Froude, Charles Lamb, Thomas Babington Macaulay, Jonathan Swift

(2) "M. Grün ... about Montaigne" (mentioned by Pattison--see [3] under "Obvious Source")

Alphonse Gruen, *La Vie Publique de M. Montaigne.* Paris: n.p., 1855.

(3) "a certain translator of Spinoza" (mentioned by Arnold--see [1] under "Obvious Source")

Robert Willis, trans., *Tractatus Theologico-Politicus* by Benedict de Spinoza. London: n.p., 1862.

(4) First quote, p. 50:

Francis Bacon, "Of Great Place." In *Essays.* 1612. Prob. ed.: *The Essays of Counsels Civil and Moral of Francis Bacon.* M. Clark, 1680.

This is listed in Holleyman; it belonged to Leslie Stephen.

Passing Allusions:

Miscellaneous writers:

(1) Aeschylus (mentioned by Butler--see [2] under "Obvious Source")

(2) John Stuart Mill (mentioned by Hutton--see [4] under "Obvious Source")

- -

MODERN FICTION (II)--*TLS,* Apr. 10, 1919, pp. 189-90; first collected in *C.R. I* (w/var.) Reading notes "Modern Novels ... , Holograph Notebook, Unsigned and Undated" (Berg)+

Supportive Sources:

   (1) William Henry Hudson, *The Purple Land*. (Orig. 1885)

   (2) William Henry Hudson, *Green Mansions*. (Orig. 1904)

   (3) William Henry Hudson, *Far Away and Long Ago*. Dent, 1918.

      Woolf reviewed this for *TLS*, Sept. 26, 1918, p. 453. (See "Mr. Hudson's Childhood.")

   (4) Arnold Bennett, *The Old Wives' Tale*. (Orig. 1908)

   (5) "Mr. Wells ... his Joans and his Peters"

      H.G. Wells, *Joan and Peter*. Cassell, 1918.

      Woolf reviewed this for *TLS,* Sept. 19, 1918, p. 438. (See "The Rights of Youth.")

   (6) James Joyce, *A Portrait of the Artist as a Young Man*. Egoist Pr., 1916.

   (7) James Joyce, *Ulysses* ([1922]; "now [1919] appearing in the *Little Review*"--periodical, 1914-20)

      I.e., March-July, Sept.-Oct., 1918: 7 sections

      This is indicated by the reading notes.+

   (8) Joseph Conrad, *Youth*. (Orig. 1902) Prob. ed.: Dent, 1917.

      Woolf reviewed this for *TLS*, Sept. 20, 1917, p. 451.

   (9) Thomas Hardy, *The Mayor of Casterbridge*. (Orig. 1886)

 (10) Anton Tchekov, "Gusev." (Orig. 1890) In Tchehov, *The Witch and Other Stories*, trans. by Constance Garnett. Chatto and Windus, 1917.

      Woolf reviewed this for *TLS,* May 16, 1918, p. 231.

 (11) Quote, p. 109:

      Elena Militsina, "The Village Priest"; in Militsina and Mikhail Saltikov, *The Village Priest and Other Stories,* trans. by Beatrix L. Tollemache.

      Woolf reviewed this for *TLS,* Dec. 19, 1918, p. 641. (See "The Russian Point of View.")

Important Allusions:

   (1) Laurence Sterne, *The Life and Opinions of Tristram Shandy*. (Orig. 1759-67)

(2) William Makepeace Thackeray, *The History of Pen-
     dennis.* 2 vol. Bradbury and Evans, 1849-50.

This is indicated by the reading notes.+

Passing Allusions:

(1) Miscellaneous English novelists: Jane Austen,
     Henry Fielding, John Galsworthy, George Mere-
     dith

(2) Various Arnold Bennett characters: George Cannon
     (*Hilda Lessways* [1911] and *These Twain* [1916]);
     Edwin Clayhanger (*Clayhanger* [1910], *Hilda Less-
     ways,* and *These Twain*)

- -

MODERN LETTERS (II)--1930; first published in *C.D.B.*

Important Allusions:

(1) "Dorothy [Osborne's] ... letters"

    (See "Dorothy Osborne's *Letters*.")

(2) "Walpole's thick packets"

    (See, e.g., "Horace Walpole" and "The Humane
    Art.")

(3) "Cowper ... writing"

    (See "Cowper and Lady Austen.")

(4) "[letters of] Edward Fitzgerald"

    E.g., *Letters and Literary Remains of Edward
    FitzGerald.* 7 vol. Macmillan, 1902-03.

    This is listed in Holleyman; it belonged to Vir-
    ginia.

Passing Allusions:

Miscellaneous writers: Aristotle, Thomas Gray

- -

MODES AND MANNERS OF THE NINETEENTH CENTURY (BP)--*TLS,*
                                                    Feb. 24,
                                                    1910, p.
                                                    64

   Obvious Source
   (stated--without author's name--in *TLS* with essay and
   in footnote):

      [Max Ulrich von Boehn], *Modes and Manners of the
      Nineteenth Century,* trans. by Marian Edwardes,
      w/introduction by Grace Rhys. 3 vol. J.M. Dent,
      1909.

   Passing Allusions:

      Miscellaneous British writers: Thomas Carlyle, Jona-
      than Swift

- -

MOMENTS OF VISION (CW)--*TLS,* May 23, 1918, p. 243

   Obvious Source
   (stated in *TLS* with essay and in headnote):

      Logan Pearsall Smith, *Trivia.* Constable, 1918.

- -

MONEY AND LOVE (III)--*Athenaeum,* March 12, 1920, pp. 332-
                      34; first collected in *G.R.*

   Obvious Source
   (stated in *Athenaeum* with essay and in footnote):

      Ernest Hartley Coleridge, *The Life of Thomas Coutts,
      Banker.* 2 vol. John Lane, 1920.

   Passing Allusion (mentioned by E. Coleridge):

      Lady Hester Stanhope

- -

MONTAIGNE (III)--*TLS,* Jan. 31, 1924, p. 57; first collect-
                  ed in *C.E. I* (w/var.)   Reading notes
                  #s20, 23, 26+

Obvious Source
(stated in *TLS* with essay and in footnote):

> *Essays of Montaigne,* trans. by Charles Cotton, edit-
> ed by William Carew Hazlitt. (Orig. 1877 in this
> trans.) 5 vol. Navarre Society, 1923.

Specific essays quoted from:

> (1) First quote, p. 18:
>
> > Book II, Essay 17, "Of Presumption"
>
> (2) Quote, pp. 18-19
>
> > Book II, Essay 6, "Use Makes Perfect"
>
> (3) Quote, pp. 19-20
>
> > Book III, Essay 6, "Of Coaches"
>
> (4) First quote, p. 20
>
> > Book III, Essay 13, "Of Experience"
>
> (5) 2nd quote, p. 20; quote, pp. 21-22
>
> > Book II, Essay 1, "Of the Inconstancy of Our Ac-
> > tions"; "in one word" (top of p. 22) should be
> > in brackets
>
> (6) Quote, near bottom of p. 21
>
> > Book II, Essay 16, "Of Glory"

Supportive Source:

> (Woolf also quotes from the French [orig. 1580].)
>
> Prob. ed.: Michel Eyquem de Montaigne, *Essais,* edit-
> ed by H. Motheau and D. Jouaret. 7 vol. Paris: E.
> Flammarion, 1886-89.
>
> This is listed in Holleyman Addendum.

Important Allusion:

> "the firm of Louis Conard is issuing ... Montaigne
> ... [edited by] Dr. Armaingaud"

I.e., Montaigne, *Oeuvres Complètes,* edited by A[r-thur] Armaingaud. 12 vol.   Paris: L. Conard, 1924-41.

Passing Allusions:

    (1) Miscellaneous writers:

        (a) Mentioned by Montaigne: Etienne de la Boétie, Catullus, Homer

        (b) Samuel Pepys, Jean Jacques Rousseau

    (2) Sir Thomas Browne, *Religio Medici.*   (Orig. 1642)

    (3) "Boswell ... in the famous biography"

        James Boswell, *The Life of Samuel Johnson, LL.D.* (Orig. 1791)

- -

MORE DOSTOEVSKY (BP)--*TLS,* Feb. 22, 1917, p. 91

Obvious Source
(stated in *TLS* with essay and in footnote):

    Fyodor Dostoevsky, *The Eternal Husband and Other Stories,* trans. by Constance Garnett.   Heinemann, 1917.

Important Allusions:

    (1) Specific stories mentioned:

        (a) "The Eternal Husband."   (Orig. 1870)

        (b) "The Double."   (Orig. 1846)

        (c) "A Gentle Spirit."   (Orig. 1876)

    (2) Fyodor Dostoevsky, *The Idiot.*   (Orig. 1882)

    (3) Fyodor Dostoevsky, *The Possessed.*   (Orig. 1873)

- -

THE "MOVIE" NOVEL (CW)--*TLS,* Aug. 29, 1918, p. 403

Obvious Source
(stated in *TLS* with essay and in headnote):

> Compton Mackenzie, *The Early Life and Adventures of Sylvia Scarlett*. Martin Secker, 1918.

Passing Allusions:

(1) Charles Dickens

(2) Various characters from English novels: George Borrow, *Lavengro* (1851)--the Flaming Tinman; Borrow, *Lavengro and the Romany Rye* (1858)-- Isopel Berners; Moll Flanders; Tom Jones

- -

MR. BENNETT AND MRS. BROWN (I)--*Criterion,* July 1924, pp. 409-30; repr. as pamphlet by Hogarth, 1924; and in *New York Herald Tribune Books* (w/var.), Aug. 23, pp. 1-3, and Aug. 30, pp. 1-4, 1925; first collected in *C.D.B.* (text in *C.D.B.* and *C.E.* from *Criterion*)

Supportive Sources:

(1) "Mr. Bennett ... in an article"

> Arnold Bennett, "Is the Novel Decaying?" *Cassell's Weekly,* March 28, 1923, p. 47.

(2) Arnold Bennett, *Hilda Lessways*. Methuen, 1911.

> This is listed in Holleyman.

Important Allusions:

(1) Samuel Butler, *The Way of All Flesh*. (Orig. 1903)

(2) Miscellaneous English novelists: John Galsworthy, H.G. Wells

(3) James Joyce, *Ulysses*. (Orig. 1922)

(4) Lytton Strachey, *Eminent Victorians*. (Orig. 1918)

(5) Lytton Strachey, *Queen Victoria*. (Orig. 1921)

Passing Allusions:

   (1) Miscellaneous writers: the Carlyles, Joseph Conrad, Charles Dickens, T.S. Eliot, E.M. Forster,
John Keats, D.H. Lawrence, Thomas Babington Macaulay, John Milton, George Bernard Shaw, William Shakespeare

   (2) "Read the *Agamemnon*"

       Aeschylus, *Agamemnon*. (Orig. 4th cent. B.C.)

   (3) Leo Tolstoy, *War and Peace*. (Orig. 1868)

   (4) William Makepeace Thackeray, *Vanity Fair*. (Orig.
1848)

   (5) Laurence Sterne, *The Life and Opinions of Tristram Shandy*. (Orig. 1759-67)

   (6) Gustave Flaubert, *Madame Bovary*. (Orig. 1857)

   (7) Jane Austen, *Pride and Prejudice*. (Orig. 1813)

   (8) Thomas Hardy, *The Mayor of Casterbridge*. (Orig.
1886)

   (9) Charlotte Brontë, *Villette*. (Orig. 1853)

  (10) Mentioned by Bennett in *Hilda Lessways*:

       Alfred Lord Tennyson, *Maud*. (Orig. 1855)

- -

MR. CONRAD: A CONVERSATION (I)--*Nation and Athenaeum*, Sept.
                              1, 1923, pp. 681-82; first
                              collected in *C.D.B.*
                              Reading notes #25

Obvious Sources
(stated in *Nation and Athenaeum* with essay):

  Works by Joseph Conrad:

   (1) *Almayer's Folly*. (Orig. 1895)

   (2) *Tales of Unrest*. (Orig. 1898)

   (3) *An Outcast of the Islands*. (Orig. 1896)

(4) *The Nigger of the "Narcissus."* (Orig. 1897)

2nd quote, top of p. 312, is from here.

(5) *Typhoon.* (Orig. 1902)

(6) *Lord Jim.* (Orig. 1900)

(7) *Youth.* (Orig. 1902)

(8) *Romance* [with Ford Madox Hueffer]. (Orig. 1903)

The essay itself refers to "six ... magnificent volumes." Woolf's reading notes indicate that she was
using Conrad, *Works.* Uniform Ed.+ J.M. Dent, 1923-.
This is listed in Holleyman Addendum. *Almayer's Folly* and *Tales of Unrest* constitute a single volume,
as do *The Nigger of the "Narcissus"* and *Typhoon.*

Important Allusions:

(1) Works by Conrad:

(a) *The Arrow of Gold.* (Orig. 1919)

(b) *The Rescue.* Dent, 1920.

Woolf reviewed this for *TLS,* July 1, 1920, p.
419.

(c) "[Conrad] praises Henry James and Anatole
France"

(i) (For Henry James, see "Joseph Conrad.")

(ii) 2 reviews by Conrad of works by France:

Of *Crainquebille* (orig. in *Speaker,*
n.s. 10 [July 16, 1904], 359-61); of
L'Ile des Pingouins (orig. in *English
Review,* 1 [Dec. 1908], 188-90)

Both repr. in Conrad, *Notes on Life and
Letters,* pp. 32-44.

(See "Joseph Conrad.")

(d) *Chance.* (Orig. 1913)   Methuen,
1914.

This is indicated by the reading notes+ and
is listed in Holleyman.

(2) "Their elegy is Milton's" (p. 311)

John Milton, *Samson Agonistes.* (Orig. 1671)

Passing Allusions:

> (1) Miscellaneous English poets: John Dryden, Alexander Pope, William Shakespeare
>
> (2) Various Conrad characters: Charles Marlow, Captain Whalley
>
> (See "Joseph Conrad" for both.)
>
> (3) "There's Mrs. Schomberg" (quote, p. 312)
>
> Conrad, *Victory*. (Orig. 1915)

- -

MR. GALSWORTHY'S NOVEL (CW)--*TLS*, Aug. 30, 1917, p. 415

Obvious Source
(stated in *TLS* with essay and in headnote):

> John Galsworthy, *Beyond*. William Heinemann, 1917.

- -

MR. HUDSON'S CHILDHOOD (CW)--*TLS*, Sept. 26, 1918, p. 453

Obvious Source
(stated in *TLS* with essay and in headnote):

> W.H. Hudson, *Far Away and Long Ago*. J.M. Dent, 1918.

Important Allusions:

> (1) Mentioned by Hudson:
>
> Serge Aksakoff, *History of My Childhood [sic]*.
>
> (See "A Russian Schoolboy.")
>
> (2) Miscellaneous autobiographers: George Borrow, Jean Jacques Rousseau, George Sand [pseud. of Amadine Aurore Lucie Dupin, Baroness Dudevant]

Passing Allusion (mentioned by Hudson):

> Charles Dickens

- -

MR. KIPLING'S NOTEBOOK (BP)--*Athenaeum,* July 16, 1920, p.
75

Obvious Source
(stated in *Athenaeum* with essay and in footnote):

Rudyard Kipling, *Letters of Travel, 1892-1913.* Macmillan, 1920.

Important Allusion:

Alfred Lord Tennyson, "A Dream of Fair Women." (Orig. 1833)

Quote, p. 64, is from here.

Passing Allusions:

Miscellaneous adventure writers: Joseph Conrad, Richard Hakluyt

- -

MR. MERRICK'S NOVELS (CW)--*TLS,* July 4, 1918, p. 311

Obvious Sources
(stated in *TLS* with essay and in headnote):

(1) Leonard Merrick, *While Paris Laughed.* Hodder
and Stoughton, 1918. (Orig. 1914)

(2) Leonard Merrick, *Conrad in Quest of His Youth,*
w/introduction by James Barrie. Hodder and
Stoughton, 1918. (Orig. 1903)

Important Allusions:

(1) Mentioned by Barrie (see above): Thomas Hardy

(2) Laurence Sterne, *A Sentimental Journey Through
France and Italy.* (Orig. 1768)

(3) Various Merrick novels:

(a) *The Man Who Was Good.* (Orig. 1892)

(b) *The House of Lynch.* (Orig. 1907)

(c) *[The Position of] Peggy Harper.* (Orig. 1911)

(d) *Quaint Companions.* (Orig. 1903)

- -

MR. NORRIS'S METHOD (CW)--*TLS,* March 4, 1920, p. 153

  Obvious Source
  (stated in *TLS* with essay and in headnote):

    W[illiam] E[dward] Norris, *The Triumphs of Sara.* Hut-
    chinson, 1920.

- -

MR. NORRIS'S STANDARD (CW)--*TLS,* Feb. 10, 1921, p. 89

  Obvious Source
  (stated in *TLS* with essay and in headnote):

    W[illiam] E[dward] Norris, *Tony the Exceptional.* Hut-
    chinson, [1921].

  Important Allusions:

    Miscellaneous novelists: Gustave Flaubert, Henry
    James

- -

MR. SASSOON'S POEMS (BP)--*TLS,* May 31, 1917, p. 259, and
                             July 11, 1918, p. 323 (two books,
                             reviewed at different times)

  Obvious Sources
  (stated in *TLS* with essays and in footnote):

    (1) Siegfried Sassoon, *The Old Huntsman and Other
        Poems.* William Heinemann, 1917.

    (2) Siegfried Sassoon, *Counter-Attack and Other Poems.*
        William Heinemann, 1918.

  Supportive Sources:

    (1) Specific poems quoted from *The Old Huntsman:*

        (a) "The Hero"

            Quote, p. 97, is from here.

        (b) Quote, p. 98

            "Stretcher Case"; "shines" should read
            "shone"

(b) Quote, p. 99

"South Wind"

(2) Specific poems quoted from *Counter-Attack:*

(a) "The General"

Quote, top of p. 100, is from here.

(b) 2nd quote, p. 100

"Suicide in Trenches"

(c) Quote, middle of p. 100

"To Any Dead Officer"

(d) "Dead Musicians"

Quote, bottom of p. 100, is from here.

Important Allusions:

Specific poems mentioned but not quoted from:

(1) "The Tomb-Stone Maker" (in *The Old Huntsman*)

(2) "Morning Express" (in *The Old Huntsman*)

- -

MRS. GASKELL (BP and WW)--*TLS,* Sept. 29, 1910, p. 349

Obvious Source
(stated in *TLS* with essay and in footnote):

Mrs. Ellis H. [Esther A.] Chadwick, *Mrs. Gaskell.*
Sir I. Pitman, 1910.

Supportive Sources:

(1) Elizabeth Gaskell, *Mary Barton.* (Orig. 1848)

Quote, pp. 138-39, is from here.

(2) Elizabeth Gaskell, *North and South.* (Orig. 1854)

Quote, pp. 139-40, is from here.

Important Allusions:

(1) Elizabeth Gaskell, *Cranford.* (Orig. 1851-53)

(2) John Galsworthy, *Strife*. (Orig. 1909)

(3) "Lady Ritchie ... hails Molly Gibson 'dearest of heroines ... '" (quoted by Chadwick)

Anne Thackeray Ritchie, "The Author of Cranford," orig. in *Cornhill Mag.*, Dec. 1906; repr. as "Mrs. Gaskell" in Ritchie, *Blackstick Papers*. Smith, Elder, 1908.

Woolf reviewed this for *TLS*, Nov. 19, 1908, p. 411.

(Molly Gibson is the heroine of Gaskell, *Wives and Daughters*. [Orig. 1864-66])

(4) "the critic's praise" (p. 140)

Cannot locate

(5) "Charlotte Brontë ... invite[d] her to Haworth, ... and Mrs. Gaskell's comment was 'Poor Miss Brontë'"

Elizabeth Gaskell to anon. correspon., June 1, 1853; repr. in Gaskell, *The Life of Charlotte Brontë*. (Orig. 1857) Prob. ed.: Smith, Elder, 1865.

This is listed in Holleyman; it belonged to Leslie Stephen.

(6) Last 2 quotes, p. 140

(a) In Ritchie (see above)

(b) Cannot locate

Passing Allusions:

Miscellaneous English writers: Charles Darwin (mentioned by Chadwick), Charles Dickens, George Meredith, Thomas Love Peacock, Percy Bysshe Shelley, William Makepeace Thackeray, Anthony Trollope

- -

MRS. THRALE (III)--*New Statesman and Nation,* March 8, 1941, p. 250; first collected in *M.* Reading notes #16

Obvious Source
(stated in *New Statesman and Nation* with essay and in footnote):

James L. Clifford, *Hester Lynch Piozzi (Mrs. Thrale)*. Oxford: Clarendon, 1941.

This is listed in the reading notes.

Supportive Source:

"One anecdote" (p. 159)

Frances Reynolds, "Recollections by Miss Reynolds," in *Johnsonian Miscellanies*, edited by George Birkbeck Hill. 2 vol. Oxford: Clarendon, 1897. Vol. II.

Important Allusions (mentioned by Clifford [see above]):

(1) "Boswell's sketch of Mrs. Thrale"

James Boswell, *The Life of Samuel Johnson, LL.D.* (Orig. 1701) *Passim.*

(2) "as Johnson said" (quoted also by Clifford)

Abraham Hayward, editor, *Autobiography ... and Literary Remains of Mrs. Piozzi.* (Orig. 1861)

Passing Allusion:

"Queen of the Blues" (identified by Clifford)

I.e., Elizabeth Montagu, "Queen" of the "Blue-Stocking Circle"; friend and rival of Hester Thrale

- -

MUMMERY (CW)--*TLS*, Dec. 19, 1918, p. 641

Obvious Source
(stated in *TLS* with essay and in headnote):

Gilbert Cannan, *Mummery*. W. Collins, [1918].

Passing Allusions (mentioned by Cannan):

Miscellaneous dramatists: Henrik Ibsen, William Shakespeare

- -

THE NARROW BRIDGE OF ART (II)--*New York Herald Tribune Books*, Aug. 14, pp. 1, 6-7, and Aug. 21, pp. 1, 6, 1927; first collected in *G.R.*

Important Allusions:

(1) Charles Algernon Swinburne, *Atalanta in Calydon*. (Orig. 1865)

(2) Percy Bysshe Shelley, *Prometheus Unbound*. (Orig. 1820)

(3) George Gordon, Lord Byron, *Don Juan*. (Orig. 1822-26)

(4) George Meredith, *The Ordeal of Richard Feverel*. (Orig. 1859)

(5) Charlotte Brontë, *Villette*. (Orig. 1853)

(6) Laurence Sterne, *The Life and Opinions of Tristram Shandy*. (Orig. 1759-67)

Passing Allusions:

(1) Various characters: Hamlet, Ophelia, Robinson Crusoe

(2) Miscellaneous writers: Robert Browning, Samuel Butler, Samuel Taylor Coleridge, Fyodor Dostoevsky, John Dryden, George Gissing, Henrik Ibsen, Walter Pater, Marcel Proust, George Bernard Shaw, Alfred Lord Tennyson, Oscar Wilde, William Wordsworth

(3) John Keats, "Ode to a Nightingale." (Orig. 1819)

(4) "the modern poet [who] talks of the nightingale"

T.S. Eliot, *The Waste Land*. (Orig. 1922)

(5) William Shakespeare, *Measure for Measure*. (Orig. 1604-05)

- -

THE NEW BIOGRAPHY (IV)--*New York Herald Tribune Books*, Oct. 30, 1927, pp. 1, 6; first collected in *G.R.*   Reading notes #14

Obvious Source
(stated in *New York Herald Tribune Books* with essay and mentioned in fifth paragraph):

Harold Nicolson, *Some People*. Constable, 1927.

This is listed in the reading notes.

Supportive Source:

"said Sir Sidney Lee"

Sir Sidney Lee, *Principles of Biography*. Cambridge: University Pr., 1911.

This is listed in the reading notes and in Holleyman Addendum; it belonged to Virginia.

Important Allusions:

(1) Sir Sidney Lee, *A Life of William Shakespeare*. (Orig. 1898)

(2) Sir Sidney Lee, *King Edward VII*. 2 vol. Macmillan, 1925, 1927.

(3) "Izaak Walton"

E.g., Izaak Walton, *The Complete Angler* [1653], *and the Lives of Donne* [1640], *Wotton* [1651], *Hooker* [1665], *Herbert* [1670] *and Sanderson* [1678], edited by A.W. Pollard. Library of English Classics ed. Macmillan, 1901.

(4) "Mrs. [Lucy] Hutchinson"

(See "Reading.")

(5) "Boswell's page"

James Boswell, *The Life of Samuel Johnson, LL.D.* (Orig. 1791)

(6) "Mr. Strachey compressed ... "

Lytton Strachey, *Eminent Victorians*. (Orig. 1918)

(7) "M. Maurois ... a [Percy Bysshe] Shelley life"

André Maurois, *Ariel*. (Orig. 1923)

(8) Harold Nicolson, *Tennyson: Aspects* ... (Orig. 1923)

(9) Harold Nicolson, *Byron. The Last Journey* ... (Orig. 1924)

Passing Allusions:

(1) Various Shakespeare characters: Hamlet, Macbeth

(2) Miscellaneous writers: Max Beerbohm, Edmund Burke, John Morley, François Marie Arouet de Voltaire

(3) "'Tears, Idle Tears'" (mentioned by Nicolson, *Some People*)

Alfred Lord Tennyson, *The Princess*. (Orig. 1847)

- -

THE NIECE OF AN EARL (I)--*Life and Letters,* Oct. 1928, pp. 356-61; first collected in *C.R. II*

Inferred Impulse
(mentioned in first paragraph):

George Meredith, "The Case of General Ople and Lady Camper." (Orig. 1890)

Important Allusions:

(1) Miscellaneous writers: Lord Byron, Geoffrey Chaucer, Charles Dickens, Benjamin Disraeli, John Keats, Marcel Proust, William Shakespeare, William Makepeace Thackeray

(2) Various women characters: Austen, *Pride and Prejudice* (1812)--Elizabeth [Bennet]; Austen, *Emma* (1816)--Emma [Woodhouse]; C. Brontë, *Jane Eyre* (1847)--Jane Eyre

(3) John Milton, *Paradise Lost*. (Orig. 1667)

- -

"NOT ONE OF US" (IV)--*New York Herald Tribune Books,* Oct. 23, 1927, pp. 1, 6; first collected in *D.M.*

Obvious Source
(stated in *New York Herald Tribune Books* with essay and
in footnote):

> Walter Edwin Peck, *Shelley: His Life and Work.* 2
> vol. Ernest Benn, 1927.

Supportive Sources:

> (1) Quoted by Peck:
>
>> (a) "Shelley said" (p. 20)
>>
>>> Percy Bysshe Shelley to Thomas Love Peacock,
>>> Apr. 6, 1819; repr. in Shelley, *Letters,* ed-
>>> ited by Roger Ingpen. 2 vol. Sir Isaac Pit-
>>> man, 1909. (See also [c] and [d] below.)
>>
>> (b) Quote about carpet (p. 21)
>>
>>> Elizabeth Grant, *Memoirs of a Highland Lady,*
>>> edited by Lady [Jane Maria] Strachey. John
>>> Murray, 1898.
>>
>> (c) "[Shelley] saw 'the likeness of what is per-
>> haps eternal'"
>>
>>> Percy Bysshe Shelley to John Gisborne, June
>>> 18, 1822
>>
>> (d) "Godwin ... complained"
>>
>>> William Godwin to Percy Bysshe Shelley, Jan.
>>> 6, 1822; paraphrased by Shelley in reply, Jan.
>>> 16, 1812
>>
>> (e) "lines which Professor Peck quotes" (p. 24)
>>
>>> Shelley, "Good Night." (Orig. 1819)
>
> (2) "Mary Shelley ... exclaimed"
>
>> From her Journal, Oct. 7, 1822. In *Shelley Me-
>> morials,* edited by Lady [Jane] Shelley. Smith,
>> Elder, 1859.
>>
>> This is listed in Holleyman Addendum.

Important Allusions:

> (1) "[Shelley] was canonized by Edward Dowden"
>
>> Edward Dowden, *Life of Percy Bysshe Shelley.* 2
>> vol. Kegan Paul, 1886.

(2) "by Matthew Arnold [Shelley] was ... reduced"

   (See "Dostoevsky the Father.")

(3) Works by Percy Bysshe Shelley:

   (a) "Epipsychidion." (Orig. 1821)

   (b) *Prometheus Unbound*. (Orig. 1820)

   (c) "To a Skylark." (Orig. 1821)

   (d) "Ode to the West Wind." (Orig. 1819)

Passing Allusions:

   Miscellaneous writers:

   (1) John Keats, Leo Tolstoy

   (2) Mentioned by Peck: Lord Byron, Leigh Hunt

- -

NOTES ON AN ELIZABETHAN PLAY (I)--*TLS,* March 5, 1925, pp.
                                 145-46; first collected
                                 in *C.R. I* (w/var.)
                                 Reading notes #s19, 25
                                 and B2o
Supportive Sources:

(1) "the first Elizabethan play that comes to hand"

   George Chapman, *Bussy d'Ambois:* II:i:119-23.
   (Orig. 1607)   In *The Works of George
   Chapman: Plays,* edited by Richard Herne Shep-
   herd. Chatto and Windus, 1874.

   This is indicated by the reading notes+ (B20)
   and is listed in Holleyman Addendum; it belonged
   to Leslie Stephen.

   Quote, p. 61, is also from here: V:iv:12-14.

(2) John Webster, *The White Devil.* (Orig. 1617) In
   The Works of John Webster, edited by Alexander
   Dyce. The Old Dramatists ser. New ed., rev.
   and corrected. George Routledge, 1871. (Orig.
   in this ed. 1830)

   This is indicated by the reading notes+ (B2o)
   and 25) and is listed in Holleyman; it belonged
   to Leslie Stephen.

2nd quote, p. 58 (II:i:168-70); quote, p. 59
(V:vi:248-49); and first 2 quotes, p. 60
(III:ii:115; V:iii;30-31), are from here.

(3) Francis Beaumont and John Fletcher, *The Maid's Tragedy*. (Orig. 1619) Prob. ed.: In *The Works of*, edited by George Darley. 2 vol. Edward Moxon, 1839-40.+

This is listed in the reading notes (#19) and in Holleyman; it belonged to Leslie Stephen.

Last quote, p. 58, is from here: II:i:76-79.

(4) John Ford, *'Tis Pity She's a Whore*. (Orig. 1633) In *John Ford*, edited by Havelock Ellis ("says Mr. Havelock Ellis"). Mermaid ser. Vizetelly, 1888.

This is indicated by the reading notes+ (#19) and is listed in Holleyman Addendum.

(5) John Ford, *The Broken Heart*. (Orig. publ. 1633) In *ibid*.

This is indicated by the reading notes+ (#19).

First quote, p. 58 (V:iii:67-70), and 3rd quote, p. 60 (III:v:13-17), are from here.

(6) Last quote, p. 60:

William Rowley, Thomas Dekker and John Ford, *The Witch of Edmonton*: IV:ii:31-32. (Orig. 1658) In *Thomas Dekker*, edited by Ernest Rhys. Mermaid ser. Vizetelly, [1894]. (Orig. in this ed. 1888)+

This is indicated by the reading notes (#19) and is listed in Holleyman.

Important Allusions:

(1) Thomas Kyd, *The Spanish Tragedy*, edited by J. Schick. Dent, 1898. (Orig. 1592[?])

This is indicated by the reading notes+ (#s19 and 25).

(2) Leo Tolstoy, *Anna Karenina*. (Orig. 1878)

Passing Allusions:

(1) Miscellaneous writers: Sir Thomas Browne, John Donne, Gustave Flaubert, Robert Greene, Ben Jonson, George Peele, Michel de Montaigne, William Shakespeare, Stendhal, Henry Taylor, Alfred Lord Tennyson

(2) Sophocles, *Antigone*. (Orig. 5th cent. B.C.)

(3) Leo Tolstoy, *War and Peace*. (Orig. 1868)

- -

NOTES ON D.H. LAWRENCE (I)--date unknown[*]; first published
in *M*.

Supportive Source:

D.H. Lawrence, *Sons and Lovers*.   (Orig. 1913)

Important Allusions:

Works by Lawrence:

(1) *"Trespassers"* [*sic*]

The Trespasser. (Orig. 1912)

(2) *The Prussian Officer and Other Stories*.   (Orig.
1914)

(3) *The Lost Girl*. (Orig. 1920)

Woolf reviewed this for *TLS,* Dec. 2, 1920, p.
795.   (See "Postscript or Prelude?")

(4) "[Lawrence's] sketches of Italian travel"

(a) *Twilight in Italy*. (Orig. 1916)

(b) *Sea and Sardinia*. (Orig. 1921)

Etruscan Places was publ. in 1932, presumably after Woolf was writing.

(5) *Nettles*. (Orig. 1930)

(6) *Pansies*. (Orig. 1929)

Passing Allusions:

(1) Arnold Bennett

(2) Marcel Proust, *Swann's Way*.   (Orig. 1914)

[*] The essay was written after Lawrence's death in 1931.

- -

THE NOVELS OF E.M. FORSTER (I)--*Atlantic Monthly,* Nov.
1927, pp. 642-48; first
collected in *D.M.*
Reading notes #15

Supportive Sources:

Works by Forster:

(1) *Where Angels Fear to Tread.* (Orig. 1903)   Edinburgh: Blackwood, 1905.

This is indicated by the reading notes.+

(2) *The Longest Journey.* (Orig. 1907)

(3) *A Room with a View.* Edward Arnold, 1908.

Woolf reviewed this for *TLS,* Oct. 22, 1908, p.
362. (See essay "A Room with a View.")

(4) *The Celestial Omnibus.* (Orig. 1911)

(5) *Howards End.* (Orig. 1910)

Both quotes, p. 345, are from here.

(6) *A Passage to India.* (Orig. 1924)

Important Allusions:

(1) Henrik Ibsen, *The Wild Duck.* (Orig. 1884)

(2) Henrik Ibsen, *The Master Builder.* (Orig. 1892)

Passing Allusions:

Miscellaneous novelists: Jane Austen, Charles Dickens, Thomas Hardy, George Meredith, Thomas Love Peacock, Leo Tolstoy, Ivan Turgenev, H.G. Wells

- -

THE NOVELS OF GEORGE MEREDITH (I)--*TLS,* Feb. 9, 1928, pp.
                                  85-86; repr. in *New
                                  York Herald Tribune*
                                  (w/var.), Feb. 12, 1928,
                                  pp. 85-86; first col-
                                  lected in *C.R. II*
                                  (w/var.)   Reading
                                  notes B2n and #26

Supportive Sources:

(1) E.M. Forster, *Aspects of the Novel.*

(See "The Art of Fiction.")

(2) Works by Meredith:

(a) *The Ordeal of Richard Feverel*. 3 vol. Chapman and Hall, 1859.

This is indicated by the reading notes+ (B2n).

(b) *The Adventures of Harry Richmond*. (Orig. 1871)

This is listed in the reading notes (B2n).

(c) *The Egoist*. (Orig. 1879) C. Kegan Paul, 1888.

This is indicated by the reading notes+ (B2n) and is listed in Holleyman Addendum.

Important Allusions:

(1) Jane Austen, *Pride and Prejudice*. (Orig. 1813)

(2) Anthony Trollope, *The Small House at Allington*. (Orig. 1864)

(3) Quote, middle of p. 231:

George Meredith to G.P. Baker, July 22, 1887; repr. in *Letters of George Meredith*.

(See "George Eliot.")

This is indicated by the reading notes+ (#26).

Passing Allusions:

Miscellaneous writers: Emily Brontë, Charles Dickens, John Donne, George Eliot, Thomas Hardy, Gerard Manley Hopkins, Thomas Love Peacock, William Shakespeare, Stendhal, Anton Tchekov, Alfred Lord Tennyson

- -

THE NOVELS OF THOMAS HARDY (I)--*TLS*, Jan. 19, 1928, pp. 33-34; first collected in *C.R. II* (w/var.)
Reading notes #20 and B2j

Supportive Sources
(all are mentioned in the reading notes [B2j]):

Works by Hardy:

(1) *Desperate Remedies*. (Orig. 1871)

This is also listed in reading notes #20.

Quote, p. 256, is orig. from Preface to 1889 ed.

(2) *Under the Greenwood Tree*. (Orig. 1872)

(3) *Far from the Madding Crowd*. (Orig. 1874)

(4) *The Woodlanders*. (Orig. 1887)

Quote, pp. 262-63, is from here.

(5) *The Return of the Native*. (Orig. 1878)

(6) *The Mayor of Casterbridge*. (Orig. 1886)

(7) "[Tess] replies"; "we see Tess"; "asks little Abraham"

Tess of the d'Urbervilles. (Orig. 1891)

This is also listed in reading notes #20.

(8) *Jude the Obscure*. (Orig. 1895)

2 poss. eds. of the "Wessex novels," as indicated by the reading notes (B2j): Osgood, McIlvaine, 1895-96;+ OR Macmillan, 1902-03.+

Important Allusions:

(1) "[Hardy] has warned us" (p. 263):

Orig. in Preface to *Tess of the d'Urbervilles* (see above), 5th ed., 1892.

(2) "and, again" (p. 263):

Orig. in Preface to *Poems of the Past and the Present,* 1902. In Hardy, *Collected Poems*. Macmillan, 1920.

This is listed in Holleyman Addendum and is indicated by the reading notes (#20).

(3) Various Hardy characters:

Far from the Madding Crowd--Fanny Robin, Frank Troy, Bathsheba Everdene, Gabriel Oak, Jan Coggan, Henry Fray, Joseph Poorgrass; *Return of the Native*--Eustacia Vye, Damon Wildeve, Diggory Venn, Clym Yeobright; *Mayor of Casterbridge*--Michael Henchard, Lucetta Le Seur, Donald Farfrae, Mrs. ("Mother") Cuxson, Mrs. Susan Henchard, Richard Newson, Elizabeth Jane Newson; *Jude the Obscure*--Sue Bridehead, Richard Phillotson; *The Woodlanders*--Edred Fitzpiers, Marty South, Giles Winterbourne [*sic*; i.e., Winterborne]

Passing Allusions:

(1) Miscellaneous writers: Jane Austen, Charles Dickens, Gustave Flaubert, George Eliot, Henry James, George Meredith, Sir Walter Scott, William Shakespeare

(2) Various characters: Tolstoy, *War and Peace*--Natasha, Pierre; Thackeray, *Vanity Fair*--Becky Sharp

- -

THE NOVELS OF TURGENEV (I)--*TLS,* Dec. 14, 1933, pp. 885-86; repr. in *Yale Review* (w/var.), Dec. 1933, pp. 276-83; first collected in *C.D.B.* (text in *C.D.B.* and *C.E.* from *TLS*)   Reading notes #1

Inferred Source
(Woolf quotes often in French):

Isaac Pavlovsky, *Souvenirs sur Tourguéneff.* Paris: A. Savine, 1887.

This is listed in the reading notes.

Supportive Sources:

(1) "the brothers Goncourt wrote" (quote in French)

Edmond and Jules Goncourt, *Journal des Goncourts. Mémoires de la vie littéraire.* 9 vol. Paris: n.p., 1887-96.

(2) "Henry James noted"

James,"Ivan Turgenieff," *Atlantic Monthly,* 53 (Jan. 1884), 42-55; repr. in James, *Partial Portraits.* (Orig. 1888) Prob. ed.: Macmillan, 1889.

This is listed in Holleyman Addendum.

(3) Works by Turgenev (all are listed in the reading notes):

(a) *Rudin.* (Orig. 1855) Trans. by Constance Garnett, w/introduction by S. Stepniak [pseud.]. Heinemann, 1895.

This is indicated by the reading notes.+

English quote, p. 253, is from here.

(b) *Fathers and Children.* (Orig. 1862) Trans. by Constance Garnett, w/introduction by Edward Garnett. Heinemann, 1895.

This is indicated by the reading notes.+

(c) *Smoke.* (Orig. 1867) Trans. by Constance Garnett, w/introduction by Edward Garnett. Heinemann, 1896.

This is indicated by the reading notes.+

(d) *On the Eve.* (Orig. 1859) Trans. by Constance Garnett. W. Heinemann, 1895.

This is indicated by the reading notes+ and is listed in Holleyman; it belonged to Leonard Woolf.

(e) *Virgin Soil.* (Orig. 1877) Trans. by Constance Garnett. W. Heinemann, 1896.

This is indicated by the reading notes.+

English quote, p. 249, and 2nd, 3rd and 4th quotes, p. 252, are from here.

(f) *A Lear of the Steppes.* (Orig. 1873) Trans. by Constance Garnet, w/introduction by S. Stepniak [pseud.]. Heinemann, 1898.

This is indicated by the reading notes.+

(g) *A House of Gentlefolk.* (Orig. 1859) Trans. by Constance Garnett. W. Heinemann, 1894.

This is indicated by the reading notes.+

Important Allusions:

Various Turgenev characters: *Fathers and Children*--Bazarov; *A House of Gentlefolk*--Lavretsky, Lisa; *Smoke*--Litvinov; *On the Eve*--Elena, Insarov; *Rudin*--Violetta

Passing Allusions:

(1) Various English characters: Dickens, *David Copperfield* (1850)--Micawber; Dickens, *Martin Chuzzlewit* (1844)--Pecksniff; Thackeray, *Vanity Fair* (1848)--Becky Sharp

(2) Emily Brontë, *Wuthering Heights.* (Orig. 1847)

(3) Thomas Hardy, *The Return of the Native.* (Orig. 1878)

(4) Herman Melville, *Moby Dick.* (Orig. 1851)

- -

THE OBSTINATE LADY (CW)--*TLS,* May 1, 1919

  Obvious Source
  (stated in *TLS* with essay and in headnote):

    W[illiam] E[dward] Norris, *The Obstinate Lady.* Hut-
    chinson, [1919].

- -

THE OLD ORDER (I)--*TLS,* Oct. 18, 1917; first collected in
                D.M.

  Obvious Source
  (stated in *TLS* with essay and in footnote):

    Henry James, *The Middle Years,* edited by Percy Lub-
    bock. W. Collins, 1917.

  Important Allusion:

    Henry James, *Notes of a Son and Brother.* Macmillan,
    1914.

  Passing Allusions:

    (1) Nathaniel Hawthorne

    (2) Miscellaneous British writers mentioned by James:
        Matthew Arnold, Robert Browning, Thomas Carlyle,
        George Eliot, James Anthony Froude, Thomas Hux-
        ley, John Stuart Mill, Herbert Spencer

    (3) Mentioned by James: Alfred Lord Tennyson, *Locks-
        ley Hall.* (Orig. 1842)

- -

OLIVE SCHREINER (WW)--*New Republic,* March 18, 1925, p.
                103   Reading notes B2o

Obvious Source
(stated in *New Republic* with essay and in headnote):

> Olive Schreiner, *The Letters of ...* , *1876-1920,*
> edited by W. Cronwright Schreiner. T. Fisher Unwin,
> 1924.
>
> This is listed in the reading notes.

Supportive Source:

> Oliver Schreiner, *The Story of an African Farm.*
> (Orig. 1883) Prob. ed.: T. Fisher Unwin, 1924.
>
> This is listed in Holleyman Addendum.

Important Allusion:

> "the Brontë[s'] novels"

- -

OLIVER GOLDSMITH (I)--*TLS,* March 1, 1934, pp. 133-34;
                      first collected in *C.D.B.*
                      Reading notes at Yale U. (Beinecke
                      Library) and in #23 and B3d

Stated Source
(stated in *TLS* with essay, in footnote and in fifth paragraph):

> Oliver Goldsmith, *"The Citizen of the World" and "The
> Bee,"* w/introduction by Richard Church, edited by
> Austin Dobson. J.M. Dent, 1934. (Orig. 1762 and
> 1759, respectively)
>
> (See pp. 13-14 for actual edition[s] used, as indicated by reading notes [B3d].)

Supportive Sources (listed in reading notes [see pp. 11-16 above]):

> (1) Works by Goldsmith:
>
>> (a) *An Enquiry into the Present State of Polite
>>   Learning.* (Orig. 1759)
>>
>>   Quotes, pp. 106, 107, 108, and one on pp.
>>   111-12, are from here.
>>
>> (b) *She Stoops to Conquer.* (Orig. 1773)
>>
>> (c) "[Goldsmith] replied" (p. 109)
>>
>>   Preface to his *Essays.* (Orig. 1765)

(d) *The Vicar of Wakefield.* (Orig. 1766)

> First quotes, pp. 111 and 112, respectively, are from here.

(e) "[Goldsmith] exclaimed" (2nd quote, p. 112)

> *The Deserted Village.* (Orig. 1770)

(f) "poetry ... that ... crystallizes itself" (3rd quote, p. 112)

> *Retaliation.* (Orig. 1774)

(g) *The Traveller.* (Orig. 1765)

> 4th and last quotes, p. 112, are from here.

See discussion, above, under "The Reading Notes" (pp. 11-16), for edition of Goldsmith used by Woolf: *The Miscellaneous Works of,* edited by James Prior. 4 vol. Murray, 1837.

(2) "open Boswell"

> James Boswell, *The Life of Samuel Johnson, LL.D.,* edited by James Birkbeck Hill. 6 vol. Oxford: Clarendon, 1887. (Orig. 1791)
>
> This is indicated by the reading notes+ (B3d and Yale).

Passing Allusions:

(1) Miscellaneous writers: William Hazlitt, Charles Lamb, Michel de Montaigne, Lady Pembroke (Mary Sidney), Philip Sidney

(2) Mentioned by Goldsmith in *The Vicar of Wakefield*:

    (a) "'Barbara Allen'" (17th-century ballad)

    (b) "Johnny Armstrong's last good night"

>   "Johnie Armstrong" (16th-century ballad)

- -

OLIVER WENDELL HOLMES (IV)--*TLS,* Aug. 26, 1909, pp. 305-06; first collected in *G.R.* Reading notes "Holograph ..., Jan. 1909-March 1911" (Berg)+

Obvious Source
(stated in *TLS* with essay):

> Lewis W. Townsend, *Oliver Wendell Holmes.* Headley, 1909.

5th quote, p. 45, is from here.

Supportive Sources:

> (1) John Torrey Morse, *Life and Letters of Oliver Wendell Holmes*. 2 vol. Sampson Low, 1896.
>
> This is listed in Holleyman; it belonged to Leslie Stephen.
>
> Specific quotes from:
>
> (a) 2nd quote, p. 45
>
> (b) 3rd quote, p. 45; there should be ellipses before "had"
>
> (c) Quotes 4, 6-9, p. 45
>
> > Holmes, autobiographical notes (in MS); 9th quote contains phrase from John Milton, *Paradise Lost* (orig. 1667)
>
> (d) Quote, top of p. 46; "this" should read "the"
>
> > Autobiographical notes, *ibid*.
>
> (2) First quote, p. 45
>
> Cannot locate
>
> (3) "Two friends have put together a picture of him" (p. 46; quoted by Townsend)
>
> (a) 2nd and 4th quotes: David Macrae, *The Americans at Home*. (Orig. 1870)
>
> (b) 3rd quote: Mary Russell Mitford, *Recollections of a Literary Life*. (Orig. 1852)
>
> (4) Oliver Wendell Holmes, *The Autocrat of the Breakfast-Table*, w/introduction by Leslie Stephen. Macmillan, 1903. (Orig. 1858)
>
> This is indicated by the reading notes.+

Important Allusions:

> (1) "Such questions as Lowell conceived" (p. 44)
>
> James Russell Lowell, "On a Certain Condescension in Foreigners," in *My Study Windows*. (Orig. 1871)

2 eds are listed in Holleyman; they belonged to Leslie Stephen:

(a) Sampson Low, Marston, 1871.

(b) 17th ed. Houghton, Mifflin, 1882.

(2) "Hawthorne rapped out" (p. 44)

Nathaniel Hawthorne, *Our Old Home.* (Orig. 1863)

(3) Works by Holmes:

(a) *The Professor at the Breakfast-Table.* (Orig. 1860) In *The Works of.* Riverside Ed. 13 vol. Sampson, Low, 1891-92. Vol. II.

This is indicated by the reading notes.+

(b) *The Poet at the Breakfast-Table.* (Orig. 1872)

(c) "the two novels"

(i) *Elsie Venner.* (Orig. 1861)

This is listed in the reading notes.

(ii) *The Guardian Angel.* (Orig. 1867)

Passing Allusions:

Miscellaneous writers: Henry James, Alexander Pope, William Shakespeare

- -

ON BEING ILL (IV)--*New Criterion,* Jan. 1926, pp. 32-45; repr. in *Forum* (w/var.), Apr. 1926, pp. 582-90, and as pamphlet (w/var.) by Hogarth, 1930; first collected in *M.* (text in *M.* and *C.E.* from pamphlet) Reading notes #18

Supportive Source:

Augustus Hare, *The Story of Two Noble Lives.* 3 vol. George Allen, 1893. (Orig. 1891)

This is indicated by the reading notes.+

Important Allusions:

(1) Thomas DeQuincey, *Confessions of an English Opium Eater.* (Orig. 1821)

(2) Edward Gibbon, *The History of the Decline and Fall of the Roman Empire.* (Orig. 1776-88)

(3) Henry James, *The Golden Bowl.* (Orig. 1904)

(4) Gustave Flaubert, *Madame Bovary.* (Orig. 1857)

(5) Quotes, p. 199:

    (a) First 2 lines: John Milton, *Comus*. (Orig. publ. 1637)

    (b) Second 2 lines: Percy Bysshe Shelley, *Prometheus Unbound*. (Orig. 1820)

(6) "Lamb's letters" (quote, p. 200)

    Charles Lamb to Bernard Barton, July 25, 1829; repr. in Lamb, *The Letters of ...* , edited by Alfred Ainger. (Orig. 1888) Prob. ed.: 2 vol. Macmillan, 1904.

    This is listed in Holleyman.

(7) "open Rimbaud"

    Arthur Rimbaud, "O Saisons, o chateaux," in Rimbaud, *Derniers Vers*. (Orig. 1872) Prob. ed.: in Rimbaud, *Oeuvres de ... vers et proses*. Paris: Mercure de France, n.d. [c. 1912].

    This is listed in Holleyman.

(8) William Shakespeare, *Antony and Cleopatra*. (Orig. publ. 1623)

Passing Allusions:

    (1) William Shakespeare, *King Lear*. (Orig. 1608)

    (2) William Shakespeare, *Macbeth*. (Orig. publ. 1623)

    (3) Miscellaneous writers: William Beckford, James Boswell, Jean de La Bruyère, Samuel Coleridge, John Donne, Thomas Hardy, John Keats, Stephane Mallarmé, Samuel Pepys, Marcel Proust

- -

ON NOT KNOWING GREEK (I)--date unknown; first published
in *C.R. I*   Reading notes
#s19, 25 and B2d, B2o

Supportive Sources:

    (1) Euripides, *The Bacchae,* edited by R.Y. Tyrrell. Macmillan, 1897. (Orig. 5th cent. B.C.)

    This is indicated by the reading notes+ (#19) and is listed in Holleyman; it belonged to Thoby Stephen.

(2) Sophocles, *Electra*, trans. by Richard C. Jebb.
2 eds. are listed in Holleyman and Holleyman Addendum. respectively:

(a) In *The Tragedies of*. Cambridge: University
Pr., 1904. (Orig. 5th cent. B.C.)
This belonged to Virginia.

(b) In *The Plays and Fragments of*. 7 vol. Cambridge: University Pr.,+ 1882-1900. Vol. VI.
This belonged to Leonard.
English quotes, pp. 1, 4, 5 and 12 are from
here.

(3) Sophocles, *Antigone*. In *ibid*. ([a] or [b--(Vol.
III)].+ (Orig. 5th cent. B.C.)
This is indicated by the reading notes (#19, B2o).

(4) Aeschylus, *Agamemnon*. (Orig. 4th cent. B.C.)
This is listed in the reading notes (#25).

(5) Plato, *Dialogues*, edited by Benjamin Jowett. 4
vol. Oxford: Clarendon, 1871. (Orig. 4th cent.
B.C.)

This is indicated by the reading notes (B2o) and
is listed in Holleyman Addendum; it belonged to
Leslie Stephen.

Specific dialogues referred to: "Protagoras" (p.
8), "The Symposium" (p. 9; see next item)

(6) "Shelley takes twenty-one words in English to
translate"

The Banquet of Plato, trans. by Percy Bysshe
Shelley. (Orig. publ. 1840)   Prob. ed.: In Shelley, *Prose Works* ... , edited by R.H. Shephard.
St. Martin's Library, 1912.

This is listed in the reading notes (B2d) and
in Holleyman; it belonged to Virginia.

Quotes, p. 9, are also from here; according to
Shelley, "this wonderful fellow's head" should
read "the wonderful head of this fellow."

(7) "Professor MacKail"

J.W. MacKail, editor and trans., *Select Epigrams
from the Greek Anthology*. New ed. Longmans,
1907. (Orig. 1890; for *Greek Anthology*, see
"Jack Mytton.")

This is listed in Holleyman.

2 quotes, bottom of p. 10, are from here:

(a) Simonides, "On the Lacadaemonian Dead at
Plataea." (Orig. 479 B.C.)

    (b) Simonides, "On the Athenian Dead at Plataea."
    (Orig 479 B.C.) "Greece" should read "Hel-
    las."

(8) Homer, *The Odyssey*. (Orig. 10th cent. B.C.)

This is listed in the reading notes (#25).

Important Allusions:

(1) Jane Austen, *Emma*. (Orig. 1816)

(2) Geoffrey Chaucer, *The Canterbury Tales*. (Orig.
1387-94)

(3) William Shakespeare, *King Lear*. (Orig. 1607)

Passing Allusions:

Miscellaneous writers: Joseph Addison, Aristophanes,
Fyodor Dostoevsky, George Eliot, Henry Fielding,
Thomas Hardy, George Meredith, William Morris, Wil-
frid Owen, Jean Racine, Sappho, Siegfried Sassoon,
William Makepeace Thackeray, Thucydides, Francois
Arouet de Voltaire, William Wycherley

- -

ON RE-READING MEREDITH (I)--*TLS,* July 25, 1918, p. 347;
                          first collected in *G.R.*

Obvious Source
(stated in *TLS* with essay and in footnote):

J.H.E. Crees, *George Meredith: A Study of His Works
and Personality*. B.H. Blackwell, 1918.

Supportive Sources (mentioned by Crees):

Works by Meredith:

(1) *The Ordeal of Richard Feverel*.   (Orig. 1859)

(2) 2 quotes, bottom of p. 235 (quoted also by Crees):

    (a) George Meredith to Frederick A. Maxse, [Dec.
    28, 1865]

    (b) Same to same, Sept. 22, 1887; should read
    "sheer Realism, breeder at best of the dung-
    fly!" (misquoted by Crees)

Both letters repr. in *Letters of George Meredith.*

(See "George Eliot.")

(3) *The Tragic Comedians.* (Orig. 1880)

(4) *The Egoist.* (Orig. 1879)

Important Allusions:

(1) Works by Meredith (mentioned by Crees):

(a) *The Shaving of Shagpat.* (Orig. 1855)

(b) *Modern Love.* (Orig. 1862)

(c) *Love in the Valley.* (Orig. 1851)

(2) Ivan Turgenev, *Fathers and Sons.* (Orig. 1862)

(3) Leo Tolstoy, *War and Peace.* (Orig. 1868)

(4) Fyodor Dostoevsky, *Crime and Punishment.* (Orig. 1867)

Passing Allusions:

(1) Various Meredith characters: *Diana of the Crossways* (1885)--Diana [Warwick]; *The Egoist*--Willoughby Patterne, Clara Middleton, Vernon Whitford

(2) Miscellaneous English writers: Charles Dickens, John Donne, George Eliot, William Shakespeare, William Makepeace Thackeray

- -

ON RE-READING NOVELS (II)--*TLS,* July 20, 1922, pp. 465-66;
                         first collected in *M.* (w/var.)
                         Reading notes #26

Stated Impulse
(stated in *TLS* with essay and mentioned in first paragraph):

"So there are to be new editions of Jane Austen and the Brontës and George Meredith"

(1) *The Novels of Jane Austen,* w/illus. by G.C.E. Brock. 5 vol. J.M. Dent, 1922.

(2) *The Novels of Charlotte, Emily and Anne Brontë.* 6 vol. J.M. Dent, 1922.

Woolf specifically mentions *Jane Eyre* (orig. 1847).

(3) *The Works of George Meredith.* 19 vol. Constable, 1922.

Woolf specifically mentions *The Adventures of Harry Richmond* (orig. 1871) and *The Egoist* (orig. 1879).

Obvious Source
(stated in *TLS* with essay):

Percy Lubbock, *The Craft of Fiction.* Jonathan Cape, 1921.

This is listed in Holleyman Addendum and in the reading notes.

Important Allusions:

(1) Mentioned by Lubbock (see above):

   (a) Gustave Flaubert, *Un Coeur Simple.* (Orig. 1877)

   (b) Marie Madeleine Motier, Countess de La Fayette, *La Princesse de Clèves.* (Orig. 1678)

   (c) Henry James, *The Ambassadors.* (Orig. 1903)

   (d) Samuel Richardson, *Clarissa Harlowe.* (Orig. 1747-48)

   (e) Henry James, *The Wings of the Dove.* (Orig. 1902)

(2) William Shakespeare, *Macbeth.* (Orig. 1609)

(3) Sophocles, *Antigone.* (Orig. 5th cent. B.C.)

Passing Allusions:

(1) Miscellaneous writers:

   (a) Mentioned by Lubbock (see above): Honoré de Balzac, Fyodor Dostoevsky, Sir Walter Scott, Leo Tolstoy

   (b) Joseph Conrad, Thomas Hardy, John Keats, Thomas Babington Macaulay, Marcel Proust, Daniel Defoe

(2) William Makepeace Thackeray, *Vanity Fair.* (Orig. 1847-48)

(3) George Moore, *Esther Waters*. (Orig. 1894)

(4) Charles Dickens, *David Copperfield*. (Orig. 1850)

- -

ONE IMMORTALITY (CW)--*TLS,* Feb. 4, 1909, p. 42

Obvious Source
(stated in *TLS* with essay and in headnote):

   H[arold] Fielding Hall, *One Immortality*. Macmillan,
   1909.

Important Allusion:

   "Mr William Watson's feeling"

   William Watson, "World-Strangeness." (Orig. publ.
   1890) Prob. ed.: Watson, *Selected Poems*. London,
   N.Y.: John Lane, 1903.

   This is listed in Holleyman Addendum.

- -

PAPERS ON PEPYS (BP)--*TLS,* Apr. 4, 1918, p. 161

Obvious Source
(stated in *TLS* with essay and in footnote):

   *Occasonal Papers Read by Members at Meetings of the
   Samuel Pepys Club,* Vol. I, 1903-14, edited by Henry
   B. Wheatley. London: n.p. [Chiswick Pr.], 1917.

Supportive Sources:

   (1) Specific papers quoted from:

      (a) Henry B. Wheatley, "The Growth of the Fame
          of Samuel Pepys," pp. 156-73.

          Quotes, p. 39, are from here.

      (b) D'Arcy Power, "Why Samuel Pepys Discontinued
          His Diary," pp. 64-77.

          Quote, p. 42, is from here.

(2) "the Diary"

    Poss. ed.: Samuel Pepys, *Diaries and Correspondence,* edited by Richard Lord Braybrooke. (Orig. 1825) 6th ed. H.G. Bohn, 1848.

    This is listed in Holleyman; it belonged to Leslie Stephen.

Important Allusions:

    Specific papers mentioned but not quoted from:

    (1) on "Pepys's portraits"

        (a) Lionel Cust, "Notes on the Portraits of Samuel Pepys," pp. 15-35.

        (b) Samuel Pepys Cockerell, "Notes on Some Distinctive Features in Pepys's Portraits," pp. 36-40.

    (2) on "Pepys's stone"

        D'Arcy Power, "Who Performed Lithotomy on Mr. Samuel Pepys?" pp. 58-63.

    (3) on "Pepys's ballads"

        Frank Sidgwick, "The Pepys Ballads," pp. 47-57.

    (4) on "Pepys's health"

        D'Arcy Power, "The Medical History of Mr. and Mrs. Samuel Pepys," pp. 178-93.

    (5) on "Pepys's musical instruments"

        Sir Frederick Bridge, "Musical Instruments Mentioned by Pepys," pp. 104-08.

Passing Allusions:

    (1) Samuel Pepys, "Beauty Retire" (1665; a song with melody by Pepys, words by Sir William Davenant in his masque *The Siege of Rhodes* [1661])

        [Cf. Henry B. Wheatley, "Davenant's Operas ... " in *Occasional Papers* (above), pp. 130-43.]

    (2) Quote, p. 40

        Cannot locate

- -

THE PARK WALL (CW)--*TLS,* Aug. 31, 1916, p. 415

Obvious Source
(stated in *TLS* with essay and in headnote):

    Elinor Mordaunt, *The Park Wall.* Cassell, 1916.

- -

THE PASTONS AND CHAUCER (III)--date unknown; first pub-
                             lished in *C.R. I*   Read-
                             ing notes B2d, B2o, B2q

Stated Source
(stated in footnote and in third paragraph from end):

  "The four thick volumes"

    The Paston Letters, edited by James Gairdner. 4 vol.
    Westminster: Archibald Constable, 1904 [*sic;* i.e.,
    1900-01].

    Actual editions used, as indicated by reading notes
    (B2d, B2q): New Ed. 3 vol. Annotated Reprints ser.
    Edward Arber, 1870-75;+ and New and Complete Library
    Ed. 6 vol. Chatto and Windus, 1904. Both were
    edited by Gairdner.

    Specific items quoted from:

    (1) 2 quotes, top of p. 1

        "Will of Sir John Fastolf," Nov. 3, 1459

    (2) Middle of p. 3

        "Sir John Fastolf's Wardrobe," 1459

    (3) 3 quotes, bottom of p. 4

        (a) Agnes Paston to John Paston [Sr.], 1458(?)

        (b) Same as (1), above

        (c) Cannot locate

    (4) 2 quotes, middle of p. 5

        (a) John Paston [Jr.] to Sir John Paston, [May]
            1469

        (b) John Paston [Sr.] to Margaret Paston *et al.,*
            [Jan. 15], 1465

(5) P. 9

Sir John Paston to John Paston [Jr.], March 1467

(6) 2 quotes, p. 7

   (a) Margaret Paston to Sir John Paston, July 11,
       1467; "though" should be in brackets

   (b) Margaret Paston to John Paston [Jr.], Nov.
       29, 1471; "of" should read "upon"

(7) Middle of p. 15

Sir John Paston to Margaret Paston, Feb. 21, 1475

(8) Bottom of p. 15

John Paston [Jr.] to Sir John Paston, July 8,
1472

(9) 2 quotes, p. 16

   (a) Margaret Paston to Sir John Paston, May 27,
       1478

   (b) Agnes Paston to John Paston [Sr.], 1451

(10) Pp. 16-17

Cecily Dawne to Sir John Paston, Nov. 3, 1463(?)

(11) 4 quotes, p. 17

   (a) Margaret Paston to John Paston [Sr.], Aug.
       18, 1465

   (b) Margaret Paston to Sir John Paston, June 5,
       1472; there should be ellipses between
       "bushes" and "and"

   (c) Same to same, March 12, 1469; "haste" should
       read "rape" [old definition: "haste"]

   (d) Margaret Paston to John Paston [Jr.], Nov.
       5, 1471; "which" should be in brackets

Supportive Source:

Geoffrey Chaucer, *The Canterbury Tales*.   (Orig. 1387-
94)

2 eds., as indicated by the reading notes (B2q and
B2o, respectively): Vol. IV of *The Complete Works of
... Chaucer*, edited by Walter W. Skeat.   6 vol.   Ox-
ford: Clarendon, 1894-1900; and in *Works*, edited by
Alfred W. Pollard, *et al.*   Globe Ed.   Macmillan,
1898.+   This belonged to Leonard.

Specific quotes from (all are listed in the reading
notes [B2q]):

(1) P. 9

   "The Nun's Priest's Tale"

(2) First quote, p. 10

   "Prologue [description of the Prioress]"

(3) 2nd quote, p. 10

   "The Knight's Tale"

(4) 3rd quote, p. 10

   "The Physician's Tale"

(5) P. 11

   "Introduction" to "The Wife of Bath's Tale"

(6) First and 2nd quotes, p. 12

   "The Nun's Priest's Tale"

(7) 3rd and 4th quotes, p. 12

   "The Merchant's Tale"

(8) 5th and 6th quotes, p. 12

   "The Knight's Tale"

(9) Pp. 14, 15

   "The Clerk's Tale"

Important Allusions:

(1) First quote, p. 13

   William Wordsworth, "Elegaic Stanzas, Suggested by a Picture of Peele Castle." (Orig. 1805)

(2) 2nd quote, p. 13

   Samuel Taylor Coleridge, *The Rime of the Ancient Mariner.* (Orig. 1798)

Passing Allusions:

(1) Miscellaneous writers: Joseph Conrad, David Garnett, John Lydgate, John Masefield, Percy Bysshe Shelley, Laurence Sterne, Alfred Lord Tennyson

    (2) Various characters: Chaucer, "The Clerk's Tale"--
Griselda; Defoe, *The Fortunes ... of the Famous
Moll Flanders* (1722)--Moll Flanders

    (3) James Joyce, *Ulysses*. (Orig. 1922)

    (4) William Shakespeare, *King Lear*. (Orig. 1607)

    (5) William Shakespeare, *Romeo and Juliet*. (Orig.
1597)

- -

PATMORE'S CRITICISM (BP)--*TLS,* May 26, 1921, p. 331

Obvious Source
(stated in *TLS* with essay and in footnote):

    Coventry Patmore, *Courage in Politics and Other Es-
says,* edited by F. Page. Humphrey Milford, 1921.

Important Allusions:

    (1) Various works mentioned by Patmore:

        (a) Sir Thomas Browne, *Religio Medici*. (Orig.
1642)

        (b) Sir Thomas Browne, *Urne Burial*. (Orig. 1658)

        (c) Sir Thomas Browne, *Christian Morals*. (Orig.
publ. 1716)

        (d) Oliver Goldsmith, *The Vicar of Wakefield*.
(Orig. 1766)

        (e) Jane Austen, *Pride and Prejudice*. (Orig.
1813)

        (f) Anthony Trollope, *Barchester Towers*. (Orig.
1857)

        (g) Lucy Bethia Walford, *The Mischief of Monica*.
(Orig. 1891)

    (2) Miscellaneous English poets mentioned by Patmore:
William Blake, Samuel Taylor Coleridge, Thomas
Hardy, Percy Bysshe Shelley

    (3) Miscellaneous critics mentioned by Page (see
above): Aristotle, Samuel Taylor Coleridge, Wil-
helm von Goethe

Passing Allusions:

    (1) Samuel Johnson, *Lives of the English Poets*.
       (Orig. 1779-81)

    (2) Miscellaneous English poets: Alfred Lord Tennyson,
       William Wordsworth

    (3) Coventry Patmore, *The Angel in the House*. (Orig.
       1854)

- -

PERSONALITIES (II)--date unknown; first published in *M*.

Inferred Impulse:

    "the opinion of J.A. Symonds"; "Symonds continues"

    John Addington Symonds to Edmund Gosse, Feb. 16,
    1878; repr. in Horatio F. Brown, *John Addington Sy-
    monds*. (Orig. 1895) Prob. ed.: 2nd ed. Smith, El-
    der, 1903.

    This is listed in Holleyman; it belonged to Leslie
    Stephen.

Important Allusions:

    (1) "Keats's 'Love Letters'" (mentioned by Symonds)

       Letters of John Keats to Fanny Brawne, edited by
       H. Buxton Forman. (Orig. 1878)

    (2) Alfred Lord Tennyson, *In Memoriam*. (Orig. 1850)

    (3) George Eliot, *Middlemarch*. (Orig. 1872-73)

    (4) Charlotte Brontë, *Jane Eyre*. (Orig. 1847)

    (5) "Mrs. Humphry Ward points out" (p. 276)

       [Mary Augusta] Ward, intro. to *Jane Eyre*, in *The
       Life and Works of Charlotte Brontë and Her Sis-
       ters*. 7 vol. Clement K. Shorter, 1899, 1900.
       Vol. I.

    (6) Miscellaneous writers: Aeschylus,
       Jane Austen, Thomas Hardy, Sappho, William
       Shakespeare, Laurence Sterne

- -

PHASES OF FICTION (II)--*Bookman,* Apr., pp. 123-32, May,
                            pp. 269-79, and June, pp. 404-17,
                            1929; first collected in *G.R.*
                            Reading notes #s13, 14, 25 and B2n

Supportive sources (star means item listed in the reading notes):

(1) Daniel Defoe, *Moll Flanders.*   (Orig. 1722)

(2) Daniel Defoe, *Robinson Crusoe.*   (Orig. 1719)

(3) Daniel Defoe, *Roxana,* edited by R. Brimley John-
    son. Abbey Classics ser. Simpson, Marshall,
    Hamilton, Kent, [1926]. This is indicated by
    the reading notes+ (#25) and is listed in Holley-
    man Addendum.

(4) "W[illiam] E[dward] Norris"

    E.g., Norris, *The Triumphs. of Sara.* Hutchin-
    son, 1920. (*#25) Woolf reviewed this for *TLS,*
    March 4, 1920, p. 153. (See "Mr. Norris's Meth-
    od.")

(5) Guy de Maupassant, *Boule de suif.*   (Orig. 1879)

(6) Lady Violet Greville, *Vignettes of Memory.* Hut-
    chinson, 1927.

(7) "the Barchester novels"

    E.g., Anthony Trollope, *Barchester Towers.*
    (Orig. 1857) Collins Clear-Type Pr., n.d.   This
    is indicated by the reading notes+ (#25).

(8) Sir Walter Scott, *The Bride of Lammermoor.*
    (Orig. 1819) In Scott, *Tales of My Landlord,* 3rd
    series. 4 vol. Edinburgh: Constable, 1819.
    Vols. I and II. This is indicated by the reading
    notes+ (#25).

(9) Robert Louis Stevenson, *The Master of Ballantrae.*
    (Orig. 1889) (*#25) In quote, "Durisdeer"
    should read "Durrisdeer."

(10) Ann Radcliffe, *The Mysteries of Udolpho.* 4 vol.
     Robinson, 1794, 1795. This is indicated by the
     reading notes+ (#s14, 25 and B2n) and is listed
     in Holleyman; it belonged to Leslie Stephen.

(11) Charles Dickens, *Bleak House.* (Orig. 1853) In
     The Works of. Authentic Ed. 22 vol. Chapman
     and Hall, 1901-[06]. Vol. XI. This is indicated
     by the reading notes+ (#14 and B2n).

(12) Jane Austen, *Pride and Prejudice.* (Orig. 1813)
     Everyman's Edition, 1906. This is indicated by
     the reading notes+ (B2n) and is listed in Holley-
     man.

(13) George Eliot, *Silas Marner*.   (Orig. 1861)   (*#25)

(14) Henry James, *What Maisie Knew*. Heinemann, 1898. This is indicated by the reading notes (14).

(15) Marcel Proust, *A la Recherche du Temps Perdu*, trans. by C.K. Scott Moncrieff. (Orig. 1914-27) Chatto and Windus. This is indicated by the reading notes: (a) *Swann's Way*. 3 vol. 1922.+ (#sl3, 14); (b) *Guermantes Way*. 2 vol. 1925+ (#14).

(16) Fyodor Dostoevsky, *The Possessed*, trans. by Constance Garnett. Heinemann, 1916. This is indicated by the reading notes+ (#14 and B2n).

(17) Thomas Love Peacock, *Crotchet Castle*. (Orig. 1831) Oxford U. Pr., 1924. This is indicated by the reading notes+ (#14).

(18) Laurence Sterne, ... *Tristram Shandy*. (Orig. 1759) In *Works*. 4 vol. Johnson, 1808. Vols. I and II. This is indicated by the reading notes+ (#14).

Quote, p. 94, is from here.

(19) Emily Brontë, *Wuthering Heights*. (Orig. 1847)

(20) Leo Tolstoy, *War and Peace*, trans. by Constance Garnett. (Orig. 1868) Heinemann, 1904. This is indicated by the reading notes+ (#sl3, 25).

Characters, p. 74, are from here.

Important Allusions:

(1) "the reality that Maupassant brings" (quotes, p. 61)

Guy de Maupassant, "Histoire d'une Fille de Ferme." (*#25) Prob. ed.: In Maupassant, *La Maison Tellier*. (See below)

(2) Jonathan Swift, *Gulliver's Travels*. (Orig. 1726)

(3) Guy de Maupassant, *La Maison Tellier*. (Orig. 1881)

(4) George Meredith, *The Ordeal of Richard Feverel*. (Orig. 1859)

(5) Thomas Hardy, *Far from the Madding Crowd*. (Orig. 1874)

(6) Herman Melville, *Moby Dick*. (Orig. 1851) Cape, 1928. This is indicated by the reading notes+ (#14) and is listed in Holleyman Addendum.

Passing Allusions:

(1) Miscellaneous writers: George Borrow, Robert
Browning, Henry Fielding, Anatole France, George
Gissing, John Lydgate, Samuel Richardson, William
Shakespeare, Percy Bysshe Shelley, Edmund Spen-
ser, William Makepeace Thackeray, Francois Arouet
de Voltaire

(2) Various characters: David Copperfield, Micawber
(Dickens, *David Copperfield* [1850]); Mrs. Gamp
(Dickens, *Martin Chuzzlewit* [1844]); Mrs. Prou-
die (Trollope, *Barchester Towers, Doctor Thorne*
[1858], *Framley Parsonage* [1861], *The Small
House at Allington* [1864; listed in reading notes
B2n], *The Last Chronicle of Barset* [1867]);
Becky Sharp (Thackeray, *Vanity Fair* [1848]); Mr.
Slope (Trollope, *Barchester Towers, Framley Par-
sonage*)

(3) George Eliot, *Middlemarch*. (Orig. 1871-72)

(4) [Mary Augusta] Ward, *Robert Elsmere*. (Orig. 1888)

(5) Harriet Beecher Stowe, *Uncle Tom's Cabin*. (Orig.
1851)

(6) Jane Austen, *Emma*. (Orig. 1816)

(7) Thomas Gray, *Elegy Written in a Country Church-
yard*. (Orig. 1751)

(8) George Gordon, Lord Byron, *Don Juan*. (Orig. 1819-
24)

- -

PHILOSOPHY IN FICTION (CW)--*TLS,* Jan. 10, 1918, p. 18

Obvious Source
(stated in *TLS* with essay and in headnote):

L[awrence] P[earsall] Jacks, *Writings by* ... 6 vol.
Williams and Norgate, 1916-17.

(Individual volumes: *Mad Shepherds, From the Human
End, Philosophers in Trouble, The Country Air, All
Men Are Ghosts, Among the Idolmakers*)

Important Allusions:

(1) "A Grave Digger's Scene" [*sic*]

I.e., "A Gravedigger Scene" in *Mad Shep-herds* (orig. 1910) and *The Country Air* (orig. 1917)

(2) "Farmer Perryman's Tall Hat" in *Mad Shepherds* and *The Country Air*

(3) "Father Jeremy and His Ways" in *All Men Are Ghosts* (orig. 1913) and *The Country Air*

(4) "The [portrait] of ... Peter Rodright"

"Made Out of Nothing" in *Among the Idolmakers* (orig. 1912)

(5) "the study of Snarley Bob in *Mad Shepherds*"

E.g., "Snarley Bob on the Stars"; "Snarley Bob's Invisible Companion"; "The Death of Snarley Bob" and *passim.*

(6) Quote, pp. 69-70

Cannot locate

(7) "The Professor's Mare" in *All Men Are Ghosts*

(8) "Piecraft is trying to live in two worlds"

E.g.,"Dr. Piecraft Becomes Confused" in *All Men Are Ghosts.*

(9) "The Castaway" in *Among the Idolmakers*

- -

PLEASANT STORIES (CW)--*TLS,* Dec. 16, 1920, p. 854

Obvious Source
(stated in *TLS* with essay and in headnote):

Joseph Hergesheimer, *The Happy End.* William Heinemann, 1920.

Important Allusions:

(1) First quote, p. 115

Dedication to *The Happy End*

   (2) Specific stories

      (a) Second quote, p. 115

         "The Flower of Spain"

      (b) "Bread"

Passing Allusions:

   (1) John Keats, "The Eve of St. Agnes." (Orig. 1820)

   (2) Anton Tchehov

- -

POE'S HELEN (IV)--*TLS,* Apr. 5, 1917, p. 162; first col-
            lected in *G.R.*

Obvious Source
(stated in *TLS* with essay and in footnote):

   Caroline Ticknor, *Poe's Helen*. John Lane, 1917.

Supportive Source:

   "Professor Woodberry thinks" (quoted by Ticknor)

   George Edward Woodberry, *The Life of Edgar Allan Poe,
   Personal and Literary*. 2 vol. Houghton, Mifflin,
   1909. Espec. Preface.

Important Allusions (mentioned by Ticknor):

   (1) "the love letters ... have already been pub-
       lished"

       *The Last Letters of Edgar Allan Poe to Sarah Hel-
       en Whitman,* edited by James A. Harrison, w/notes
       by Charlotte F. Dailey. N.Y.: G.P. Putnam's,
       1909.

   (2) Edgar Allan Poe, "To Helen." (His 2nd poem by
       that name; orig. written c. 1848)

   (3) Edgar Allan Poe, "The Raven." (Orig. 1845)

Passing Allusions (mentioned by Ticknor):

   (1) Miscellaneous writers: Ralph Waldo Emerson, Marg-
       aret Fuller, Percy Bysshe Shelley

(2) Various works mentioned by Harrison (see above):

   (a) "Letters of Abelard and Eloise"

> E.g., Petrus Abelardus, *Letters of Abelard
> and Heloise to Which Is Prefix'd, a Particu-
> lar Account of Their Lives, Amours, and Mis-
> fortunes ...* (Orig. English trans. 1718)

   (b) Elizabeth Barrett Browning, *Sonnets from the
   Portuguese.* (Orig. 1850)

- -

POSTSCRIPT OR PRELUDE? (CW)--*TLS,* Dec. 2, 1920, p. 795

Obvious Source
(stated in *TLS* with essay and in headnote):

> D.H. Lawrence, *The Lost Girl.* Martin Secker, 1920.

Important Allusions:

> Miscellaneous novelists: Arnold Bennett, Thomas Har-
> dy, George Meredith, Leo Tolstoy

- -

PRAETERITA (BP)--*T.P.'s Weekly,* Dec. 3, 1927; repr. in
              New Republic (w/var.), Dec. 28, 1927, pp.
              165-66 (text in *BP* from *New Republic*)
              Reading notes #14

Inferred Impulse
(stated in first paragraph):

> "an abridgement of 'Modern Painters' [has] lately
> ... been published"

> John Ruskin, *Modern Painters,* abridged and edited by
> A.J. Finberg. G. Bell, 1927.

Obvious Source:

> John Ruskin, *Praeterita: Outlines of Scenes and
> Thoughts Perhaps Worthy of Memory in My Past Life.*
> 3 vol. George Allen, 1899.

> This is listed in the reading notes.

Important Allusion:

> "the first volume of 'Modern Painters' [was written] before he was twenty-four" (i.e., orig. publ. 1843)

- -

THE PURSUIT OF BEAUTY (CW)--*TLS,* July 8, 1920, p. 437

Obvious Source
(stated in *TLS* with essay and in headnote):

> Joseph Hergesheimer, *Linda Condon.* William Heine-mann, 1920.

- -

QUEEN ADELAIDE (BP)--*TLS,* Jan. 13, 1916, p. 19

Obvious Source
(stated in *TLS* with essay and in footnote):

> Mary F. Sandars, *The Life and Times of Queen Adelaide.* Stanley Paul, 1915. (Queen Adelaide, 1792-1849, was the wife of William IV.)

Passing Allusions:

> Miscellaneous English novelists: Charles Dickens, George Eliot

- -

RAMBLING ROUND EVELYN (III)--*TLS,* Oct. 28, 1920, pp. 689-
90; first collected in
C.R. I (w/var.)

Obvious Source
(stated in *TLS* with essay):

> *The Early Life and Education of John Evelyn, 1620-1641,* edited by H. Maynard Smith. Oxford: Clarendon, 1920.

Supportive Sources:

(1) "In 1652 [in Diary]"; "In 1658, too"

> *The Diary of John Evelyn.* (Orig. publ. 1818)
> Prob. ed.: edited by William Bray. 2 vol. J.M.
> Dent, 1911.

> This is listed in Holleyman.

(2) "Pepys ... sums up our case"

> Samuel Pepys, *Diary.* Quote from Nov. 5, 1665.

> (See "Papers on Pepys.")

Important Allusions:

Various works by Evelyn:

(1) "a history of the Dutch war"

> Only the first part, *Navigation and Commerce,*
> was published. Benjamin Tooke, 1674.

(2) "a sincere and touching biography" of Margaret
Godolphin

> *The Life of Mrs. Godolphin,* edited by Samuel
> [Wilberforce], Bishop of Oxford. Chiswick, 1847.

Passing Allusions:

(1) William Shakespeare

(2) Alfred Lord Tennyson, *The Princess.* (Orig. 1847)

- -

READING (II)--1919; first published in *C.D.B.*   Reading
                 notes B2d

Supportive Sources:

(1) "Lady Fanshawe ... wrote"

> *The Memoirs of Lady Anne Fanshawe ...* Prob. ed.:
> Lane, 1907. (Orig. 1829; Lady Fanshawe's dates
> were 1600-72)

> Woolf reviewed this for *TLS,* July 26, 1907, p.
> 234.

(2) "Lucy Hutchinson ... writes"

Memoirs of the Life of Colonel Hutchinson ... to Which Is Prefixed the Life of Mrs. Hutchinson, Written by Herself. (Orig. 1806)

(3) "the Leghs ... at Lyme"

Lady Newton [Evelyn Legh], *The House of Lyme from Its Foundation to the End of the Eighteenth Century.* William Heinemann, 1917.

Woolf reviewed this for *TLS,* March 29, 1917, p. 150.

(4) "Froude says"

James Anthony Froude, *English Seamen in the Sixteenth Century.* (Orig. 1895) New ed. Longmans, Green, 1896.

This is indicated by the reading notes.+

Woolf reviewed a later edition for *TLS,* Dec. 12, 1918, p. 618.

(5) "[Richard] Hakluyt's book"

The Hakluyts' Principal Navigations, Voyages, Traffiques and Discoveries of the English Nation. (Orig. 1598-1600) Everyman ed. 8 vol. J.M. Dent; N.Y.: E.P. Dutton, 1907-08.

This is indicated by the reading notes Vols. II and III are listed in Holleyman Addendum.

(6) Sir Thomas Browne, *Vulgar Errors [Pseudodoxia Epidemica].* (Orig. 1646)

(7) Sir Thomas Browne, *Religio Medici.* (Orig. 1642) In *Works.*

(See "The Elizabethan Lumber Room.")

This is indicated by the reading notes.+

Quotes, pp. 27-29, are from here.

(8) Miguel de Cervantes, *Don Quixote de la Mancha.* (Orig. 1605) Prob. ed.: trans. w/introduction and notes by John Ormsby. 4 vol. Smith, Elder, 1885.

This is listed in Holleyman; it belonged to Leslie Stephen.

(9) Sir Thomas Browne, *Urne Burial [Hydriotaphia]*.
(Orig. 1658) Prob. ed.: see "The Elizabethan
Lumber Room" under *Religio Medici*.

Important Allusions:

(1) "the Verneys"

During the Seventeenth Century, edited by Lady
Frances Parthenope Verney and Lady Margaret
Maria Verney. 2 vols. Longmans, Green, 1904.
(Orig. 1892, 1899, as *Memoirs of the Verney
Family* ...)
This is indicated by the reading notes+ (#19)
for "The Elizabethan Lumber Room," *q.v.*

(2) "the Pastons"

(See "The Pastons and Chaucer.")

(3) "Margaret, Duchess of Newcastle"

(See "The Duchess of Newcastle.")

(4) "Lord Herbert of Cherbury heard it"

Edward Herbert, Lord of Cherbury, *Autobiography
of* ... Prob. ed.: Edited by Sidney Lee. J.C.
Nimmo, 1886. (Orig. 1764; Lord Herbert's dates
were 1583-1648.)

This is listed in Holleyman.

(5) Quotes from Hakluyt [cf. "The Elizabethan Lumber
Room"]:

(a) P. 18: Richard Hakluyt, describing Master
Hore's voyage

(b) Top of p. 19: Sir Humphrey Gilbert, urging discovery of a Northwest Passage

(c) Bottom of p. 19: Anthony Jenkinson, describing Russia

(d) First quote, p. 20: William Hareborne's am-
bassage to Constantinople

(e) 2nd quote, p. 20: Letter from Sultan Murad
Can to Queen Elizabeth

Passing Allusions:

(1) Miscellaneous writers: Matthew Arnold, Robert
Burns, Geoffrey Chaucer, William Cowper, John
Dryden, Euripides, Edward Fitzgerald, Thomas

> Hardy, George Herbert, Homer, Ben Jonson, John
> Keats, Christopher Marlowe, Alexander Pope, Sir
> Walter Scott, William Shakespeare, Edmund Spen-
> ser, Horace Walpole, John Webster, William
> Wordsworth

(2) John Milton, *Paradise Lost*. (Orig. 1667)

- -

A REAL AMERICAN (CW)--*TLS,* Aug. 21, 1919, p. 446

Obvious Sources
(stated in *TLS* with essay and in headnote):

    (1) Theodore Dreiser, *Free and Other Stories*. N.Y.:
        Boni and Liveright, 1918.

    (2) Theodore Dreiser, *Twelve Men*. N.Y.: Boni and
        Liveright, 1919.

Important Allusions:

    Specific stories:

    (1) "Free" (orig. in *Sat. Eve. Post,* March 1918)

    (2) Quote, middle of p. 136:

        "Nigger Jeff" (orig. in *Ainslee's Magazine,* Nov.
        1901); there should be ellipses between "pathos"
        and "'I'll'"

Passing Allusions:

    (1) William Shakespeare

    (2) "One of these [12] men writes songs"

        I.e., Paul Dresser (1857-1911; Dreiser's brother)

- -

REFLECTIONS AT SHEFFIELD PLACE (I)--*New Statesman and Na-*
                                           tion, June 19, 1937,
                                           pp. 1001-03; first
                                           collected in *D.M.*
                                           Reading notes #6

Inferred Sources:

(1) "[Gibbon] reflected" (p. 124)

Edward Gibbon, *Miscellaneous Works. With Memoirs ... ; Illustrated from His Letters,* w/notes by John Lord Sheffield. 2 vols. Strahan, Cadell, and Davies, +1796.

This is indicated by the reading notes and is listed in Holleyman; it belonged to Leslie Stephen.

First 2 Gibbon quotes, p. 125, are also from here:

(a) Gibbon to Lord Sheffield, July 21, 1797

(b) Same to same, 1786-90, *passim;* "soft" always refers to the other daughter, Louise

(2) "Maria Holroyd observed"

The Girlhood of Maria Josepha Holroyd, Lady Stanley of Alderley. Recorded in Letters of a Hundred Years Ago ... , edited by J[ane[H. Adeane. Longmans, 1896.

This is listed in the reading notes.

Quotes from:

(a) "a girl saw"; "but" should be in brackets

Maria to Martha Sarah Holroyd, Sept. 1, 1786

(b) "[she] remarked" (last quote, p. 124); "person" should read "persons"; there should be ellipses after "walk"; "and" should be in brackets

Maria to Ann Firth, July 2, 1793

(c) "he could forecast" (p. 125)

Gibbon to Maria, Nov. 10, 1792

(d) *Re* Madame da Silva

Maria to Martha Sarah Holroyd, Dec. 9, 1791

(e) *Re* "Fred North and Mr. [Sylvester] Douglas"; "serious" and "trifling" should be reversed

Maria to Ann Firth, Oct. 1, 1793

(f) *Re* turtles (p. 125) and quote, top of p. 126

Same to same, Oct. 20, 1793, and Jan. 1, 1795

    (h) "Serena [Sarah Martha Holroyd] wrote to Maria"
        (p. 130)

        Jan. 17, 1794

  (3) "[Gibbon] wrote" (p. 127; 2 quotes, p. 129)

    (a) To Dorothea Gibbon, May 24, 1774

    (b) To Lord Sheffield, May 10, 1786

    (c) To same, Sept. 8, [1788]; "it might" should
        read "she might"

    All are repr. in *Memoirs* (see above)

  (4) First 3 quotes, p. 128 (*re* Hester Gibbon)

    Gibbon to Lord Sheffield, Aug. 7, 1790; repr. in
    Private Letters ... , edited by R.E. Prothero

    (See "The Historian and the Gibbon.")

  (5) 4th quote, p. 128, and quote, pp. 128-29 (*re* Cath-
    erine Porten)

    In *Memoirs* (see above)

Important Allusion:

  Edward Gibbon, *The History of the Decline and Fall
  of the Roman Empire.* (Orig. 1776-88)

  This is listed in the reading notes.

  (See "The Historian and the Gibbon.")

Passing Allusions:

  (1) "Marlowe's [line]" (quote, p. 124)

    Christopher Marlowe, *The Famous Tragedy of the
    Rich Jew of Malta:* II:[iii]:786. (Orig. 1633)
    In Marlowe, *Works,* edited by C.F. Tucker Brooke.
    Oxford: Clarendon, 1910.

    This is indicated by the reading notes and is
    listed in Holleyman Addendum.

  (2) Mentioned by Gibbon in *Memoirs:*

    (a) William Law

    (b) "*The Cavern of the Winds,* ... *the Palace of
        Felicity* ... [in] a favourite tale"

I.e., [Catherine La Mothe], *Historie d'Hypo-lite*. (Orig. 1699; first English trans. by "Aeneas Sylvius," 1708)

(c) "Pope's *Homer*"

(i) Homer, *The Iliad*, trans. by Alexander Pope. 6 vol. 1715-18, 1720.

(ii) Homer, *The Oydssey*, trans. by Alexander Pope. 5 vol. 1725-26.

(d) *The Arabian Nights*. (Orig. trans. into French in 18th cent.)

(3) Bertrand Russell

- -

THE REV. JOHN SKINNER (III)--date unknown;[*] first pub-lished in *C.R. II*

Inferred Source:

"the diary"

Journal of a Somerset Rector: John Skinner ... 1772-1839, edited by Howard Coombs and Arthur N. Bax. John Murray, 1930.

Passing Allusions (mentioned by Skinner):

(1) Miscellaneous writers: Diodorum [*sic;* i.e., Dio-dorus] Siculus, Thomas Moore, Seneca, Tacitus

(2) Ptolemy (Claudius Ptolemaeus), *Geography*. (Orig. 2nd cent. A.D.)

[*] Presumably written about the time of "All About Books" (1931), *q.v.*

- -

THE REV. WILLIAM COLE: A LETTER (III)--*New Statesman and Nation,* Feb. 6, 1932; first collect-ed in *D.M.* Reading notes #8

Obvious Source
(stated in *New Statesman and Nation* with essay):

The Blecheley Diary of the Rev. William Cole, ... 1765-67, edited by Francis Griffin Stokes, w/introduc-tion by Helen Waddell. Constable, 1931. [Woolf's spelling, Bletchley, is incorrect.]

Important Allusions:

(1) "when [Cole] went to Paris"

(See "All About Books.")

(2) Miscellaneous English writers: Jane Austen, Henry Fielding, Thomas Gray, John Skinner, Horace Walpole, James Woodforde

- -

REVIEWING (II)--Hogarth pamphlet, 1939; first collected in *C.D.B.*

Supportive Sources:

(1) *"Times History"*

History of the Times, 1785-1948. N.Y.: Macmillan; London: The Times, 1935-52.

According to Holleyman, the Woolfs had Vols. I-III and part of Vol. IV. (III and IV were published after Virginia's death.)

(2) "Thackeray ... said"

William Makepeace Thackeray to Captain Robert F. Atkinson, Dec. 27, 1858; orig. in *The Leisure Hour*, 1883 (a London periodical, 1852-99)

Henry Esmond was reviewed in *The Times,* Dec. 22, 1852. (Review mentioned in *History of the Times* [see above], Vol. II [1939].)

(3) Cannot locate

(a) "Dickens demanded"

(b) 2 footnoted items:

(i) advertisement (?) in *The New Statesman,* Apr. 1939

(ii) Harold Nicolson in *The Daily Telegraph,* March 1939

Important Allusion:

"according to Matthew Arnold"

Arnold, "The Study of Poetry"

(See "How It Strikes a Contemporary.")

Passing Allusions:

(1) William Shakespeare, *Hamlet*. (Orig. 1603)

(2) John Milton, *Paradise Lost*. (Orig. 1667)

(3) Miscellaneous writers: Jane Austen, Samuel Taylor Coleridge, John Keats, Michel de Montaigne, Alfred Lord Tennyson

- -

REVOLUTION (CW)--*TLS,* Jan. 27, 1921, p. 58

Obvious Source
(stated in *TLS* with essay and in headnote):

J[ohn] D[avys] Beresford, *Revolution*. W. Collins, 1921.

Important Allusions:

(1) Miscellaneous novelists: Thomas Hardy, Leo Tolstoy

(2) Various novels by Beresford:

(a) [*The Early History of*] *Jacob Stahl*. (Orig. 1911)

(b) *The House in Demetrius Road*. (Orig. 1914)

(c) *These Lynnekers*. (Orig. 1916)

- -

THE RIGHTS OF YOUTH (CW)--*TLS,* Sept. 19, 1918, p. 439

Obvious Source
(stated in *TLS* with essay and in headnote):

H.G. Wells, *Joan and Peter*. Cassell, 1918.

- -

ROBINSON CRUSOE (I)--*Nation and Athenaeum,* Feb. 6, 1926,
                    pp. 642-43; first collected in
                    C.R. II (w/var.)   Reading notes
                    #4 and B2p

Obvious Source:

Daniel Defoe, ... *Robinson Crusoe.*

2 eds, as indicated by the reading notes (#4 and B2p,
respectively):

(1) Stated in *Nation and Athenaeum* with essay:

The Life and Adventures of Robinson Crusoe;
Further Adventures of Robinson Crusoe; Serious
Reflections of Robinson Crusoe, w/introduction
by Charles Whibley. 3-vol. set. Constable,
1925. (Orig. 1719, 1719, 1720)

(2) Edited by Austin Dobson. Facsimile repr.
Elliot Stock, 1883.+

Important Allusion:

Daniel Defoe, ... *Moll Flanders.* (Orig. 1732)

Passing Allusions:

(1) Philip Sidney, *The Countess of Pembroke's Arca-*
dia. (Orig. 1593)

(2) Miscellaneous novelists: Jane Austen, Thomas
Love Peacock, Marcel Proust, Sir Walter Scott

(3) Thomas Hardy, *Jude the Obscure.* (Orig. 1895)

- -

ROMANCE AND THE HEART (CW)--*Nation and Athenaeum,* May 19,
                    1923, p. 229

Obvious Sources
(stated in *Nation and Athenaeum* with essay and in headnote):

(1) Romer Wilson [pseud. of Florence Roma Wilson],
The Grand Tour. Methuen, 1923.

(2) Dorothy Richardson, *Revolving Lights.* Duckworth, 1923.

Important Allusions:

(1) Henrik Ibsen

(2) Maggie Tulliver (in George Eliot, *The Mill on*
the Floss [1860])

Passing Allusions:

    Miscellaneous English writers: Geoffrey Chaucer,
Charles Dickens, John Donne, George Meredith

- -

A ROOM WITH A VIEW (CW)--*TLS,* Oct. 22, 1908, p. 362

    Obvious Source
(stated in *TLS* with essay and in headnote):

      E.M. Forster, *A Room with a View.* Edward Arnold,
1908

- -

ROYALTY (WW)--*Time and Tide,* Dec. 1, 1934, pp. 1533-34;
        first collected in *M.;* not in *C.E.*

    Obvious Source
(stated in *Time and Tide* with essay and mentioned in
first paragraph):

      Marie, Queen of Roumania, *The Story of My Life.* 3
vol. Cassell, 1934.

- -

RUPERT BROOKE (BP)--*TLS,* Aug. 8, 1918, p. 371

    Obvious Source
(stated in *TLS* with essay and in footnote):

      Rupert Brooke, *The Collected Poems of* ... , [w/"Mem-
oir" by Edward Marsh]. Sidgwick and Jackson, 1918.

    Important Allusions:

      Specific items from:

      (1) "in Mrs. Brooke's words"

         M[ary] R[uth] Brooke, p. ix

(2) "As Mrs. [Frances] Cornford says" (quoted by Marsh, p. xii)

(3) "[Brooke's] first book of poems"

Rupert Brooke, *Poems*. Sidgwick and Jackson, 1911.

(4) Rupert Brooke, "Town and Country." (Orig. c. 1910[?])

(5) Quote, bottom of p. 88

Marsh, p. xlii

(6) "as he said of himself" (p. 89)

Rupert Brooke to Edward Marsh, March 1914 (in MS); p. cxv

(7) "as he wrote" (p. 89)

Rupert Brooke to Frances Cornford, February 1911 (in MS); p. lvii

(8) 3rd quote, top of p. 89

Marsh, p. xlii

(9) Quote, middle of p. 89

Denis Browne to Edward Marsh, June 2, 1915 (in MS); p. clix

Passing Allusion:

John Donne

- -

RUSKIN (I)--date unknown; first published in *C.D.B.*

Supportive Sources:

(1) "according to Professor Norton" ("that" should be in brackets); "to quote Professor Norton again"

Charles Eliot Norton to G.W. Curtis, July 22, 1869; repr. in Norton, *Letters of ...* , edited by Sara Norton and M.A. DeWolfe Howe. Constable, 1930.

(2) John Ruskin, *Praeterita: Outlines of Scenes and Thoughts Perhaps Worthy of Memory in My Past Life.*

(See "Praeterita.")

Important Allusions:

Various works by Ruskin:

(1) *Modern Painters.* (Orig. 1843)

(2) *Fors Clavigera: Letters to the Workmen and Labourers of Great Britain.* (Orig. 1871-76)

(3) *Stones of Venice.* (Orig. 1851, 1853)

(4) *Sesame and Lilies.* (Orig. 1865)

Passing Allusions:

(1) Miscellaneous writers: Thomas Carlyle, Dante Alighieri (mentioned by Ruskin), Charles Darwin

(2) Edward Gibbon, *History of the Decline and Fall of the Roman Empire.* (Orig. 1776-88)

- -

THE RUSSIAN BACKGROUND (BP)--*TLS,* Aug. 14, 1919, p. 435

Obvious Source
(stated in *TLS* with essay and in footnote):

Anton Tchehov, *The Bishop and Other Stories,* trans. by Constance Garnett. Chatto and Windus, 1919.

Supportive Sources:

Specific stories:

(1) "The Steppe" (orig. 1888)

Quote, p. 127, is from here.

(2) Quote, p. 125

"The Murder" (orig. 1895)

- -

THE RUSSIAN POINT OF VIEW (I)--date unknown; first published in *C.R. I*

Supportive Sources:

(1) "Dr. Hagberg Wright finds"

In E[lena] Militsina and M[ikhail] Saltikov, *The
Village Priest and Other Stories,* trans. by Beatrice L. Tollemache, w/introduction by C. Hagberg Wright. T. Fisher Unwin, 1918.

Woolf reviewed this for *TLS,* Dec. 19, 1918, p.
641.

Quote, p. 239, is also from here: Militsina,
"The Village Priest."

(2) "Tchekov ... story after story"

(a) "The Lady with the Dog" (1899); in *The Lady
with the Dog and Other Stories,* trans. by
Constance Garnett. Chatto and Windus, 1917.

This is listed in Holleyman Addendum.

First quote, p. 240, is from here.

(b) "The Post" (1887); in *The Witch and Other
Stories,* trans. by Constance Garnett. Chatto and Windus, 1918.

Woolf reviewed this for *TLS,* May 16, 1918, p.
231.

2nd quote, p. 240, is from here.

(c) Quote, p. 241

Cannot locate

(d) "The Wife" (1892); in *The Wife and Other Stories,* trans. by Constance Garnett. Chatto
and Windus, 1918.

Woolf reviewed this for *TLS,* May 16, 1918, p.
231.

Quote, p. 242, is from here.

(3) Fyodor Dostoevsky, *The Brothers Karamazov.* (Orig.
1880) Poss. ed.: Trans. by Constance Garnett.
W. Heinemann, 1912.

This is listed in Holleyman; it belonged to Virginia.

(4) Fyodor Dostoevsky, *The Possessed*. (Orig. 1873) Poss. ed.: Trans. by Constance Garnett. W. Heinemann, 1913.

> This is listed in Holleyman; it belonged to Leonard.

(5) Leo Tolstoy, *War and Peace*. (Orig. 1864-69)

(6) Leo Tolstoy, *Family Happiness*. (Orig. 1859)

(7) Leo Tolstoy, *The Kreutzer Sonata*. (Orig. 1889-90)

Important Allusions:

Various characters:

(1) In Dostoevsky: *The Gambler* (1866)--Polina, Marquis de Grieux

> Woolf reviewed this (trans. by Constance Garnett. W. Heinemann, 1917) for *TLS*, Oct. 11, 1917, p. 489.

(2) In Tolstoy: *The Cossacks* (1863)--[Dimitri] Olenin; *Anna Karenina* (1873-77)--Pierre [Bezrakhov], [Konstantin] Levin

> Woolf reviewed *The Cossacks* (trans. by Louise and Aylmer Maude, World's Classics ser. [Oxford U. Pr., 1917]) for *TLS,* Feb. 1, 1917, p. 55.

Passing Allusions:

Miscellaneous writers: John Galsworthy, Henry James, William Shakespeare, George Bernard Shaw

- -

A RUSSIAN SCHOOLBOY (BP)--*TLS,* Nov. 8, 1917, p. 539

Obvious Source
(stated in *TLS* with essay and in footnote):

Serge Aksakoff, *A Russian Schoolboy,* trans. by J.D. Duff. Edward Arnold, 1917. (Orig. 1856 [*Recollections*] and 1858 [*Butterfly Collecting*])

Specific quotes from:

(1) Pp. 102-03; "is," 1. 3, should be in brackets; "the time" should read "that time"

(2) P. 103; first line should read "As before I took
my cat to bed with me; she was so attached to me
that ... "; line 5 needs no ellipses

Supportive Sources:

(1) "the previous volumes of this chronicle"

(a) *Years of Childhood,* trans. by J.D. Duff.
Edward Arnold, 1916. (Orig. 1858)

(b) *A Russian Gentleman,* trans. by J.D. Duff.
Edward Arnold, 1917. (Orig. 1856)

(2) Quote, pp. 101-02

Cannot locate

(3) "As Mr. Duff says" (quote, p. 103)

"Translator's Preface," *A Russian Schoolboy.*

Important Allusions:

(1) Fyodor Dostoevsky

(2) "[Aksakov] has been compared ... with Gilbert
White"   [Cf. "White's Selborne."]

Prince [Petr] Kropotkin, *Russian Literature.*
(Orig. 1905) Poss. ed.: 2nd ed. Duckworth,
1916.

- -

SARA COLERIDGE (III)--*New Statesman and Nation,* Oct. 26,
1940, pp. 418, 420; first collected
in *D.M.*   Reading notes B5b

Obvious Source
(stated in *New Statesman and Nation* with essay and in
footnote):

Earl Leslie Griggs, *Coleridge Fille: A Biography of
Sara Coleridge.* Oxford U. Pr., 1940.

Supportive Source (mentioned by Griggs):

"her autobiography"

Sara Coleridge, *Memoirs and Letters,* edited by Edith
Coleridge. 2 vol. H.S. King, 1873.

This is listed in the reading notes.

Quotes by Sara, pp. 222-23, are from here; "twelve or one" should read "twelve and one"; "never" should read "not"; there should be ellipses between "pocket" and "long"

Important Allusions:

(1) Quoted by Griggs (see above)

    (a) "Coleridge wrote" (p. 222)

        Samuel Taylor Coleridge to wife Sara Coleridge, Feb. 15, 1804; repr. in *Unpublished Letters of Samuel Taylor Coleridge,* edited by E.L. Griggs. 2 vol. Constable, 1932.

        Unpublished Letters is listed in the reading notes and in Holleyman Addendum.

    (b) "Hartley [Coleridge] wrote" (p. 223)

        Hartley Coleridge to Derwent Coleridge, Aug. 30, [1830]; repr. in *Letters of Hartley Coleridge,* edited by G.E. and E.L. Griggs. Oxford U. Pr., 1936.

    (c) "Wordsworth wrote" (p. 223)

        William Wordsworth to Thomas Poole, March 13, 1815; repr. in *The Letters of William and Dorothy Wordsworth. The Middle Years,* edited by E. Selincourt. 2 vol. Oxford: Clarendon, 1937.

    (d) "Lamb wrote" (p. 223)

        Charles Lamb to Bernard Barton, [Feb. 17, 1823]; repr. in *The Letters of Charles Lamb,* edited by E.V. Lucas. 3 vol. J.M. Dent and Methuen, 1935.

    (e) "as Mrs. Wordsworth called her" (p. 224)

        Mary Wordsworth to Henry Crabb Robinson, [Feb. 24, 1849]; repr. in *The Correspondence of Henry Crabb Robinson.* 2 vol. Oxford: Clarendon, 1927.

    (f) First quote, p. 226

        Sara Coleridge, unpublished diary

(g) 3rd quote, p. 226

Sara Coleridge, last line of untitled poem (in MS) *re* Samuel Taylor Coleridge's "Work Without Hope" (orig. publ. 1828)

(h) 5th quote, p. 226

Sara Coleridge, first 2 lines of untitled poem (see [g] above)

(2) Miscellaneous English writers (mentioned by Sara): Thomas DeQuincey, Robert Southey

(3) Reprinted in Sara Coleridge, *Memoirs and Letters* (see above)

(a) Quote, middle of p. 224

Sara Coleridge to Mrs. L. Plummer, 1835

(b) 2nd quote, p. 226

Aubrey de Vere to Edith Coleridge, n.d. given

(c) 4th quote, p. 226

Sara Coleridge to Aubrey de Vere, 1849

Passing Allusions:

(1) Samuel Taylor Coleridge, *Christabel*. (Orig. 1816)

(2) Miscellaneous writers (mentioned by Sara): Aristophanes, Jane Austen, Thomas Carlyle, George Crabbe, Richard Crashaw, Dante Alighieri, John Keats, Thomas Babington Macaulay, Percy Bysshe Shelley, Virgil

(3) [Henry Nelson Coleridge], *Six Months in the West Indies* ... J. Murray, 1826.

- -

A SCRIBBLING DAME   (BP and WW)--*TLS,* Feb. 17, 1916, p. 78

Obvious Source
(stated in *TLS* with essay and in footnote):

George F. Whicher, *The Life and Romances of Mrs. Eliza Haywood*. N.Y.: Columbia U. Pr., 1915.

Important Allusions:

   (1) Mentioned by Whicher

      (a) "the disgusting stanzas in the 'Dunciad'"

         Alexander Pope, *The Dunciad*. (Orig. 1728)
         See espec. Book II, ll. 137-48; Book III, ll.
         149-53.

      (b) Miscellaneous women authors of Restoration
         period: Aphra Behn, the Duchess of Newcastle
         (Margaret Cavendish)

      (c) Plot details and characters in Haywood nov-
         els (p. 127):

           (i) *The Lucky Rape* (1727): Berinthus, Emi-
             lia, Henriquez

           (ii) *The Agreeable Caledonian* (1728): Clem-
             entina, Don Jaque[s] di Morella

           (iii) *The Fair Hebrew* (1729): Dorante, Keziah

           (iv) *The Injur'd Husband* (1723): Baron de
             Tortilles [*sic*; i.e., Tortillee], Mlle.
             la Motte

      (d) Eliza Haywood, *History of Miss Betsy Thought-
         less*. (Orig. 1751)

      (e) Eliza Haywood, *History of Jemmy and Jenny
         Jessamy*. (Orig. 1753)

      (f) *The Parrot,* edited by Eliza Haywood (periodi-
         cal, Aug. 2-Oct. 14, 1746)

   (2) "Mr. Gosse ... compares Mrs. Haywood to Ouida"

      Edmund Gosse, "What Ann Lang Read," *Gossip in a
      Library*. W. Heinemann, 1891.

Passing Allusions (mentioned by Whicher):

   (1) Miscellaneous English novelists: Jane Austen,
      Fanny Burney, Henry Fielding, Samuel Richardson

   (2) Various Haywood characters (p. 127): *Love in Ex-
      cess* (1729)--Melliora; *Philidore and Placentia*
      (1727)--Placentia; *The Fruitless Enquiry* (1727)--
      Montrano, Miramillia

- -

SELINA TRIMMER (III)--*New Statesman and Nation,* July 6,
                    1940, p. 16; first collected in
                    C.D.B.

Obvious Source
(stated in *New Statesman and Nation* with essay and in
footnote):

> *Hary-O: The Letters of Lady Harriet Cavendish, 1796-
> 1809,* edited by Sir George Leveson Gower and Iris
> Palmer. John Murray, 1940.

Specific letters quoted from:

(1) "Lady Harriet wrote" (p. 213)

   To Selina Trimmer, n.d. [Dec. 1809]

(2) "Hary-o wrote" (p. 214)

   To Lady Georgiana Morpeth, n.d. [Nov. or Dec.
   1803]

(3) "a description" (p. 215); "and" (l. 2) should
                            read "or"; "a" (l. 6)
                            should be omitted; "in-
                            toxicating" should read
                            "intoxication of"; "sort
                            of" should be omitted

   To same, n.d. [March 1807]

(4) "Hary-o ... owned to her sister" (quotes 4-5, p.
                            215);there should
                            be ellipses be-
                            tween "not" and
                            "prudent"; "sit-
                            uation" should
                            read "situations"

   To same, Nov. 29, 1803

(5) Quotes 6-7, p. 215; "supplanting" should read
                       "having supplanted"

   To same, Nov. 16 [-17], 1803

(6) Quote, top of p. 216

   To same, Nov. 10, 1807

(7) 2nd quote, p. 216; "about giving the" should read
                      "of giving his"

   To same, Oct. 30, 1807

(8) 4th quote, p. 216 (letter quoted but not reproduced; quoted also in Granville Leveson Gower
   [see below])

   To same, n.d. given ["she wrote as a bride"; Harriet and Granville were married Dec. 24, 1809]

Supportive Source:

"Lady Bessborough lamented" (quotes 2-3, p. 215)

Henrietta, Countess of Bessborough, to Granville
Leveson Gower, Oct. 27 [-28], 1807; repr. in Lord
Granville Leveson Gower, *Private Correspondence
1781-1821,* edited by Castalia Countess Granville.
(Orig. 1916)

Passing Allusions:

Miscellaneous English writers:

(1) Charlotte Brontë

(2) "Miss Weeton" (i.e., Ellen Weeton, *Journal of a
Governess 1807-1811,* edited by Edward Hall. 2
vol. Oxford U. Pr., 1936, 1937)

(3) "the famous Mrs. Trimmer of the *Tales*" (Selina's
sister-in-law: Sarah Trimmer, *Instructive Tales,*
early 19th cent.--several editions)

- -

THE "SENTIMENTAL JOURNEY" (I)--*New York Herald Tribune
                              Books,* Sept. 23, 1928,
                              pp. 1, 6; first collected
                              in *C.R. II* (w/var.)
                              Reading notes B2n

Obvious Source:

Laurence Sterne, *A Sentimental Journey Through France
and Italy.* (Orig. 1768) [This essay was written
as the introduction to the "World's Classics" edition of Sterne's novel (Oxford: University Pr.; London: Humphrey Milford, 1928); but text does not duplicate exactly either version listed above.]

Supportive Sources:

(1) "[Sterne] told Lord Shelburne"

Laurence Sterne to Lord Shelburne (William
Petty), Nov. 28, 1767; repr. in *Letters of
Laurence Sterne.* (Orig. 1775) New ed. Ox-
ford: Basil Blackwell, 1927.

This is indicated by the reading notes.

(2) "Thackeray lashed [Sterne]"

William Makepeace Thackeray, *The English Humourists.* (Orig. 1853) Prob. ed.: Smith,
Elder, 1877.

This is listed in Holleyman Addendum.

Important Allusion:

Laurence Sterne, *The Life and Opinions of Tristram Shandy.* (Orig. 1759-67)

Passing Allusions:

Miscellaneous novelists: Henry Fielding, Samuel Richardson, Leo Tolstoy

- -

THE SENTIMENTAL TRAVELLER (CW)--*TLS,* Jan. 9, 1908, p. 14

Obvious Source
(stated in *TLS* with essay and in headnote):

Vernon Lee [pseud. of Violet Paget], *The Sentimental Traveller.* John Lane, 1908 [1907].

Important Allusion (mentioned by Lee):

Johann Wolfgang von Goethe

Passing Allusions:

Miscellaneous essayists: Henry James, Charles Lamb

- -

SEPTEMBER (CW)--*TLS,* Sept. 25, 1919, p. 513

Obvious Source
(stated in *TLS* with essay and in headnote):

Frank Swinnerton, *September.* Methuen, 1919.

Important Allusion:

Frank Swinnerton, *Shops and Houses.*

(See "Honest Fiction.")

- -

SHELLEY AND ELIZABETH HITCHENER (BP)--*TLS,* March 5, 1908, pp. 76-77

Obvious Source
(stated in *TLS* with essay and in footnote):

Percy Bysshe Shelley, *Letters from P.B. [sic] Shelley to Elizabeth Hitchener,* edited by [Bertram Dobell]. Bertram Dobell, 1908.

Supportive Source:

"Professor Dowden gives us a singular picture"

(See "Not One of Us.")

Important Allusions:

(1) "Shelley's letters to Miss Hitchener have ... been printed ... privately"

2 vol. London: n.p., 1890.

(2) "Shelley's first letter [to Miss Hitchener]"

I.e., June 5, 1811

Passing Allusions:

(1) Mentioned in Shelley's first letter (see above)

(a) John Locke

(b) Robert Southey, *The Curse of Kehama.* (Orig. 1810)

(c) George Ensor, *National Education.* (Orig. 1811)

(2) Elizabeth Hitchener, "Ode on the Rights of Women" (in MS; mentioned by Dowden)

(See "Not One of Us.")

- -

SHERIDAN (BP)--*TLS,* Dec. 2, 1909, pp. 461-63   Reading
notes "Holograph ..., Jan. 1909-March 1911" (Berg)+
Obvious Source
(stated in *TLS* with essay and in footnote):

Walter Sichel, *Sheridan.* 2 vol. Constable, 1909.

Supportive Sources:

Various plays by Sheridan:

(1) *The Rivals*. (Orig. 1775)

Quotes, p. 47 and middle of p. 48, are from here:
IV:i:17-22; V:i:155-59.

(2) *The School for Scandal*. (Orig. 1781)

Quotes, top of p. 48, are from here: IV:i:97-99,
161-62.

(3) *The Critic*. (Orig. 1781)

Quotes, bottom of p. 48 and top of p. 49, are
from here: III:i:293-99 (quoted by Sichel);
II:i:152, 148 (latter quoted by Sichel)

Important Allusions (quoted by Sichel):

(1) "[Sheridan's] speech at the trial of Warren Hastings"

First printed in *Speeches of the Managers and
Counsel in the Trial of Warren Hastings*, edited
by E.A. Bond. Longmans, 1859.

(2) "wrote Byron" (p. 45)

George Gordon, Lord Byron, Journal, Oct. 15,
1821; repr. in Byron, ... *Letters and Journals*
(see below)

(3) "[Sheridan's] sister ... confessed" (p. 45)

Alicia Sheridan LeFanu to Esther Ogle Sheridan,
July 1816; repr. in Thomas Moore, *Memoirs of the
Life of the Rt. Hon. Richard Brinsley Sheridan*.
(Orig. 1825)

(4) "two letters from Sheridan at Harrow"

To Richard Chamberlaine, March 2, [1766(?)] and
[Oct. 1766]; repr. in W. Fraser Rae, *Sheridan*.
(Orig. 1896)

(5) "Sir Henry Irving found"

In Rae, *ibid*.

(6) Richard Brinsley Sheridan, *Affectation* . (Orig.
1781; incomplete)

(7) "a boyish essay"

Richard Brinsley Sheridan, "Remarks on Black-stone," 1772 (in MS)

2nd quote, p. 50, is from here.

(8) "[Sheridan's] speech upon the Begums of Oude"

Speech of Richard Brinsley Sheridan Esquire, on Wednesday, February 7, 1787 ... Reported by a Member of the House of Commons. J. French, 1787.

(9) "[Sheridan] considered his situation" (p. 52)

Richard Brinsley Sheridan to Georgiana, Duchess of Devonshire, and Lady Henrietta Frances Bess-borough, [May 7], 1792 (in MS)

(10) "[Sheridan] wrote" (near bottom of p. 52)

To Samuel Rogers, May 15(?), 1816; repr. in Moore (see above)

(11) "Byron murmured" (p. 53)

George Gordon, Lord Byron, to Thomas Moore, June 1, 1818; repr. in Byron, ... *Letters and Journals,* edited by Rowland E. Prothero. 6 vol. John Murray, 1898-1901.

Passing Allusions (quoted by Sichel):

(1) 2nd quote, p. 46

Sheridan, "Parade Coffee House" letter, [May 5, 1772]; repr. in Moore (see above)

(2) Last 3 quotes, p. 46

Richard Brinsley Sheridan to Thomas Grenville: Aug. 30, 1772; *Ibid.*; Oct. 30, 1772--"that" should be in brackets; both repr. in Rae (see above)

(3) Mentioned by Sheridan in letter of Oct. 30 to Grenville, *ibid.*

(a) Philip Sidney, *The Countess of Pembroke's Arcadia.* (Orig. 1593)

(b) Edmund Spenser, *The Faery Queen.* (Orig. 1590, 1596)

(c) Miscellaneous 18th-century English novelists: Henry Fielding, Tobias Smollett

(4) "Johnson declared"

   James Boswell, *The Life of Samuel Johnson, LL.D.*
   (Orig. 1791)

(5) Miscellaneous writers: Edmund Burke, William
    Congreve, Homer, Sir John Vanbrugh

(6) George Villiers, *The Rehearsal.* (Orig. 1671)
    This is listed in the reading notes.+
(7) Last 2 quotes, p. 50

   Richard Brinsley Sheridan to Charles Sheridan,
   Apr. 2, 1782

(8) Quote, top of p. 51

   William Shakespeare, *King Lear:* III:iy:106-07.
   (Orig. publ. 1608)

(9) "the Duchess of Devonshire's diary" (p. 51)

   Georgiana, Duchess of Devonshire: her diary, Nov.
   20, 1788-Jan. 12, 1789, is appended to Sichel, II.

   (a) Nov. 20, 1788

   (b) *Ibid.*

   (c) Nov. [29], 1788

(10) Last 2 quotes, p. 51

   Thomas Creevey, *The Creevey Papers.* (Orig. publ.
   1901; Creevey's dates were 1768-1838)

(11) "the beautiful Mrs. Sheridan ... wrote"

   Elizabeth Sheridan to Richard Brinsley Sheridan,
   1782(?) (in MS)

(12) Last quote, p. 53; "strange" should read "strange-
     looking"

   William ["Tutor"] Smyth, *Memoir of Mr. Sheridan.*
   Privately printed, 1840.

- -

SIR WALTER RALEIGH (III)--*TLS,* March 15, 1917, p. 127;
                     first collected in *G.R.*

Obvious Source
(stated in *TLS* with essay and mentioned in first paragraph):

> *Sir Walter Raleigh: Selections from His "Historie of
> the World," His Letters, Etc.*, edited by G.E. Hadow.
> Oxford: Clarendon, 1917. (*Historie* orig. 1614; *Let-
> ters* orig. 1657)

Specific quotes from:

(1) Quotes 2-6, p. 28; quotes 1-7, p. 29; first and
    3rd quotes, p. 31

> From *Historie of the World*

(2) 8th quote, p. 29; "of other" should read "or
    other"

> *Ibid.*

(3) P. 30

    (a) First and 2nd quotes

> *Ibid.*

    (b) 3rd quote

> Sir Walter to Lady Elizabeth Raleigh, [Dec.
> 9, 1603]

> 2nd quote, p. 31, is also from here.

Important Allusions:

(1) "Hakluyt's pages"

> (See "Reading" and "The Elizabethan Lumber
> Room.")

(2) "the words of Sir Humfrey Gilbert"

> In Hakluyt (above): "A Report of the Voyage ...
> Attempted in the Yeere of Our Lord 1583 by Sir
> Humfrey Gilbert Knight, ... Written by M. Edward
> Hale"

Passing Allusions:

> Miscellaneous 16th-century English writers: Christo-
> pher Marlowe, William Shakespeare, Edmund Spenser

- -

SONIA MARRIED (CW)--*TLS,* Aug. 28, 1919, p. 460

Obvious Source
(stated in *TLS* with essay and in headnote):

Stephen M[a]cKenna, *Sonia Married.* Hutchinson,
[1919].

Important Allusion:

E[dward] F[rederic] Benson, *Dodo.* (Orig. 1893)

Passing Allusion (mentioned by MacKenna):

Percy Bysshe Shelley

- -

SOUTH WIND (CW)--*TLS,* June 14, 1917, p. 283

Obvious Source
(stated in *TLS* with essay and in headnote):

Norman Douglas [pseud. of George Norman Douglass],
South Wind. Martin Secker, 1917.

Important Allusions:

(1) Thomas Love Peacock, *Nightmare Abbey.* (Orig.
1818)

(2) Thomas Love Peacock, *Crotchet Castle.* (Orig.
1831)

(3) Oscar Wilde

Passing Allusions (mentioned by Douglas):

(1) "Perrelli, *Antiquities*"

I.e., Johannis Perrelli, "De Ratione Lunae" and
[from Theodorus Gaza] "De Mensibus," in Vol. IX
of *Thesaurus Antiquitatum,* edited by Jacobus Gronovius. (Orig. 1697)

(2) Virgil

- -

STERNE (III)--*TLS,* Aug. 12, 1909, pp. 289-90; first col-
                lected in *G.R.*   Reading notes "Holograph
                ... Jan. 1909-March 1911" (Berg)+

Obvious Source
(stated in *TLS* with essay and in footnote):

   Wilbur L. Cross, *The Life and Times of Laurence
   Sterne.* N.Y.: Macmillan, 1909.

Supportive Source:

   Laurence Sterne, *The Life and Opinions of Tristram
   Shandy.* (Orig. 1759-67) In *Works.*

   (See "Phases of Fiction.")

   This is indicated by the reading notes.+

Important Allusions:

   (1) Laurence Sterne, *A Sentimental Journey Through
       France and Italy.* (Orig. 1768) In *Works, ibid.*

       This is indicated by the reading notes.+

   (2) "*Journal to Eliza*"

       (See "Eliza and Sterne.")

Passing Allusions:

   Miscellaneous writers:

   (1) Mentioned by Sterne: Aphra Behn, Guillaume Bou-
       chet, Bruscambille (a.k.a. Deslauriers), Robert
       Burton, Miguel de Cervantes Saavedra, Homer, Mi-
       chel de Montaigne, Rabelais, Earl of Rochester
       (John Wilmot), Theocritus, Virgil

   (2) Samuel Johnson, Charles Lamb, George Meredith,
       William Makepeace Thackeray.

- -

STERNE'S GHOST (III)--*Nation and Athenaeum,* Nov. 7, 1925,
                pp. 207-09; first collected in *M.*
                Reading notes #18

Inferred Source:

   "the second Mrs. [Charles] Mathews said"

   Memoirs of Charles Mathews, Comedian, edited by Anne
   Mathews. (Orig. 1838-39) 2nd ed. 4 vol. R. Bentley. 1839.

   As shown by Woolf's reading notes, the account of
   the "ghost" is from Vol. I.

Important Allusions:

> (1) Eliza Mathews, *What Has Been*. Date obscure;
> Amer. ed.: Alexandria, Va.: Cottom and Stewart,
> 1803)
>
> (2) "[Eliza] wrote ... novels, sonnets, elegies, love
> songs"
>
>> E.g., *Argus, the House-Dog at Eadlip* (1789); *Po-
>> ems* (1802); *Anecdotes of the Clairville Family
>> ...* (1802); *Griffith Abbey* (1807); *Afternoon
>> Amusements, or, Tales of Birds* (1809). 16 ti-
>> tles, in all, are listed in catalogues of British
>> Museum and Library of Congress.

Passing Allusions (mentioned by A. Mathews):

> (1) Laurence Sterne, *The Life and Opinions of Tris-
> tram Shandy*. (Orig. 1759-67)
>
> (2) Miscellaneous writers: Tate Wilkinson, William
> Wordsworth
> (3) Quoted by A. Mathews: "Shakespeare said ...
> 'marriage comes of [*sic*; i.e., by] destiny'"
>
>> *All's Well That Ends Well*: I:iii:63. (Orig.
>> publ. 1623)

- -

THE STRANGE ELIZABETHANS (III)--c. 1930; first published
                          in *C.R. II*   * Reading
                          notes #sll, 12

Inferred Sources:

> (1) "letters of ... Gabriel Harvey"
>
>> *Letter-Book of Gabriel Harvey,* edited by Edward
>> John Long Scott. Camden Society, 1884.
>
>> Specific quotes from:
>
>> (a) 2nd quote, p. 37
>
>>> To Edmund Spenser, _(?)_ [in summer] 10,
>>> 1579
>
>> (b) Middle of p. 38
>
>>> To same, n.d.; "last letter" should read
>>> "last week's letter"

(2) "Harvey left ... a commonplace book"

In *Gabriel Harvey's Marginalia,* edited by G.C. Moore Smith. Stratford:+ Shakespeare Head Pr., 1913.

Both are listed in the reading notes.

Supportive Sources (mentioned by Smith [see above]):

(1) Gabriel Harvey, *Works,* edited by Alexander B. Grosart. 3 vol. Huth Library. London: n.p., 1884-85.

This is listed in the reading notes.

Specific quotes from:

(a) First quote, p. 37 (quoted also by Smith)

Harvey, *Pierces Supererogation.* (Orig. 1595)

(b) Quote, pp. 37-38

From *ibid.*

(c) 2nd quote, p. 38; "for" should read "of"

Harvey, *Foure Letters ... , Especially Touching Robert Greene.* (Orig. 1592)

To Christopher Bird, Sept. 5, [1592]

(2) "Nash admitted" (p. 39)

Thomas Nash[e], *Have with You to Saffron-Walden.* (Orig. 1596)

(3) "Queen Elizabeth ... said" (p. 39)

Reported by Thomas Nash[e], *Strange Newes ...* (Orig. 1592)

(4) "Spenser saw [Harvey]" (p. 40)

Edmund Spenser, "Commendatory Sonnet I" (1586); repr. also in Harvey, *Foure Letters* (see above)

Important Allusions:

(1) "letters of ... Sir Henry Wotton"

The Life and Letters of ... , edited by Logan Pearsall Smith. 2 vol. Oxford: Clarendon, 1907. (Sir Henry's dates were 1568-1639)

This is indicated by the reading notes.+

(2) Philip Sidney

(3) "Mary Sidney ... wrote"

Lady Mary Dudley Sidney to Edmund Molyneux,
Oct.(?) 1578; reproduced in part in:

(a) William Percy Addleshaw, *Sir Philip Sidney*.
Methuen, 1909.

This is listed in the reading notes (Berg
#20) for "'The Countess of Pembroke's Ar-
cadia,'" *q.v.*

(b) Mona Wilson, *Sir Philip Sidney*. Duckworth,
1931.

This is listed in the reading notes.

Passing Allusions:

(1) William Shakespeare, *Hamlet*. (Orig. 1603)

(2) Miscellaneous writers: Aristotle (mentioned by
Harvey), Joseph Conrad, Alexander Pope, Alfred
Lord Tennyson

* Reading notes in #12 are holograph notes of typed ones
in #11.

- -

THE SUPERNATURAL IN FICTION (I)--*TLS,* Jan. 31, 1918, p.
55; first collected in
G.R.

Obvious Source
(stated in *TLS* with essay and in footnote):

Dorothy Scarborough, *The Supernatural in Modern English Fiction*. N.Y.: G.P. Putnam's, 1917.

Important Allusions:

(1) Various works mentioned by Scarborough:

(a) Henry James, *The Turn of the Screw*. (Orig.
1898)

    (b) Ann Radcliffe, *The Mysteries of Udolpho*.
        (Orig. 1794)

    (c) Rudyard Kipling, "The Mark of the Beast."
        (Orig. 1891)

(2) Miscellaneous authors mentioned by Scarborough,
    with titles mentioned by Woolf:

    (a) Samuel Taylor Coleridge, *The Rime of the Ancient Mariner*. (Orig. 1798)

    (b) Sir Walter Scott, *Redgauntlet*. (Orig. 1824)

    (c) Rudyard Kipling, "The Return of Imray."
        Both this and (c) above were published in
        Kipling, *Life's Handicap. Being Stories of
        Mine Own People*. (Orig. 1891)

- -

SWIFT'S *JOURNAL TO STELLA* (III)--*TLS,* Sept. 24, 1925, pp.
                              605-06; first collected
                              in *C.R. II* (w/var.)
                              Reading notes #5 and B2p

Obvious Source:

    Jonathan Swift, *Journal to Stella*. (Orig. 1768)

    (1) As indicated by reading notes B2p:

        Edited by J.K. Moorhead, w/introduction by Sir
        Walter Scott. Everyman's Edition. J.M. Dent,
        [1924].

        This is listed in Holleyman.

    (2) 2 poss. eds., as indicated by reading notes #5:

        (a) In Swift, *The Prose Works of,* edited by T.
            Scott. 12 vol. Bohn's Standard Library ed.
            Bell, 1890-1908. Vol. II.+ OR:

        (b) Edited by Frederick Ryland. Bohn's Popular
            Library ed. G. Bell, 1924.

Supportive Source:

    Quotes, p. 78:

    Swift, *Works,* w/notes ... by Walter Scott. 19 vol.
    Edinburgh: Archibald Constable, 1814. Vol. XIX es-
    pec., for Esther Vanhomrigh's letters.

    This is indicated by the reading notes (#5) and is
    listed in Holleyman; it belonged to Leslie Stephen.

Passing Allusions:

>   Miscellaneous authors (mentioned by Swift): Joseph
>   Addison, Matthew Prior

- -

SYLVIA AND MICHAEL (CW)--*TLS,* March 20, 1919, p. 150

Obvious Source
(stated in *TLS* with essay and in headnote):

>   Compton Mackenzie, *Sylvia and Michael.* Martin Seck-
>   er, 1919.

Important Allusion:

>   "Sylvia Scarlett is ... 'still running'"

>   [Cf. "The 'Movie' Novel."]

- -

A TALK ABOUT MEMOIRS (IV)--*New Statesman,* March 6, 1920,
                     pp. 642-43; first collected in
                     G.R.

Obvious Sources
(stated in *New Statesman* with essay and in footnotes):

>   (1) *Recollections of Lady Georgiana Peel,* compiled
>   by Ethel Peel. John Lane, 1920.

>   (2) John A. Bridges, *Victorian Recollections.* G.
>   Bell, 1919.

>   (3) Charlotte L.H. Dempster, *The Manners of My Time,*
>   edited by Alice Knox. Grant Richards, 1920.

>   (4) Dorothea Conyers, *Sporting Reminiscences.* Methu-
>   en, 1920.

>   (5) *John Porter of Kingsclere. An Anthology [sic;
>   i.e., Autobiography],* written in collaboration
>   with Edward Monkhouse *[sic;* i.e., Moorhouse*].*
>   Grant Richards, 1919.

Passing Allusions:

(1) Miscellaneous English writers: John Milton, Lytton Strachey

(2) "Mrs. Browning's lines" (quoted by Dempster); according to her, "trail" should read "trial"

Cannot locate

(3) "tell me how Orme was poisoned"

Described by Porter; Orme was a racehorse belonging to the Duke of Westminster.

- -

TAYLORS AND EDGEWORTHS (IV)--*London Mercury,* Jan. 1924, pp. 261-68; repr. in *Dial,* (w/var.), May 1925, pp. 381-90; first collected in *C.R. I* (w/var.)

Inferred Sources:

(1) "Mrs. Ann Gilbert ... the young Taylors"

Autobiography ... of Mrs. Gilbert, Formerly Ann Taylor, edited by Josiah Gilbert. 2 vol. London: n.p., 1874.

(2) "Richard Lovell Edgeworth ... two volumes of memoirs"

Maria Edgeworth, *Memoirs of R.L.E. [sic] ... Begun by Himself, and Concluded by His Daughter.* (Orig. 1820)

Supportive Sources:

(1) "Rev. Henry ... Elman [*sic*] ... reflects"

Edward Ellman, *Recollections of a Sussex Parson.* Skeffington, 1912.

(2) "little Miss Frend"

Sophia Elizabeth [Frend] DeMorgan, *Threescore Years and Ten ... ,* edited by Mary A. DeMorgan. E. Bentley, 1895.

(3) "Sir George Newnes"

> Hulda Friedrichs, *The Life of George Newnes, Bart.*
> Hodder and Stoughton, 1911.

Important Allusions:

(1) "men like Haydon"

> (See "Genius: B.R. Haydon.")

(2) "men like ... Mark Pattison"

> Mark Pattison, *Memoirs,* edited by Mrs. [Emilia]
> Pattison. Macmillan, 1885.

(3) "men like ... the Rev. Blanco White"

> *The Life of the Rev. Joseph Blanco White,* edited
> by John Hamilton Thoms. 3 vol. John Chapman,
> 1845.

(5) "Byron's bore" (p. 123; *re* R.L. Edgeworth)

> George Gordon, Lord Byron, to John Murray, Nov.
> 4, 1820; repr. in *The Works of Lord Byron,*
> w/notes by Thomas Moore, *et al.* John Murray,
> 1837.

> This is listed in Holleyman; it belonged to Leo-
> nard.

Passing Allusions:

Miscellaneous writers:

(a) Mentioned by Taylor: James Montgomery, Robert
  Montgomery

(b) Mentioned by Ellman: John Henry Newman

(c) Mentioned by Frend: William Blake, Charles Lamb

(d) Mentioned by Edgeworth: Jean Jacques Rousseau

- -

A TERRIBLY SENSITIVE MIND (I and WW)--*New York Herald
                              Tribune Books,* Sept.
                              18, 1927, pp. 1-2;
                              first collected in
                              G.R.

Obvious Source
(stated in *New York Herald Tribune Books* with essay):

    The Journal of Katherine Mansfield, 1914-1922, edited
by J. Middleton Murry. Constable, 1927.

- -

"THESE ARE THE PLANS" (BP)--*Athenaeum,* Aug. 1, 1919, pp.
                       682-83

Obvious Source
(stated in *Athenaeum* with essay and in footnote):

    Charles Hamilton Sorley, *Marlborough and Other Poems.*
(Orig. 1916) 4th ed. Cambridge: University Pr.,
1919.

Supportive Sources:

    (1) Specific poems quoted from:

        (a) First quote, p. 95

            "Stones" (orig. 1913)

        (b) 2nd quote [two verses], p. 93

            "Marlborough" (orig. 1914)

        (c) "A Call to Action" (orig. 1912)

            First quote, p. 94, is from here; the 2 ver-
ses are not consecutive

        (d) 2nd quote, p. 94

            Untitled ["#XXX"], (n.d.)

        (e) Quote, p. 95

            "The Song of the Ungirt Runners" (n.d.)

    (2) Specific letters quoted from (recipients not
named):

        (a) Quote, bottom of p. 94

            July 1914

        (b) First quote, p. 95

            First sentence, June 2, 1914, remainder,
Oct. 1914

(c) 2nd quote, p. 95

June 16, 1915

Important Allusions (mentioned by Sorley in letters):

> (1) Miscellaneous poets: Robert Browning, Johann Wolfgang von Goethe, Thomas Hardy, Henrik Ibsen, John Masefield
>
> (2) Homer, *The Odyssey*. (Orig. 10th cent. B.C.)

- -

THOMAS HOOD (BP)--*TLS,* Jan. 30, 1908, p. 35

Obvious Sources
(stated in *TLS* with essay and in footnote):

> (1) Walter Jerrold, *Thomas Hood: His Life and Times.* Alston Rivers, 1907.
>
> (2) Thomas Hood, *Poems,* edited by F.C. Burnand. "Red Letter Library" ed. Blackie, 1907.

Supportive Sources:

> (1) Specific poems quoted from:
>
>> (a) First quote, p. 56
>>
>> "Faithless Sally Brown" (orig. 1822)
>>
>> (b) "one of his most serious poems, that on Melancholy"
>>
>> "Ode to Melancholy" (orig. 1827)
>>
>> (c) "The Song of the Shirt" (orig. 1843)
>
> (2) Thackeray's "paper 'On a joke I once heard from the late Thomas Hood'"
>
> In William Makepeace Thackeray, *Roundabout Papers.* (Orig. 1863) Prob. ed.: Smith, Elder, 1877.
>
> This is listed in Holleyman Addendum.

Important Allusions:

> (1) Specific poems mentioned but not quoted from:
>
>> (a) "The Dream of Eugene Aram" (orig. 1829)

(b) "The Haunted House" (orig. 1844)

(c) "The Last Man" (orig. 1826)

(d) "The Bridge of Sighs" (orig. 1844)

(e) "Ruth" (orig. 1827)

(f) "The Death Bed" (orig. 1831)

(g) Mentioned by Jerrold (see above):

Hood's "long poem on the town of Dundee, in imitation of the 'New Bath Guide'"

This piece of juvenilia, "Dundee Guide," first published in the 1869 *Memorials* (see below), is quoted by Jerrold. *The New Bath Guide* (orig. 1766) was written by Christopher Anstey.

(2) "the Memorials by [Hood's] son and daughter"

[Frances Freeling Broderip and Tom Hood], *Memorials of Hood Collected by His Daughter, with a Preface and Notes by His Son.* 2 vol. E. Moxon, 1860; rev. ed., 1869.

Passing Allusions (mentioned by Jerrold):

Miscellaneous English writers: Samuel Taylor Coleridge, Thomas DeQuincey, John Keats, Charles Lamb

- -

THOREAU (BP)--*TLS,* July 12, 1917, pp. 325-26

Inferred Source:

"his biographers" (p. 72)

E.g., H[enry] S. Salt, *Life of Henry David Thoreau.* Richard Bentley, 1890.

2nd quote, p. 72 (*re* father; there should be ellipses before "man") and 4th quote, p. 73, are from here.

Supportive Sources:

(1) Quoted by Salt (see above):

(a) "as [Thoreau] says" (first quote, p. 72)

Henry David Thoreau to Daniel Ricketson, Feb. 1, 1855 (in MS)

(b) "to the penetrating eye of the Rev. John Weiss"

Weiss, "Thoreau," *Christian Examiner,* 79 (July 1865), 97-117.

(c) "[Thoreau's] diary ... journal" (in MS)

Specific quotes from:

    (i) 2nd quote, p. 73: June 26, 1852

    (ii) First quote, middle of p. 74: March 3, 1841

    (iii) First quote, p. 77: March 26, 1842

    (iv) 2nd quote, p. 77: Nov. 11, 1851; "to" should read "of"

    (v) First quote, p. 78: Apr. 11, 1852

(d) 3rd quote, p. 73

Thoreau, "Of Keeping a Private Journal" (in MS); student theme written at Harvard, 1835

(e) 5th quote, p. 73

Ellery Channing, *Thoreau, The Poet-Naturalist.* (Orig. 1873)

(f) Quote, bottom of p, 73

David Greene Haskins, *Ralph Waldo Emerson* (orig. 1886), quoted by Henry Williams, "Henry David Thoreau," in *Memorials of the Class of 1837 of Harvard University.* Boston: George H. Ellis, 1887.

(g) 2nd Thoreau quote, p. 74

Thoreau, *A Week on the Concord and Merrimack Rivers.* (Orig. 1849)

(h) Last quote, p. 76

Cannot locate; as quoted by Salt, there should be ellipses before "insignificant"

(i) Quote, p. 79

> Thoreau to Myron B. Benton, March 21, 1862;
> repr. in Thoreau, *Letters to Various Per-*
> *sons,* [edited by Ralph Waldo Emerson]. Bos-
> ton: Ticknor and Fields, 1865.

(2) Thoreau, *Walden*. (Orig. 1854)

> Quotes, bottom of p. 74, bottom of p. 75, first
> 3 on p. 76, and last 2 on p. 77 ("him" should be
> in brackets) are from here.

> The first two are quoted by Salt.

Important Allusions:

(1) "Lowell has recorded [his views of Transcendental-
ism]"

> E.g., James Russell Lowell, "Thoreau," orig. as
> "Thoreau Letters," *North American Review,* 101
> (Oct. 1865), 397 ff.; repr. in Lowell, *My Study*
> *Windows*. (Orig. 1871)

> This is mentioned by Salt.

(2) Margaret Fuller Ossoli, *Memoirs of* ... (Orig.
1852)

(3) "as [Ralph Waldo] Emerson expresses it" (p. 74)

> Cannot locate

Passing Allusions:

> Miscellaneous English nature-writers: Richard Jeffer-
> ies, Gilbert White

- -

THE THREE BLACK PENNYS (CW)--*TLS,* Dec. 12, 1918, p. 620

Obvious Source
(stated in *TLS* with essay and in headnote):

> Joseph Hergesheimer, *The Three Black Pennys*. Will-
> iam Heinemann, 1918.

- -

THE TUNNEL (CW)--*TLS,* Feb. 13, 1919, p. 81

   Obvious Source
   (stated in *TLS* with essay and in headnote):

      Dorothy Richardson, *The Tunnel.* Duckworth, 1919.

- -

TWELFTH NIGHT AT THE OLD VIC (I)--*New Statesman and Na-*
                               tion, Sept. 30, 1933,
                               pp. 385-86; first col-
                               lected in *D.M.*

   Supportive Source:

      William Shakespeare, *Twelfth Night.* (Orig. 1601)

      Quotes, pp. 28 and 30, are from here:

      (1) I:i:6

      (2) I:i:36

      (3) I:iii:15-16

      (4) I:ii:3-4

      (5) II:iv:42

      (6) III:i:14-15

      (7) II:iii:181

      (8) V:i:378

      (9) V:i:379

   Important Allusions:

      Actors and director referred to: Leon Quartermaine,
      Lydia Lopokova, Athene Seyler, Roger Livesey, Ursula
      Jeans, Ernest Hare, "Mr. Morland" [*sic;* i.e., Morland
      Graham],Tyrone Guthrie

   Passing Allusions:

      (1) Anton Chekhov, *The Cherry Orchard.* (Orig. 1903-
      04)

      (2) William Shakespeare, *Measure for Measure.* (Orig.
      1604)

(3) William Shakespeare, *Henry the Eighth*. (Orig.
1613)

- -

TWO ANTIQUARIES: WALPOLE AND COLE (III)--*Yale Review,*
                                      March 1939, pp.
                                      530-39; first
                                      collected in *D.M.*

Obvious Source
(stated in *Yale Review* with essay and mentioned in first
paragraph):

   *Horace Walpole's Correspondence with the Rev. Will-
   iam Cole.* Vols. I and II of The Yale Edition of
   Horace Walpole's Correspondence, edited by Wilmarth
   Sheldon Lewis and A.D. Wallace. Oxford U. Pr., 1937.

Important Allusion:

   Mentioned by Walpole: Thomas Gray

Passing Allusions:

   Miscellaneous authors mentioned by Walpole: Thomas
   Chatterton, Alexander Pope

- -

TWO WOMEN (IV)--*Nation and Athenaeum,* Apr. 23, 1927, pp.
               78-79; repr. in *New Republic* (w/var.),
               May 18, 1927, pp. 358-59; first collected
               in *M.* (text in *M.* and *C.E.* from *Nation and
               Athenaeum*)

Obvious Sources
(stated in *Nation and Athenaeum* with essay and in footnotes):

   (1) Lady Barbara Stephen, *Emily Davies and Girton
       College.* Constable, 1927.

   (2) *Letters of Lady Augusta Stanley: A Young Lady at
       Court, 1849-1863,* edited by the Dean of Windsor
       [Albert Baillie] and Hector Bolitho. Gerald
       Howe, 1927.

Important Allusions:

    (1) Mentioned by Lady Stephen:

        (a) "Charlotte Yonge wrote"

            Yonge, *Womankind.* (Orig. 1887)

        (b) "Queen Victoria [was] ... furious"

            Sir Theodore Martin, *Queen Victoria as I Knew Her.* William Blackwood, 1908.

        (c) "Mr. Greg"

            William Rathbone Greg, "Why Are Women Redundant?" in Greg, *Literary and Social Judgments.* London: n.p., 1868.

        (d) "Trollope's picture of four girls"

            Anthony Trollope, *Miss Mackenzie.* (Orig. 1865)

        (e) "Miss Martineau ... hailed"

            Harriet Martineau, *Autobiography.* (Orig. 1877)

        (f) "Miss Garrett herself said"

            Elizabeth Garrett to Emily Davies, Apr. 12, 1862 (in MS)

        (g) "The *Saturday Review*"

            "Feminine Wranglers," *Saturday Review* (London), July 23, 1864; according to Stephen, "accomplished" should read "over-accomplished," "one of" should precede "the most," and "monster" should read "monsters"

    (2) "Miss Nightingale said" (p. 62)

        [Florence Nightingale], "Cassandra," in her *Suggestions for Thought to the Searchers After Truth* ... Eyre and Spottiswoode, 1860.

Passing Allusions:

    Miscellaneous writers (mentioned by Lady Stanley): Victor Hugo, Alphonse Lamartine, Prosper Mérimée, Ernest Renan, Charles Augustin Sainte-Beuve, Ivan Turgenev

- -

VISITS TO WALT WHITMAN (IV)--*TLS,* Jan. 3, 1918, p. 7; first collected in *G.R.*

Obvious Source
(stated in *TLS* with essay and in footnote):

> John Johnston and J.W. Wallace, *Visits to Walt Whitman in 1980-91.* George Allen and Unwin, 1917.

Important Allusion:

> Earlier versions of same book:

> (1) *Notes of a Visit to Walt Whitman ... in July, 1890.* T. Brimelow, 1890.

> (2) *Diary Notes of a Visit to Walt Whitman and Some of His Friends.* T. Brimelow, 1898.

Passing Allusions:

> Miscellaneous writers (mentioned by Johnston and Wallace): Aeschylus, Thomas Carlyle, Ralph Waldo Emerson, William Shakespeare, John Addington Symonds, Alfred Lord Tennyson

- -

WALTER RALEIGH (I)--*Vogue* (London), early May 1926, pp. 69, 94; first collected in *C.D.B.*

Obvious Source
(stated in *Vogue* with essay):

> *The Letters of Sir Walter Raleigh,* edited by Lady [Lucie Gertrude] Raleigh, w/preface by D. Nichol Smith. 2 vol. Methuen, 1926.

Specific letters quoted from:

(1) P. 314

> (a) *Re* Geoffrey Chaucer and William Wordsworth
>
> To W.P. Ker, Dec. 1, 1900; "doing" should be in brackets

> (b) *Re* Sir Walter Scott
>
> To Jessie Raleigh, Apr. 29, 1889

> (c) *Re* William Blake
>
> To John Sampson, Nov. 17, 1905

> (d) *Re* Wordsworth and William Shakespeare
>
> To same, May 16, 1901

(2) P. 315

> (a) To Jessie Raleigh, Nov. 28, 1889

    (b) To J.M. Mackay, Nov. 30, 1889

    (c) *Re* John Keats

       To Jessie Raleigh, Apr. 29, 1889; "examinations" should read "Examination"

  (3) Bottom of p. 316

    (a) "he wrote"

       Cannot locate

    (b) "He really believed, he said"

       To Lucie Jackson, Oct. 5, 1889

  (4) Bottom of p. 317

    (a) "he said"

       To Alice Raleigh, Nov. 14, 1899

    (b) "he asked"

       To W.P. Ker, March 30, 1897; there should be ellipses between "at" and "mess"

  (5) P. 318

    (a) To Mrs. A.H. Clough, March 29, 1908

    (b) To Émile Legouis, Oct. 4, 1911

    (c) "he bursts out"

       To W. Macneile Dixon, Sept. 8, 1913

    (d) "he exclaimed"

       To Mrs. Walter Crum, Aug. 8, 1914

Important Allusions:

  Works by Raleigh:

  (1) *The English Novel.* (Orig. 1891)

  (2) *Style.* (Orig. 1897)

  (3) *Shakespeare.* (Orig. 1907)

  (4) "[Raleigh] was made historian of the Air Force"

The War in the Air: Being the Story of the Part
Played in the Great War by the Royal Air Force.
Vol. I [only]. Oxford: [Clarendon], 1922.

Passing Allusions:

(1) "the letters of Keats"

Prob. ed.: John Keats, *Letters of* ... , edited
by Sidney Colvin. [Rev. ed.] Macmillan, 1918.
(Orig. 1891)

This is listed in Holleyman.

Quote, p. 315, is from here: To John Taylor, Feb.
27, [1818].

(2) "the diary of the Goncourts"

(See "The Novels of Turgenev.")

(3) "the letters of Lamb"

E.g., Charles Lamb, *The Letters of* ... , edited
by Alfred Ainger. 2nd ed. 2 vol. Macmillan,
1904. (Orig. 1888)

This is listed in Holleyman.

(4) Miscellaneous writers: Samuel Taylor Coleridge,
Gustave Flaubert, Alfred Lord Tennyson

- -

WAR IN THE VILLAGE (CW)--*TLS,* Sept. 12, 1918, p. 426

Obvious Source
(stated in *TLS* with essay and in headnote):

Maurice Hewlett, *The Village Wife's Lament.* Martin
Secker, 1918.

- -

THE WAY OF ALL FLESH (CW)--*TLS,* June 26, 1919, p. 347

Obvious Source:

("the impression before us is the eleventh of the
second edition")

Samuel Butler, *The Way of All Flesh*.   A.C. Fifield,
1919. (Orig. 1903)   e

Important Allusions:

(1) 2nd and 3rd quotes, p. 33

Cannot locate

(2) "the note-book which, according to Butler, every
one should carry"

[Cf. "A Man with a View."]

- -

WHITE'S SELBORNE (III)--*New Statesman and Nation,* Sept.
30, 1939, pp. 460-61; first col-
lected in *C.D.B.*   Reading
notes #24

Obvious Source:

Gilbert White, *The Natural History of Selborne.*
(Orig. 1789) New ed. 2 vol. Arch, 1822.+

This is indicated by the reading notes.+

Supportive Source:

"[White's] biography"

A[lfred] N[ewton], "White, Gilbert," *Dictionary of
National Biography.*

This is listed in the reading notes.

Holleyman lists an edition of the *DNB,* edited by
Leslie Stephen and Sidney Lee: 68 vol. Smith, Elder, 1885-1904: "Leslie Stephen's own copy."

- -

WILCOXIANA (BP and WW)--*Athenaeum,* Sept. 19, 1919, pp.
913-14

Obvious Source
(stated in *Athenaeum* with essay and in headnotes):

Ella Wheeler Wilcox, *The Worlds and I*. Gay and Hancock, [1919].

Important Allusions (mentioned by Wilcox):

Works by Wilcox:

(1) "The Queen's Last Ride" (orig. 1901)

(2) "Solitude" (orig. 1883)

Quote, bottom of p. 146, is from here.

(3) "*Songs [sic] of Purpose, Passion, and Power*"

(a) *Poems of Purpose*. (Orig. 1916)

(b) *Poems of Passion*. (Orig. 1883)

(c) *Poems of Power*. (Orig. 1901)

(4) "Hello, Boys." (Orig. [during World War I])

(5) *Sonnets of Sorrow and Triumph*. (Orig. 1918)

Passing Allusions:

Miscellaneous writers:

(1) Anne Louise de Staël

(2) Mentioned by Wilcox: Théophile Gauthier [*sic; i.e., Gautier*], Robert Ingersoll, Ouida [Marie Louise de la Ramée], William Shakespeare

- -

WILLIAM HAZLITT (I)--*New York Herald Tribune Books*, Sept. 7, 1930, pp. 1, 4; repr. in *TLS* (w/var.), Sept. 18, 1930, pp. 721-22; first collected in *C.R. II* (w/var.) Reading notes #22

Stated Source
(stated in *New York Herald Tribune Books* with essay):

The Complete Works of William Hazlitt, edited by P.P. Howe. Vols. I, IV and V.* J.M. Dent, 1930.

Supportive Sources:

(1) First quote, p. 155

"Why Distant Objects Please"; orig. collected in
Hazlitt, *Table Talk,* edited by William Hazlitt
the Younger. 3rd ed. 2 vol. Templeman, 1845,
1846. (Orig. 1821-22)

This is indicated by the reading notes+ and is
listed in Holleyman; it belonged to Leslie Stephen.

(2) "We see [Hazlitt] as Coleridge saw him"

Samuel Taylor Coleridge to Thomas Wedgwood, Sept.
18, 1803; repr. in Coleridge, *Unpublished Letters,* edited by E.L. Griggs.

(See "Sara Coleridge.")

(3) 3rd quote, p. 155; "become" should read "being"

"Is Genius Conscious of Its Powers?"; orig. collected in Hazlitt, *The Plain Speaker,* edited by
William Hazlitt the Younger. 2 vol. Colburn,
1826.

This is indicated by the reading notes.+

(4) "Blackwood's reviewers called him 'pimply [*sic;*
i.e., pimpled] Hazlitt'"

Anon. review of Charles Lamb, *Works* (2 vol.; C.
and J. Ollier, 1818), in *Blackwood's,* August
1818; quoted in Patmore (see below) and in
William Carew Hazlitt, *Memoirs of William Hazlitt.* 2 vol. Richard Bentley, 1867.

Memoirs is listed in the reading notes (as "Life.
1867") and in Holleyman Addendum.

(5) First quote, p. 156

"Why Distant Objects Please" (see above)

(6) 2nd quote, p. 156

"On the Conduct of Life"; orig. collected in
Hazlitt, *Literary Remains of the Late William
Hazlitt,* edited by E.L. Bulwer and Sergeant Tal-
fourd. 2 vol. Saunders and Otley, 1836.

This is listed in the reading notes.

(7) 3 quotes, bottom of p. 156

"Project for a New Theory of Civil and Criminal
Legislation"; orig. collected in *ibid.*

(8) Quote, middle of p. 157

William Carew Hazlitt, *Memoirs of William Hazlitt* (see above)

(9) First quote, p. 158

William Hazlitt, *Liber Amoris,* w/introduction by
Richard Le Gallienne. Privately printed, 1895.
(Orig. 1823)

This is indicated by the reading notes.

(10) "Mrs. Hazlitt ... faced the fact"

Sarah Hazlitt, diary, Apr. 10, 1822; quoted by
William Carew Hazlitt, *Memoirs of William Hazlitt* (see above)

(11) "[Hazlitt] chooses some abstract idea" (p. 159)

"[On] Envy"; "[On] Egotism"; "[On] Reason and
Imagination"; all orig. collected in *The Plain
Speaker* (see above)

(12) First quote, p. 159

"On Swift, Young, Gray, Collins, Etc."; orig.
collected in Hazlitt, *Lectures on the English
Poets.* (Orig. 1813) 2nd ed. Taylor and Hessey,
1819.

This is indicated by the reading notes and is
listed in Holleyman; it belonged to Leslie Stephen.

(13) "[Hazlitt's] passion for prize-fighting and
Sarah Walker"

(a) "The Fight"; in Hazlitt, *Selected Essays,* edited by George Sampson. Cambridge: University Pr., 1917. (Orig. collected 1836)

This is indicated by the reading notes+ and
is listed in Holleyman; it belonged to Leonard Woolf.

(b) *Liber Amoris* (see above)

(14) "The famous [passage] about reading [Congreve's]
Love for Love [orig. 1695]"

In "Is Genius Conscious of Its Powers?" (see
above)

(15) "The famous [passage] about ... reading [Rous=
seau's] *La Nouvelle Héloïse* [orig. 1761]"

In "On Going a Journey"; orig. collected in *Table Talk* (see above)

(16) Quote, p. 160; "Faces" should read "face"

     "On the Past and Future"; orig. collected in *ibid.*

(17) First quote, p. 161; "the" should read "this"

     "On Genius and Common-Sense, Part I"; orig. collected in *ibid.*

(18) 2nd quote, p. 161; 2nd quote, p. 162

     Cannot locate

(19) Quote, pp. 161-62

     "On Genius and Common-Sense, Part II"; orig. collected in *Table Talk* (see above)

(20) First quote, p. 162; "of" should read "in"

     "On Poetry in General"; orig. collected in *Lectures on the English Poets* (see above)

(21) 3rd quote, p. 162

     "On the Ignorance of the Learned"; orig. collected in *Table Talk* (see above)

(22) "Hazlitt had read only one poem by Donne"

     "On Dryden and Pope"; orig. collected in *Lectures on the English Poets* (see above)

(23) "[Hazlitt] found Shakespeare's sonnets unintelligible"

     "On Milton's Sonnets"; orig. collected in *Table Talk* (see above)

(24) "[Hazlitt] never read a book through after he was thirty"

     Cannot locate

(25) "[Hazlitt] came ... to dislike reading altogether"

     "Is Genius Conscious of Its Powers?" (see above)

(26) 2nd quote from bottom, p. 162

     "On Criticism"; orig. collected in *Table Talk* (see above)

(27) Quote, pp. 162-63

"On Swift, Young, Gray, Collins, Etc." (see above)

The poem praised is William Collins, "Ode on the Poetical Character." (Orig. 1746)

(28) First quote, p. 163 (*re* Geoffrey Chaucer)

"On Chaucer and Spenser"; orig. collected in *Lectures on the English Poets* (see above)

(29) 2nd quote, p. 163 (*re* George Crabbe)

"On Thomson and Cowper"; orig. collected in *ibid.*

(30) "[Hazlitt's] criticism of Scott"

Sir Walter Scott occupies 3 columns of fine print in the Index (Vol. XXI) to Howe's completed edition of Hazlitt (see above).

(31) 3rd quote, p. 163 (*re* Edmund Burke)

"On Reading Old Books" in Hazlitt, *Selected Essays,* edited by George Sampson (see above). (Orig. collected 1826)

This is indicated by the reading notes.+

(32) Last quote, p. 163

"On Old English Writers and Speakers"; orig. collected in *The Plain Speaker* (see above)

(33) Peter George Patmore, *My Friends and Acquaintances.* 3 vol. Saunders and Otley, 1854.

This is indicated by the reading notes.+

(34) Quote, middle of p. 164

"Is Genius Conscious of Its Powers?" (see above)

The 3 contemporary critics addressed by Hazlitt in this quote: William Blackwood, John Wilson Croker, Thomas Moore.

(35) Last quote, p. 164

In William Carew Hazlitt, *Memoirs of William Hazlitt* (see above)

Important Allusions:

(1) Specific Hazlitt essays mentioned but not quoted from:

(a) *Essay on the Principles of Human Action.* (Orig. 1802)

(b) "Hot and Cold"; orig. collected in *The Plain Speaker* (see above)

(c) "'The Picturesque and the [*sic*] Ideal'"

"On the Picturesque and Ideal"; orig. collected in *Table Talk* (see above)

(2) William Hazlitt, *The Life of Napoleon Buonaparte.* (Orig. 1828-30)

This is listed in the reading notes.

(3) William Hazlitt, *Conversations of James Northcote.* (Orig. 1830)

This is listed in the reading notes.

Passing Allusions:

(1) Mentioned by Hazlitt: *The Letters of Junius.* (Orig. 1769-72)

(2) Michel de Montaigne, *Essais.*

(See "Montaigne.")

(3) Charles Lamb, *Essays of Elia.*

(See "The Duchess of Newcastle.")

(4) Joseph Addison, *Sir Roger de Coverley.*

(See "Addison.")

* Of the specific titles employed by Woolf, only "Essay on the Principles of Human Action" and *Lectures on the English Poets* are in the Howe volumes listed: I and V respectively. The reading notes do not indicate either volume.

- -

WINGED PHRASES (CW)--*TLS,* Oct. 30, 1919

Obvious Source
(stated in *TLS* with essay and in headnote):

George Moore, *Avowals.* Privately printed, 1919.

Important Allusions:

   (1) Mentioned by Moore:

      (a) "as Henry James said" (p. 141)

         Henry James, letter to George Moore, n.d. given

         The novel referred to was Moore, *A Mummer's Wife*. (Orig. 1884)

      (b) "Edmund Gosse's statement" (p. 142)

         Moore: "It must have been in some essay or preface"

         Cannot locate

      (c) Jane Austen, *Sense and Sensibility*. (Orig. 1811)

      (d) Miscellaneous writers: John Lloyd Balderston, Honoré de Balzac, Charles Dickens, Fyodor Dostoieffsky, Henry Fielding, Théophile Gautier, the Goncourts, Rudyard Kipling, Stephane Mallarmé, Guy de Maupassant, Walter Pater, Sir Walter Scott, William Makepeace Thackeray, Anthony Trollope, Leo Tolstoy, Ivan Turgenev

      (e) Joris Karl Huysmans, *En Route*. (Orig., in French, [1895])

   (2) George Moore, *Esther Waters*.

      (See "A Born Writer.")

- -

WITHIN THE RIM (1)--*TLS,* March 27, 1919, p. 163; first collected in *D.M.*

Obvious Source
(stated in *TLS* with essay):

   Henry James, *Within the Rim and Other Essays, 1914-15*. W. Collins, 1919.

- -

WOMEN AND FICTION (II)--*Forum,* March 1929, pp. 179-83;
first collected in *G.R.*

Supportive Sources:

(1) "Lady Murasaki, writing"

Lady Shikib[u] Murasaki, *The Tale of Genji.* (Orig. 11th cent.) Prob. ed.: trans. by Arthur Waley. 4 vol. G. Allen and Unwin, 1925-28.

Woolf reviewed Vol. I for *Vogue* (London), 66 (late July 1925), 53, 80. It is listed in Holleyman Addendum.

(2) Jane Austen, *Pride and Prejudice.* (Orig. 1813)

(3) Emily Brontë, *Wuthering Heights.* (Orig. 1847)

(4) Charlotte Brontë, *Villette.* (Orig. 1853)

(5) George Eliot, *Middlemarch.* (Orig. 1872-73)

(6) Charlotte Brontë, *Jane Eyre.* (Orig. 1847)

Important Allusions:

(1) Miscellaneous writers: George Henry Lewes, Sappho

(2) Leo Tolstoy, *War and Peace.* (Orig. 1868)

Passing Allusions:

(1) Miscellaneous male writers: Thomas Carlyle, Joseph Conrad, Charles Dickens, Gustave Flaubert, Samuel Johnson, John Keats, John Milton, William Shakespeare

(2) Quote, p. 142:

George Macaulay Trevelyan, *History of England.* Longmans, 1926.

This is listed in Holleyman.

- -

WOMEN NOVELISTS (CW) and WW)--*TLS,* Oct. 17, 1918, p. 495

Obvious Source
(stated in *TLS* with essay and in headnotes):

R[eginald] Brimley Johnson, *The Women Novelists.* W. Collins, 1918.

Important Allusions (mentioned by Johnson [see above]):

Miscellaneous women writers: Jane Austen, Charlotte Brontë, Fanny Burney, George Eliot

Passing Allusions:

Various characters: Thackeray, *Vanity Fair* (1848)-- Becky Sharp; Austen, *Emma* (1816)--Mr. [Henry] Woodhouse

- -

Part IV
The Appendices

A NOTE ON THE APPENDICES

A. *COLLECTIONS OF ESSAYS BY VIRGINIA WOOLF*

The 10 collections of Woolf's essays, with their contents,
are listed here in chronological order.   (A brief account
of their history will be found in the foreword to this
study.)

B. *AN ADDENDUM TO HOLLEYMAN:* *
"Books on Literature in the Woolf Library Owned by Wash-
ington State University and the University of Texas"

This list constitutes the "Holleyman Addendum" that is
mentioned frequently in the charts. For making its contents possible I offer my sincere gratitude to Leila Luedeking of Washington State University, Pullman, Washington, for her kind help on the several occasions when I
visited the campus to work in the Woolf collection there;
and to Helen S. Dunlap of the Humanities Research Center,
University of Texas (Austin), who generously shared with
me, by mail, bibliographical information concerning the
purchases made by the University of Texas from the Woolf
library at a Sotheby's sale in the early 1970s. Both libraries have catalogued the books involved. At the University of Texas, Austin, they form part of the special
Humanities Collection; at Washington State, part of the
Library of Rare Books.

The phrase "on literature" is slightly misleading in a
very few cases where I have listed books on subjects
like Lepidoptera and the solar universe, which Virginia
Woolf scholars will recognize as important to her personal, creative imagery.

C. *INDEX OF AUTHORS AND WORKS NAMED IN THE COLLECTED ESSAYS*

More than once, when the 4 volumes of *Collected Essays*
were issued in the 1960s, reviewers complained of the fact
that they lacked an index--so that someone wishing to
read Virginia Woolf's comments on, say, William Shakespeare
or James Joyce would be unable to, --except by scanning each
page separately. The Index presented here is an attempt
to remedy such a situation for all 7 basic collections.

---

*For complete title, see Table of Contents, *infra.*

It also serves as an index to the charts just completed, emphasizing again the authors and titles of literary works, rather than pedestrian studies.

COLLECTIONS OF ESSAYS BY VIRGINIA WOOLF

The Common Reader [*C.R. I*]. 1925.

   Contents: Preface ("The Common Reader"), The Pastons
   and Chaucer, On Not Knowing Greek, The Elizabethan
   Lumber Room, Notes on an Elizabethan Play, Mon-
   taigne, The Duchess of Newcastle, Rambling Round
   Evelyn, Defoe, Addison, Lives of the Obscure (Tay-
   lors and Edgeworths, Laetitia Pilkington, Miss Or-
   merod [Amer. ed. only]), Jane Austen, Modern Fiction,
   Jane Eyre and *Wuthering Heights*, George Eliot, The
   Russian Point of View, Outlines (Miss Mitford, Dr.
   Bentley, Lady Dorothy Nevill, Archbishop Thomson),
   The Patron and the Crocus, The Modern Essay, Jo-
   seph Conrad, How It Strikes a Contemporary

The Common Reader: Second Series [*C.R. II*]. 1932.
(Called in America and in Penguin ed. [1944] *The Second
Common Reader*)

   Contents: The Strange Elizabethans, Donne After Three
   Centuries, *The Countess of Pembroke's Arcadia*, *Rob-
   inson Crusoe*, Dorothy Osborne's *Letters*, Swift's
   Journal to Stella, *The Sentimental Journey*, Lord
   Chesterfield's Letters to His Son, Two Parsons (James
   Woodforde, The Rev. John Skinner), Dr. Burney's Eve-
   ning Party, Jack Mytton, De Quincey's Autobiography,
   Four Figures (Cowper and Lady Austen, Beau Brummell,
   Mary Wollstonecraft, Dorothy Wordsworth), William
   Hazlitt, Geraldine and Jane, *Aurora Leigh*, The Niece
   of an Earl, George Gissing, The Novels of George Mer-
   edith, "I Am Christina Rossetti," The Novels of Thom-
   as Hardy, How Should One Read a Book?

The Death of the Moth [*D.M.*]. 1942. Edited by Leonard
Woolf. (Asterisks indicate so-called personal essays.)

   Contents: *The Death of the Moth, *Evening Over Sussex: Reflections in a Motor Car, *Three Pictures,
   *Old Mrs. Gray, *Street Haunting: A London Adven-
   ture, Jones and Wilkinson, *Twelfth Night* at the Old
   Vic, Madame de Sévigné, The Humane Art, Two Antiquaries: Walpole and Cole, The Rev. William Cole:
   A Letter, The Historian and "The Gibbon," Reflections at Sheffield Place, The Man at the Gate, Sara

Coleridge, "Not One of Us," *Within the Rim*, The Old
Order, *The Letters of Henry James*, George Moore, The
Novels of E.M. Forster, Middlebrow, The Art of Biog-
raphy, Craftsmanship, A Letter to a Young Poet, Why?,
Professions for Women, *Thoughts on Peace in an Air
Raid

The Moment [*M.*]. 1947. Edited by Leonard Woolf.

Contents: *The Moment: Summer's Night, On Being Ill,
The Faery Queen, Congreve's Comedies, Sterne's
Ghost, Mrs. Thrale, Gas at Abbotsford, *The Antiquary*,
Lockhart's Criticism, *David Copperfield*, Lewis Car-
roll, Edmund Gosse, Notes on D.H. Lawrence, Roger
Fry, The Art of Fiction, American Fiction, The Lean-
ing Tower, On Re-reading Novels, Personalities, Pic-
tures, Harriette Wilson, Genius: B.R. Haydon, The En-
chanted Organ: Anne Thackeray, Two Women: Emily Da-
vies and Lady Augusta Stanley,Ellen Terry, *To Spain,
Fishing, The Artist and Politics, *Royalty [1939],
Royalty [1934]

The Captain's Death Bed [*C.D.B.*]. 1950. Edited by Leonard Woolf.

Contents: Oliver Goldsmith, White's Selborne, Life
Itself [cf. "James Woodforde" in *Second Common Read-
er*], Crabbe, Selina Trimmer, The Captain's Death Bed,
Ruskin, The Novels of Turgenev, Half of Thomas Hardy,
Leslie Stephen, Mr. Conrad: A Conversation, The Cos-
mos, Walter Raleigh, Mr. Bennett and Mrs. Brown, All
About Books, Reviewing, Modern Letters, Reading, The
Cinema, Walter Sickert, *Flying Over London, *The
Sun and the Fish, *Gas, *Thunder at Wembley, Memories
of a Working Women's Guild

Granite and Rainbow [*G.R.*]. 1958. Edited by Leonard
Woolf.

Contents: The Narrow Bridge of Art, Hours in a Li-
brary, "Impassioned Prose," Life and the Novelist,
On Re-reading Meredith, The Anatomy of Fiction, Goth-
ic Romance, The Supernatural in Fiction, Henry James's
Ghost Stories, A Terribly Sensitive Mind, Women and
Fiction, An Essay in Criticism, Phases of Fiction,
The New Biography, A Talk About Memoirs, Sir Walter
Raleigh, Sterne, Eliza and Sterne, Horace Walpole,
A Friend of Johnson, Fanny Burney's Half-sister, Mon-
ey and Love, The Dream, *The Fleeting Portrait (Wax-
works at the Abbey, The Royal Academy), Poe's Helen,
Visits to Walt Whitman, Oliver Wendell Holmes

Contemporary Writers [*CW*]. 1965. Edited by Jean Guiguet.

> Contents: The Claim of the Living, Caution and Crit-
> icism, In a Library, Women Novelists, A Man with a
> View, The Way of All Flesh, Journeys in Spain, The
> Sentimental Traveller, The Inward Light, One Im-
> mortality, A Room with a View, The Park Wall, Before
> Midnight, South Wind, Books and Persons, Mr. Gals-
> worthy's Novel, Philosophy in Fiction, The Green
> Mirror, Moments of Vision, Mr. Merrick's Novels, The
> "Movie" Novel, Sylvia and Michael, War in the Vil-
> lage, The Rights of Youth, Mr. Hudson's Childhood,
> Honest Fiction, September, The Three Black Pennys,
> Java Head, Gold and Iron, The Pursuit of Beauty,
> Pleasant Stories, Mummery, The Tunnel, Romance and
> the Heart, The Obstinate Lady, Mr. Norris's Method,
> Mr. Norris's Standard, A Real American, Sonia Mar-
> ried, Winged Phrases, A Born Writer, Cleverness and
> Youth, Freudian Fiction, Revolution, Postscript or
> Prelude?

Collected Essays [*C.E.*]. 4 vol. 1966-67. Edited by Leonard Woolf. (For contents, see charts, *infra.*)

Books and Portraits [*BP*]. 1977. Edited by Mary Lyon.

> Contents: *In the Orchard, *A Woman's College from
> Outside, *On a Faithful Friend, English Prose, *Im-
> pressions at Bayreuth, Modes and Manners of the Nine-
> teenth Century, Men and Women, Coleridge as Critic,
> Patmore's Criticism, Papers on Pepys, Sheridan, Thom-
> as Hood, Praeterita, Mr Kipling's Notebook, Emerson's
> Journals, Thoreau, Herman Melville, Rupert Brooke,
> The Intellectual Imagination, "These Are the Plans,"
> Mr Sassoon's Poems, A Russian Schoolboy, A Glance at
> Turgenev, A Giant with Very Small Thumbs, Dostoevsky
> the Father, More Dostoevsky, Dostoevsky in Cranford,
> The Russian Background, A Scribbling Dame, Maria
> Edgeworth and Her Circle, Jane Austen and the Geese,
> Mrs Gaskell, The Compromise, Wilcoxiana, The Genius
> of Boswell, Shelley and Elizabeth Hitchener, Liter-
> ary Geography, Flumina Amem Silvasque, Haworth No-
> vember 1904, The Girlhood of Queen Elizabeth, The
> Diary of a Lady in Waiting, Queen Adelaide, Eliza-
> beth Lady Holland, Lady Hester Stanhope, The Mem-
> oirs of Sarah Bernhardt, Lady Strachey, John Delane,
> Body and Brain

Women and Writing [*WW*]. 1979. Edited by Michèle Barrett.

> Contents: Women and Fiction, Women and Leisure [a
> letter], The Intellectual Status of Women [a letter],
> Professions for Women, Men and Women, Women Novel-
> ists, Indiscretions, The Duchess of Newcastle, Aphra

Behn [extract from *A Room of One's Own*], A Scribbling
Dame, Mary Wollstonecraft, Jane Austen Practising,
Jane Austen, Haworth November 1904, *Jane Eyre* and
Wuthering Heights, *Aurora Leigh*, Mrs. Gaskell,
George Eliot, "I Am Christina Rossetti," The Compro-
mise, Wilcoxiana, Olive Schreiner, A Terribly Sensi-
tive Mind, Dorothy Richardson, Royalty [1934]

AN ADDENDUM TO HOLLEYMAN:
BOOKS ON LITERATURE IN THE WOOLF LIBRARY
OWNED BY WASHINGTON STATE UNIVERSITY
AND THE UNIVERSITY OF TEXAS

(Asterisks indicate Texas holdings)

*Abercrombie, Lascelles. *Emblems of Love*. J. Lane, 1912.

Abercrombie, Lascelles, comp. *New English Poems*. V. Gollancz, 1931.

Abercrombie, Lascelles. *Thomas Hardy*. M. Secker, 1919.

Acland, Sir Arthur Herbert Dyke, ed. *A Guide to the Choice of Books for Students and General Readers*. E. Stanford, 1891.

Addison, Joseph. *The Dramatic Works of the Right Honourable Joseph Addison, Esq.* Glasgow: R. and A. Foulis, 1752.

Addison, Joseph. (See Pope, Alexander. *Letters*.)

Addison, Joseph. *Essays,* ed. by Russell David Gillman. George Newnes, n.d.

Adès, Albert. *Le Livre de Goha le Simple,* w/preface by Octave Mirabeau. Paris: Calmann-Levy, 1919(?).

Aeschylus, ed. by Frederick A. Paley. G. Bell, 1874. Belonged to Leonard.

Aeschylus. *Eschyle,* trans. by Leconte de Lisle. Paris: A. Lemerre, 1889(?).

Aeschylus. *Eumenides,* ed. by A. Sidgwick. Oxford: Clarendon, 1895. Belonged to Leonard.

Aeschylus. *Prometheus Bound,* trans. by Janet Case. J.M. Dent, 1905.

Aikin, W.A., and H.W. Fowler. *English Vowel-Sounds* by W.A. Aikin, w/introduction by Robert Bridges. AND *On "ing," A Reply to Dr. Jespersen's Paper in [S.P.E.] Tract 25* by H.W. Fowler. Oxford: Clarendon, 1927.

Akenside, Mark. *The Pleasures of Imagination. A Poem.*
R. Dodsley, 1744.

*Aldington, Richard. *Very Heaven.* W. Heinemann, 1937.

Anderson, Hans Christian. *Stories and Fairytales,* trans.
by H. Oskar Summer. G. Allen, 1893. [2 vol.] Vol.
II only.

Anstey, F. (See Guthrie, Thomas Anstey.)

Anstey, John. (See Chalmers, George.)

*An Apology for the Life of Mr. T[heophilus] C[ibber],
Comedian.* J. Mehell, 1740. Belonged to Leslie Stephen.

[*Arabian Nights*.] *Le livre des mille nuits et une nuit,*
trans. from the Arabic by J.C. Mardrus. Paris: La
Revue Blanche, 1900-04. 16 vol. Vols.I through VIII
only.

[*Arabian Nights*.] *Le livre des mille nuits et une nuit,*
trans. from the Arabic by J.C. Mardrus. Paris: E.
Fasquelle, 1908-12. 16 vol. Vol. I only. "V.S.
from J.R." [Jacques Raverat?].

Aristotle, *Metaphysica,* ed. by W. Christ. Leipzig: Teubner, 1895. Belonged to Leonard.

Arnold, Matthew. *Poems.* Macmillan, 1869. 2 vol. Belonged to Leslie Stephen.

Arnot, R. Page. *William Morris, A Vindication.* Martin
Lawrence, 1934.

Astell, Mary. (See *Reflections Upon Marriage*.)

Aungerville, Richard. (See Richard de Bury.)

Aurelius Antoninus, Marcus. *The Emperor Marcus Antoninus
His Conversation with Himself. Together with the Pre-
liminary Discourse of the Learned Gataker,* trans. by
Jeremy Collier. 2nd ed. R. Sare, 1708. Belonged
to Leslie Stephen.

Austen, Jane. *The Complete Novels of,* w/introduction by
J.C. Squire. William Heinemann, 1928.

Austen, Jane. *Five Letters from Jane Austen to Her Niece
Fanny Knight.* Oxford: Clarendon, 1924.

Austen, Jane. *Lady Susan.* Oxford: Clarendon, 1925.

Austen, Jane. *Pride and Prejudice.* 3rd ed. T. Egerton,
1817. 2 vol. "Virginia from J.M.K. [John Maynard
Keynes] ... "

Austen, Jane. *Two Chapters of Persuasion Printed from Jane Austen's Autograph.* Oxford: Clarendon, 1926. 2 copies of this, one printed on "hand-made paper" and w/facsimile of Austen's MS bound in.

Austen, Jane. *Volume the First.* Oxford: Clarendon, 1933.

Austen-Leigh, James Edward. *Memoir of Jane Austen, by Her Nephew,* ed. by R.W. Chapman. Oxford: Clarendon, 1926.

Austen-Leigh, Mary Augusta. *Personal Aspects of Jane Austen.* John Murray, 1920.

Aytoun, William Edmonstoune, ed. *The Ballads of Scotland.* Edinburgh: W. Blackwood, 1858. [2 vol.] Vol. II only.

Ball, Sir Robert Stawell. *A Popular Guide to the Heavens.* 3rd ed. G. Phillip, 1910.

Baring, Maurice, comp. *Algae, an Anthology of Phrases.* W. Heinemann, 1928.

*Baring, Maurice. *C.* Garden City, N.Y.: Doubleday, Page, 1924. 2 copies of this; one is author's presentation copy to Virginia Woolf.

Baring, Maurice. *Comfortless Memory.* W. Heinemann, 1928.

Baring, Maurice. *Passing By.* Martin Secker, 1921. "Virginia Woolf from Maurice Baring ... "

Baring, Maurice. *The Puppet Show of Memory.* W. Heinemann, 1922.

Baring, Maurice. *R.F.C.H.Q. 1914-1918.* G. Bell, 1920. "Virginia Woolf from Maurice Baring ... "

*Baring, Maurice. *Sarah Bernhardt.* P. Davies, 1933. Author's presentation copy to Virginia Woolf.

Barker, Granville. *Waste: A Tragedy.* Sidgwick and Jackson, 1905.

Barnes, William. *Select Poems of,* ed. by Thomas Hardy. Henry Frowde, 1908.

Barrès, Maurice. *Mes Cahiers.* *Tome III.* Paris: Plom, 1931.

Baudelaire, Charles. *Les Fleurs du Mal,* w/introduction by Théophile Gautier. New ed. Paris: Calmann Levy, 1890. Belonged to Leonard.

*Baudelaire, Charles. *Intimate Journals,* trans. by Chris-
  topher Isherwood; w/introduction by T.S. Eliot.
  Blackamore, 1930. Presentation copy to Virginia
  Woolf from T.S. Eliot.

Baynard, Edward. *Health of a Poem.* [J. Roberts, 1749].

     (BOUND WITH Akenside, Mark. *The Pleasures ... , q.v.)*

Bayne, Alicia. (See Pryme, Jane Townley.)

Beckford, Peter. *Thoughts of Hunting,* w/introduction by
  Charles Richardson. Chapman and Dodd, n.d.

[Beckford, William]. *Recollection of an Excursion to the
  Monasteries of Alcobaca and Batalha.* R. Bentley,
  1835. "Virginia from Lytton [Strachey] ... "

Beddoes, Thomas Lovell. *Death's Jest Book: or The Fool's
  Tragedy.* William Pickering, 1850.

Beddoes, Thomas Lovell. *Poems.* William Pickering, 1851.

Beerbohm, Max. *And Even Now.* William Heinemann, 1920.

Beethoven, Ludwig von. *Beethoven's Letters,* ed. by A.C.
  Kalischer and A. Eaglefield-Hull; trans. by J.S.
  Shedlock. J.M. Dent, 1926.

Bell, Clive. *An Account of French Painting.* Chatto and
  Windus, 1931.

*Bell, Clive. *Ad Familiares.* [Pelican Pr., 1917]. Author's presentation copy to Virginia.

Bell, Clive. *Art.* Chatto and Windus, 1914.

Bell, Clive. *Civilization, an Essay.* Chatto and Windus,
  1928. 2 copies of this, one inscribed "Virginia
  from Clive."

Bell, Clive. *Peace at Once.* Manchester and London: National Labour Pr., 1915. 2 copies of this.

Bell, Clive. *Pot-Boilers.* Chatto and Windus, 1918.

Bell, Clive. *Since Cézanne.* Chatto and Windus, 1922.

Bell, Clive. *War Mongers.* The Peace Pledge Union, 1938.

Bell, Gertrude Lowthian. *The Letters of,* ed. by Lady
  [Florence] Bell. Ernest Benn, 1930. Belonged to
  Leonard.

Bell, Julian. *Winter Movement and Other Poems*. Chatto
and Windus, 1930. " ... to my dear Aunt Virginia ...
[from author]."

Bennett, Arnold. *Anna of the Five Towns*. Methuen, 1912.

Benson, Stella. *Goodbye, Stranger*. N.Y.: Macmillan,
1926.

Beresford, John. *Gossip of the Seventeenth and Eighteenth
Centuries*. R. Cobden-Sanderson, 1923. Review slip.

Beresford, John. *The Hampdenshire Wonder*. Martin Secker,
1926.

Beyle, Marie Henri (Stendhal). *Armance,* ed. by Raymond
Lebèque; w/preface by André Gide. Paris: E. Champion,
1925. Review slip.

Beyle, Marie Henri (Stendhal). *De l'Amour,* ed. by Daniel
Muller and Pierre Jourda; w/preface by Etienne Rey.
Paris: H. Champion, 1926. Review slip.

Beyle, Marie Henri (Stendhal). *Histoire de la Peinture
en Italie,* ed. w/preface by Paul Arbelet. Paris: E.
Champion, 1924. 2 vol. Review slip.

Beyle, Marie Henri (Stendhal). *Journal,* Vol. I, ed. by
Henry Debraye and Louis Royer. Paris: E. Champion,
1923. Review slip.

Beyle, Marie Henri (Stendhal). *Lucien Leuwen,* ed. by
Henry Debraye; w/preface by Paul Valéry. Paris: H.
Champion, 1926-27. [4 vol.] Vol. II only. Review
slip.

Beyle, Marie Henri (Stendhal). *Napoleon,* ed. by Louis
Royer; w/preface by Albert Pingaud. Paris: H.
Champion, 1929. 2 vol.

Beyle, Marie Henri (Stendhal). *Racine et Shakespeare,* ed.
w/preface by Pierre Martino. Paris: E. Champion,
1925. 2 vol.

Beyle, Marie Henri (Stendhal). *Le Rouge et le Noir,* ed.
by Jules Marsan; w/preface by Paul Bourget. Paris:
E. Champion, 1923. 2 vol. Review slip.

Beyle, Marie Henri (Stendhal). *Vie de Rossini,* ed/w
preface by Henry Prunières. Paris: E. Champion,
1922. 2 vol. Review slip.

Bible, O.T. (See Book of Job.)

Binyon, Laurence. *The Sirens, An Ode*. Macmillan, 1925.
Review slip.

Biriukoff, Paul (Pavel Biryukov). *The Life of Tolstoy,* trans. and abridged from the Russian [by ?]. Cassell, 1911.

Birkhead, Edith. *Christina Rossetti and Her Poetry.* G.G. Harrap, 1930.

Blake, William. *The Lyrical Poems of,* ed. by John Sampson; w/introduction by Walter Raleigh. Oxford: Clarendon, 1905.

Blake, William. *The Poems of,* [ed. by R.H. Shepherd]. Basil Montagu Pickering, 1874.

Blake, William. *Songs of Innocence and of Experience,* ed. by R.H. Shepherd. Basil Montagu Pickering, 1868.

Blake, William. *William Blake,* ed. by Edward Thompson. Augustan Books of English Poetry ser. E. Benn, n.d.

*Blanche, Jacques Emile. *Cahiers d'un Artiste.* Paris: Emile-Paul Frères, 1915-17. Vols. I and II only. Author's presentation copies to Virginia Woolf.

Blessington, Marguerita, Countess of, [Marguerite (Power) Farmer Gardiner]. *Conversations of Lord Byron with the Countess of Blessington.* R. Bentley, 1834.

Blunden, Edmund. *English Poems.* Richard Cobden-Sanderson, 1925. Belonged to Leonard.

Boileau-Despréaux, Nicolas. *Oeuvres,* ed. by Claude Brossette. Geneva: Fabri Barriot, 1716. 2 vol.

The Book of Job According to the Authorized Version. George Bell, 1900. Belonged to Leonard.

Borrow, George Henry. *Wild Wales--Its People, Language and Scenery.* J. Murray, 1924.

Bosanquet, Theodora. *Harriet Martineau, An Essay in Comprehension.* Frederick Etchells and Hugh Macdonald, 1927. "Virginia Woolf ... [from] Theodora Bosanquet."

Boswell, James. *The Journal of a Tour to Corsica; and Memoirs of Pascal Paoli,* ed. by S.C. Roberts. Cambridge: University Pr., 1923. "To Victoria [*sic*] Woolf from Augustine Birrell ... "

Boswell, James. *The Journal of a Tour to the Hebrides with Samuel Johnson.* J.M. Dent, 1902.

*Bowen, Elizabeth. *The Cat Jumps, and Other Stories.* Victor Gollancz, 1934.

*Bowen, Elizabeth. *The Death of the Heart.* Victor Go-
    llancz, 1938. Inscribed by author to Virginia.

*Bowen, Elizabeth. *Friends and Relations.* Constable, 1931.

*Bowen, Elizabeth. *The House in Paris.* Victor Gollancz,
    1935. Inscribed by author to Virginia.

*Bowen, Elizabeth. *The Last September.* Constable, 1929.

*Bowen, Elizabeth. *To the North.* Victor Gollancz, 1932.

Bowes-Lyon, Lilian Helen. *The White Hare and Other Poems.*
    J. Cape, 1934.

Bowles, Edward Augustus. *A Handbook of Crocus and Colchi-
    cum for Gardeners.* M. Hopkinson, 1924.

Brailsford, Henry Noel. *Shelley, Godwin, and Their Cir-
    cle.* Williams and Norgate, 1913 . Belonged to Leo-
    nard.

Bridges, J.H. *The Unity of Comte's Life and Doctrine.* N.
    Trübner, 1866. (BOUND WITH Stephen, Leslie, *The
    "Times"* ... , *q.v.*)

Bridges, Robert. (See Fowler, H.W. Also Paget, Sir Rich-
    ard.)

Bridges, Robert, ed. *The Spirit of Man.* Longmans, Green,
    1917.

*Brittain, Vera Mary. *Testament of Friendship.* Macmillan,
    1940. "For Virginia Woolf ... from Vera Brittain
    ... "

Brontë, Charlotte. *The Professor* by Currer Bell. Smith,
    Elder, 1857. 2 vol.

Brontë, Charlotte. *Shirley* by Currer Bell. Smith, Elder,
    1849. 3 vol.

Brontë, Charlotte. *Twelve Adventurers and Other Stories.*
    Hodder and Stoughton, 1925.

Brontë, Charlotte. *Villette* by Currer Bell. Smith, El-
    der, 1853. 3 vol.

Brontë, Charlotte, and family. *Life* [by Elizabeth Gas-
    kell] *and Works of Charlotte Brontë and Her Sisters,*
    w/introductions by Mrs. Humphry Ward [Mary Augusta
    Arnold Ward]. "Haworth Edition." John Murray, 1924.
    [7 vol.] Vol. IV only. (Includes *The Professor* by
    Charlotte, and *Poems* by Charlotte, Emily, Anne, and
    the Reverend Patrick Brontë.)

Brooke, Rupert, *Letters from America,* w/preface by Henry
    James. Sidgwick and Jackson, 1916.

Browne, Sir Thomas. *Hydriotaphia, Urn Burial,* [and *Bromp-*
    ton ... Urns], w/introduction and notes by Sir John
    Evans. C. Whittingham, 1893.

Browne, Sir Thomas. *Religio Medici and Urn-Burial.* Tem-
    ple Classics ser. J.M. Dent, 1897. Belonged to Leo-
    nard.

Browning, Elizabeth Barrett. *The Letters of,* ed. by Fred-
    eric G. Kenyon. 3rd ed. Smith, Elder, 1898. 2
    vol.

Browning, Elizabeth Barrett. *Letters of ... Addressed to*
    Richard Hengist Horne ... , ed. by S.R. Townshend
    Mayer. Richard Bentley, 1877. 2 vol.

Browning, Robert. *Pocket Volume of Selections from the*
    Poetical Works of. Smith, Elder, 1894. "For Vir-
    ginia from G.H.D. [George Herbert Duckworth] ... "

Browning, Robert. *The Poetical Works of.* Smith, Elder,
    1900. [2 vol.] Vol. II only. Belonged to Leslie
    Stephen.

Browning, Robert. *Red Cotton Night-Cap Country, or Turf*
    and Towers. Smith, Elder, 1873.

Browning, Robert and Elizabeth Barrett. *The Letters of,*
    [ed. by Robert Barrett Browning]. John Murray, 1930.
    2 vol. in one.

Buffon, George Louis Leclerc. *Oeuvres Choisies.* Tours:
    A. Maure, 1858. Belonged to Julia Jackson, Virgin-
    ia's mother.

Bunyan, John. *The Pilgrim's Progress from This World to*
    That Which Is to Come, ed. by James Blanton Wharey.
    Oxford: Clarendon, 1928. Belonged to Leonard.

[Burges, George]. *Cato to Lord Byron on the Immorality of*
    His Writings. W. Wotton, 1824.

Burke's Peerage. 85th ed. 1927.

Burton, Robert. *Anatomy of Melancholy,* ed. by A.R. Shil-
    leto. G. Bell, 1893. 3 vol. Belonged to Leonard.

Bury, J.B. *A History of Greece to the Death of Alexander*
    the Great. Macmillan, 1900.

Butcher, S.H. *Some Aspects of the Greek Genius.* [2nd
    ed.] Macmillan, 1893.

[Byron, Lord, George Gordon]. *Astarte: A Fragment of Truth Concerning George Gordon Byron, Sixth Lord Byron. Recorded by His Grandson, Ralph Milbanke, Earl of Lovelace.* Chiswick Pr., 1905. Belonged to Thoby Stephen.

Byron, Lord, George Gordon. (See Blessington, Marguerite, Countess of.)

Cabell, James Branch. *Ballades from the Hidden Way.* N.Y.: Crosby Gaige, 1928.

Caesar, Julius. *Commentaries.* (In Latin.) Oxford and London: Jacob Parker, 1875. Belonged to Leonard.

Caine, T. Hall. *Recollections of Dante Gabriel Rossetti.* Elliot Stock, 1882.

Canton, William. *William Canton.* The Augustan Books of Modern Poetry ser. E. Benn, n.d.

Carew, Bampfylde Moore. *The Surprising Adventures of Bampfylde Moore Carew, King of the Beggars. Containing ... a Dictionary of the Cant Language ...* New ed. Taunton, 1812. Belonged to Leslie Stephen.

Carlyle, Thomas. *History of Friedrich the Second, ... Called Frederick the Great.* Chapman and Hall, 1869. 7 vol.

Carlyle, Thomas. *Past and Present.* Chapman and Hall, 1843.

Carter, Elizabeth. *Memoirs of the Life of Mrs. Elizabeth Carter,* ed. by Montagu Pennington. F.C. and J. Rivington, 1807.

Carter, Reginald. *He and His.* J. Cape, 1940.

Casanova de Seingalt, Giacomo. *Mémoires de Jacques Casanova de Seingalt..* Brussels: Rozez, 1887. 6 vol.

Case, Janet E. *Country Diaries.* Salisbury: River Pr., 1939.

Catalogue of the Principal English Books in Circulation at Mudie's Select Library. Mudie's, 1918.

Cecil, Lord David. *Jane Austen.* Cambridge: University Pr., 1935.

Cecil, Lord David. *The Young Melbourne, and the Story of His Marriage with Caroline Lamb.* Constable, 1939. "Dear Virginia ... Yr David Cecil."

Céline, Louis Ferdinand.   (See Destouches, Louis Ferdi-
     nand.)

Centlivre, Susannah, Sir John Vanbrugh, and John Gay.
     The Busy Body, a Comedy, by Mrs. Centlivre ...   J.
     Bell, 1776.   BOUND WITH *The Provok'd Wife, a Comedy,*
     by Sir John Vanbrugh ...   J. Bell, 1776.   BOUND WITH
     The Beggar's Opera, by John Gay ...   J. Bell, 1777.
     BOUND WITH *A Bold Stroke for a Wife, a Comedy,* by
     Mrs. Centlivre.   J. Bell, 1776.

Cervantes Saavedra, Miguel de.   *The History of the Valor-
     ous and Witty Knight-Errant Don Quixote of the Man-
     cha,* trans. by Thomas Skelton.   Macmillan, 1908.   3
     vol.

Chalmers, George.   *The Life of Daniel Defoe.*   J. Stock-
     dale, 1790.   BOUND WITH *The Pleader's Guide, a Di-
     dactic Poem,* by John Surrebutter [John Anstey].   T.
     Cadell and W. Davies, 1796-1803.   2 parts.   BOUND
     WITH *Cupid and Psyche, A Mythological Tale,* [by Hud-
     son Gurney].   J. Wright, 1799.

The Chapbook (A Yearly Miscellany), ed. by Harold Monro.
     Jonathan Cape, 1925.   [Contains "Obscurity" by Leo-
     nard Woolf.]

Chapman, George.   (See Marlowe, Christopher.)

Chapman, George.   *The Works of ... : Plays,* ed. by Rich-
     ard Hearne Shepherd.   Chatto and Windus, 1874.   Be-
     longed to Leslie Stephen.

Charteris, Evans.   *The Life and Letters of Sir Edmund
     Gosse.*   William Heinemann, 1931.

Chateaubriand, Francois Auguste René.   *Mémoires d'Outre
     Tombe.*   Paris: Legrand, Troussel et Pomey, n.d.   6
     vol.

Chaucer, Geoffrey.   *The Complete Works of,* ed. by Walter
     W. Skeat.   Oxford: Clarendon, 1894-1900.   6 vol.

Chaucer, Geoffrey.   *The Complete Works of,* ed. by Walter
     W. Skeat.   Oxford: Clarendon, 1901.

Chekhov, Anton.   *The Bishop and Other Stories,* trans. by
     Constance Garnett.   Chatto and Windus, 1919.

Chekhov, Anton.   *The Chorus Girl and Other Stories,* trans.
     by Constance Garnett.   Chatto and Windus, 1922.

Chekhov, Anton.   *The Darling and Other Stories,* trans. by
     Constance Garnett.   Chatto and Windus, 1916.

Chekhov, Anton. *Izbrannye Razskazy. [Collected Tales].*
Vol. II. N.Y.: [publ.?], n.d. (Includes "Khirur-
gia" ["Surgery" (1884)], "Vanka" (1886), "Chelovek
v futliare" ["The Man in a Case" (1898)], "V'more"
["At Sea, or, A Sailor's Story" (1883)].)

Chekhov, Anton. *The Lady with the Dog and Other Stories,*
trans. by Constance Garnett. Chatto and Windus, 1917.

Chekhov, Anton. *The Wife and Other Stories,* trans. by
Constance Garnett. Chatto and Windus, 1918.

Chekhov, Anton. [See also Tchekoff.]

Chesterton, G.K. *Robert Browning.* English Men of Letters ser. Macmillan, 1903. Belonged to Leonard.

Church of England. *Book of Common Prayer.* Eyre and Spot-
tiswoode, 1936(?).

Cicero, Marcus Tullius. *De Finibus Bonorum et Malorum,
Libri quinque,* ed. by C.F.W. Muller. Leipzig: Teubner, 1897. Belonged to Leonard.

Clemens, Samuel Langhorne. *The Choice Humorous Works of
Mark Twain.* Chatto and Windus, 1877.

Clifford, James Lowry. *Hester Lynch Piozzi (Mrs. Thrale).*
Oxford: Clarendon, 1941.

Clough, Arthur Hugh. *Poems.* [9th ed. Macmillan, 1880(?)].

Clough, Arthur Hugh. *Poems.* New ed. Macmillan, 1898.

Cobbett, William. *Selections, with Hazlitt's Essay,* w/in-
troduction by A.M.D. Hughes. Oxford: Clarendon,
1923.

Cohen, Victor. *Jeremy Bentham.* Fabian Tract ser. The
Fabian Society, 1927.

Cole, William. *The Blecheley Diary of the Rev. William
Cole, ... 1765-67,* ed. by Francis Griffin Stokes,
w/introduction by Helen Waddell. Constable, 1931.
"Virginia Woolf, from Helen Waddell ... "

Coleman, William Stephen. *British Butterflies, Figures
and Descriptions of Every Native Species ...* Routledge, Warne, and Routledge, 1860.

Coleridge, Samuel Taylor. *Coleridge's Poems,* ed. by
James Dykes Campbell; w/preface by W. Hale Wright.
Westminster: A. Constable, 1899.

Coleridge, Samuel Taylor. *Coleridge the Talker,* w/intro-
duction by Richard W. Armour and Raymond F. Howes.
Ithaca, N.Y.: Cornell University Pr., 1940.

Coleridge, Samuel Taylor. *The Literary Remains of,* ed. by
Henry Nelson Coleridge. W. Pickering, 1836. Vols.
I and II. Belonged to Leslie Stephen. (For Vols.
III and IV see Holleyman).

Coleridge, Samuel Taylor. *Lyrical Ballads, with a Few
Other Poems.* Noel Douglas, 1926.

Coleridge, Samuel Taylor. *The Poems of,* ed. by Derwent
and Sara Coleridge. New ed. E. Moxon, 1852. Belonged to Herbert Duckworth, first husband of Virginia's mother.

Coleridge, Samuel Taylor. *Unpublished Letters of,* ed.
by Earl Leslie Griggs. Constable, 1932. 2 vol.

*Colette, Sidonie Gabrielle. *Discours de Réception à
l'Académie Royale Belge de Langue et de Littérature
Francaises.* [Paris]: Grasset, 1936(?). Inscribed
by author to Virginia Woolf.

Colette, Sidonie Gabrielle. *Duo, Roman.* Paris: Ferenczi,
1938.

Collins, William. *Odes on Several Descriptive and Alle-
goric Subjects.* Noel Douglas, 1926.

Collins, William. *The Poetical Works of,* w/preface by
Mrs. [Anna L.] Barbauld. T. Cadell and W. Davies,
1802.

Congreve, William. (See Wycherley, William.)

Congreve, William, *et al. Memoirs of the Life, Writings
and Amours of William Congreve,* comp. by Charles
Wilson. 2nd ed. E. Curll, 1730.

Conrad, Joseph. *The Shadow-Line.* J.M. Dent, 1917.

*Conrad, Joseph. *Some Reminiscences.* Eveleigh Nash, 1912.

Conrad, Joseph. *Within the Tides.* J.M. Dent, 1915.

Conrad, Joseph. *Works.* J.M. Dent, 1923-28. 22 vol.
Vol. XVI (*The Shadow Line* and *Within the Tides*) and
Vol. XXI (*Victory*) missing.

Costelloe, Ray. *The World at Eighteen.* T. Fisher Unwin,
1907. "Virginia Stephen from M.C.S. [Marjorie C.
Strachey?] ... "

Coulton, George Gordon. *Inquisition and Liberty*. London, Toronto: W. Heinemann, 1938. Belonged to Leonard.

Coward, Noel. *Three Plays: The Rat Trap, The Vortex, Fallen Angels. With the Author's Reply to His Critics*. Ernest Benn, 1926. "For Virginia Wolff [*sic*] from Noel Coward."

Cowley, Abraham. *The Essays of Abraham Cowley. With Life by the Editor*, ed. by Dr. [Richard] Hurd *et al*. Sampson Low and Marston, 1868. Belonged to Leslie Stephen.

Cowley, Abraham. *A Selection of Poems*, ed. by G.D.H. and M.I. Cole. Noel Douglas, 1927.

[Crabbe, George]. *Readings in Crabbe's "Tales of the Hall*," ed. by E[dward] Fitzgerald. B. Quaritch, 1882. Belonged to Leslie Stephen.

Cundall, Herbert Minton. *Bygone Richmond*. John Lane, 1925.

Daniel, George. *Recollections of Charles Lamb*. Baskerville ser. Elkin Mathews, 1927.

Dante Alighieri. *La Divina Commedia*, ed. by Pietro Fraticelli. New ed. Florence: G. Barbèra, 1898. "Adeline Virginia Stephen fm CES [Caroline Emilia Stephen] ... "

Dante Alighieri. *The New Life of Dante Alighieri*, trans. by Charles Eliot Norton. Boston: Ticknor and Fields, 1867. Belonged to Leslie Stephen.

Dante Alighieri. *The Purgatorio*, [trans. by Thomas Okey]. Temple Classics ser. 3rd ed. J.M. Dent, 1903.

Darley, George. *The Complete Poetical Works of*, ed. by Ramsay Colles. George Routledge, n.d. "Virginia from Saxon [Sydney-Turner] ... "

Darwin, Charles Robert. *Autobiography*. Watts, 1929.

Dashwood, Jane. *Three Daughters*. J. Murray, 1930.

Davidson, John. *John Davidson*. The Augustan Books of Modern Poetry ser. E. Benn, n.d.

Davies, William H. *New Poems*. Elkin, Mathews, 1913.

Defoe, Daniel. *The Novels and Miscellaneous Works of Daniel De Foe*, ed. by Sir Walter Scott [*et al*.]. G. Bell, 1887-99. [7 vol.] Vol. II only. (Includes *Memoirs of a Cavalier; Memoirs of Captain Carleton; Dickory Cronke; Everybody's Business* ...)

Defoe, Daniel. *Roxana,* ed. by R. Brimley Johnson. Abbey Classics ser. Simpkin, Marshall, Hamilton, Kent, n.d.

De La Mare, Walter. *Memoirs of a Midget.* W. Collins, 1926.

De La Mare, Walter. *Peacock Pie, A Book of Rhymes.* Constable, 1924.

De La Mare, Walter. *Rupert Brooke and the Intellectual Imagination, A Lecture.* Sidgwick and Jackson, 1919.

De La Mare, Walter. *Stories, Essays and Poems.* Everyman ed. J.M. Dent, 1938.

Destouches, Louis Ferdinand (Céline). *Voyage au Bout de la Nuit, Roman.* Paris: Denoël et Steele, 1932.

Deutsch, Babette, ed. *Modern Russian Poetry,* trans. by Babette Deutsch and Avraham Yarmolinsky. John Lane, 1923. Review slip.

Dicey, Albert Venn. *The Statesmanship of Wordsworth.* Oxford: Clarendon, 1917. Belonged to Leonard.

Diderot, Denis. *Oeuvres de Théâtre.* Amsterdam: n.p., 1771. 2 vol.

Dobson, Austin. *Horace Walpole, a Memoir. With an Appendix of Books Printed at the Strawberry Hill Press.* 4th ed., rev. and enl. by Paget Toynbee. Humphrey Milford, 1927.

Donne, John. *The First and Second Anniversaries.* Noel Douglas, 1926. Review slip.

Donne, John. *John Donne.* The Augustan Books of English Poetry ser. E. Benn, n.d.

Doolittle, Hilda. *Palimpsest.* Paris: Contact Editions, 1926.

Dostoevsky, Feodor. *New Dostoevsky Letters,* trans. by S.S. Koteliansky. Mandrake Pr., n.d. Review slip.

Doughty, Charles Montagu. *Travels in Arabia Deserta.* J. Cape and the Medici Society, 1923 . 2 vol. Belonged to Leonard.

Douglas, Lord Alfred. *Lord Alfred Douglas.* The Augustan Books of Modern Poetry ser. E. Benn, n.d.

Douglas, Norman. *South Wind.* Modern Library ed. N.Y.: Random House, n.d.

Douglas, Norman. *Together*. Chapman and Hall, 1923.

Drayton, Michael. *A Selection of Shorter Poems,* ed. by
G.D.H. and M.I. Cole. Noel Douglas, 1927.

Drayton, Michael. *Selections from the Poems of,* ed. by
A[rthur] H[enry] Bullen. Chilworth: Unwin, 1883.
"V.W. from WRML [Walter Lamb?] ... "

Drinkwater, John. *John Drinkwater*. The Augustan Books
of Modern Poetry ser. E. Benn, n.d.

Dudley, Dorothy. *Forgotten Frontiers: Dreiser and the
Land of the Free*. N.Y.: H. Smith and R. Haas, 1932.
"For Miss Virginia Woolf. Dorothy Dudley ... "

*Duff, Charles. *A Handbook on Hanging*. John Lane, 1938.

Eardley-Wilmot, Sir John E. *Reminiscences of the Late
Thomas Assheton Smith Esq., or the Pursuits of an
English Country Gentleman*. John Murray, 1860.

Earle, John, Bishop of Salisbury. *Microcosmographie; Or
a Piece of the World Discovered in Essays and Characters*. J.M. Dent, 1899.

Eastman, Max. *The Literary Mind: Its Place in an Age of
Science*. N.Y.: Charles Scribner's, 1931.

An Eighteenth Century Anthology, w/introduction by Alfred
Austin. Standard English Classics ser. Blackie, n.d.

Eliot, George. *Adam Bede*. Edinburgh: W. Blackwood, 1859.
3 vol.

Eliot, George. *Middlemarch*. Edinburgh: W. Blackwood,
1871-72. 2 vol.

Eliot, George. *Works*. Cabinet ed. Edinburgh: W. Blackwood, 1878-85. 24 vol. Vol. VI (*Essays* and *Leaves
from a Notebook*), Vol. IX (*Impressions of Theophras-
tus Such*), and Vol. XVI (last part of *Middlemarch*)
missing.

*Eliot, Thomas Stearns. *Collected Poems, 1909-1935*. Faber
and Faber, 1936. Author's presentation copy to Virginia Woolf.

*Eliot, Thomas Stearns. *East Coker*. Faber and Faber, 1939.

*Eliot, Thomas Stearns. *The Family Reunion*. Faber and Faber, 1939. Author's presentation copy to Virginia
Woolf.

*Eliot, Thomas Stearns. *The Idea of a Christian Society*.
Faber and Faber, 1939. Belonged to Leonard.

*Eliot, Thomas Stearns. *Journey of the Magi*. [Faber and Gwyer, 1927].

*Eliot, Thomas Stearns. *Old Possum's Book of Practical Cats*. Faber and Faber, 1939. Author's presentation copy to Virginia Woolf.

*Eliot, Thomas Stearns. *Poems, 1909-1925*. Faber and Gwyer, 1925.

*Eliot, Thomas Stearns. *A Song for Simeon*. [Faber and Gwyer, 1928].

*Eliot, Thomas Stearns. *Triumphal March*. [Faber and Faber, 1931]. Author's presentation copy to Virginia Woolf.

*Eliot, Thomas Stearns. *Two Poems*. Cambridge: University Pr., 1935.

*Eliot, Thomas Stearns. *Words for Music*. Privately printed, 1934. Author's presentation copy to Virginia Woolf.

Erasmus, Desiderius. *Twenty Select Colloquies*, trans. by Sir Roger L'Estrange; w/introduction by Charles Whibley. Chapman and Dodd, 1923.

Euripides. *The Electra*, w/introduction by Charles Haines Keene. (In Greek). G. Bell, 1893.

Evans, B. Ifor. *A Short History of English Literature*. Penguin Books, 1940.

Evelyn, John. *The Life of Margaret Godolphin*. A. Moring, 1904.

Exquemelin, Alexandre Olivier. *The Buccaneers of America*, ed. by William Swan Stallybrass. G. Routledge, 1924. 2 vol. in one.

Farquhar, John. (See Wycherley, William.)

Ferenczi, Sandor, *et al*. *Psycho-Analysis and the War Neuroses*, w/introduction by Sigmund Freud. London, Vienna, N.Y.: The International Psychoanalytical Pr., 1921.

Firbank, Ronald. *Caprice*. [New ed.] Duckworth, 1929.

Firbank, Ronald. *Concerning the Eccentricities of Cardinal Pirelli*. [New ed.] Duckworth, 1929.

Firbank, Ronald. *Inclinations*. [New ed.] Duckworth, 1929.

Firbank, Ronald. *The Princess Zoubaroff.* [New ed.] Duckworth, 1930.

Firbank, Ronald. *Vainglory.* [New ed.] Duckworth, 1930.

Firbank, Ronald. *Valmouth.* [New ed.] Duckworth, 1929.

Fitzgerald, Edward. *Dictionary of Madame de Sévigné,* ed.
by Mary Eleanor Fitzgerald Kerrich. Macmillan, 1914.
2 vol.

Flaubert, Gustave. *Correspondance.* Paris: Charpentier,
1905-07. 4 vol.

Flaubert, Gustave. *Correspondance,* ed. by Caroline Com-
manville. Paris: L. Conard, 1926-33. 9 vol. "V.W.
from L.W. ... "

Flaubert, Gustave. *Madame Bovary, Moeurs de Province.*
Paris: Charpentier, 1922.

Flaubert, Gustave. *Madame Bovary, Moeurs de Province.*
Paris: L. Conard, 1930.

Flecker, James Elroy. *Hassan: The Story of Hassan of Bag-
dad and How He Came to Make the Golden Journey to
Samarkand: A Play in Five Acts.* William Heinemann,
1922. "V.W. from V.S.W. [Vita Sackville West]."

Flügel, John Carl. *The Psycho-Analytic Study of the Family.* London, N.Y.: The International Psycho-Analytical
Pr., 1921.

Foote, Samuel. *The Dramatic Works of Samuel Foote, Esq.,
to Which Is Prefixed a Life of the Author.* J.F. Rivington *et al.,* 1788. 4 vol. Vols. I, II and IV.
(For Vol. III see Holleyman.)

Ford, John. *John Ford,* ed. by Havelock Ellis. Vizetelly,
1888.

*Forster, Edward Morgan. *Alexandria.* Alexandria: White-
head Morris, 1922. Inscribed by author to Virginia.

Forster, Edward Morgan. *Credo.* [The Field Pr., 1938].

*Forster, Edward Morgan. *Goldsworthy Lowes Dickinson.* Edward Arnold, 1934 . Inscribed by author to Virginia.

Forster, Edward Morgan. *Nordic Twilight.* Macmillan War
Pamphlets. Macmillan, 1940.

*Forster, Edward Morgan. *A Passage to India.* Edward Arnold, 1924. Inscribed by author to Virginia.

Forster, John. *The Life of Charles Dickens,* w/introduction by G.K. Chesterton. Everyman ed. J.M. Dent, 1927.

Fowler, H.W. (See Aikin, W.A. Also Paget, Sir Richard.)

Fowler, H.W., and Robert Bridges. *The Split Infinitive* by H.W. Fowler; AND *Pictorial, Picturesque* by Robert Bridge. Oxford: Clarendon, 1923.

*Freud, Sigmund. *Selbstdarstellung. 2.* Vienna: Internationale Psychoanalytischer Verlag, 1936.

Froude, James Anthony. *History of England from the Fall of Wolsey to the Defeat of the Spanish Armada.* Longmans, Green, 1870-75(?). 12 vol. Belonged to Leslie Stephen.

Froude, James Anthony. *Short Studies on Great Subjects.* Longmans, Green, 1897-98. 4 vol.

Froude, James Anthony. *Thomas Carlyle, A History of the First Years of His Life, 1795-1835.* Longmans, Green, 1882. 2 vol.

Fry, Roger Eliot. *Architectural Heresies of a Painter.* Chatto and Windus, 1921. "To Virginia with love from Roger."

*Fry, Roger Eliot. *Art-History as an Academic Study.* Cambridge: University Pr., 1933. Author's presentation copy to Virginia.

[Fry, Roger Eliot]. *[Catalogue of the] Second Post-Impressionist Exhibition, Oct. 5-Dec. 31, 1912.* Ballantyne, 1912.

*Fry, Roger Eliot. *Flemish Art.* Chatto and Windus, 1927. "Virginia ... from Roger."

Fry, Roger Eliot. *Last Lectures,* w/introduction by Kenneth Clark. Cambridge: University Pr., 1939.

Fry, Roger Eliot. *Vision and Design.* Chatto and Windus, 1920.

*Fry, Roger Eliot. *Vision and Design.* New and rev. ed. Chatto and Windus, 1923. Author's presentation copy to Virginia.

Fry, Roger Eliot, and E.A. Lowe. *English Handwriting, with Thirty-Four Facsimile Plates and Artistic and Paleographical Criticisms.* Oxford: Clarendon, 1926.

Galsworthy, John. *Plays: Vol. III.* Duckworth, 1914. (Includes *The Fugitive, The Pigeon, The Mob.*)

Galsworthy, John. *The Silver Spoon.* W. Heinemann, 1926. Belonged to Leonard.

Galsworthy, John. *The White Monkey.* Collins, 1928(?).

Gammer Gurton's Needle, ed. by H.F.B. Brett-Smith. Oxford: B. Blackwell, 1920.

Gandhi, M.K. *Speeches and Writings of.* Madras: G.A. Nalesant, n.d. Belonged to Leonard.

*Garnett, David. *The Grasshoppers Come.* Chatto and Windus, 1931.

*Garnett, David. *Lady into Fox.* Chatto and Windus, 1922.

*Garnett, David. *A Man in the Zoo.* Chatto and Windus, 1924.

*Garnett, David. *A Rabbit in the Air.* Chatto and Windus, 1932.

Garth, Sir Samuel. *The Dispensary.* [John Nutt, 1700]. (BOUND WITH Akenside, Mark. *The Pleasures ... , q.v.*)

Gaskell, Elizabeth Cleghorn. *Mary Barton,* w/introduction by Clement K. Shorter. Oxford University Pr., 1906.

Gauguin, Paul. *Noa Noa,* trans. into German by Luise Wolf. Berlin: Br. Cassirer, n.d.

Gaultier, Bon. (See Martin, Sir Theodore.)

Gay, John. (See Centlivre, Susannah. Also Pope, Alexander. *Letters.*)

Gay, John. *Fables.* K. Paul Trench, 1882. Belonged to Leslie Stephen.

Gibbon, Edward. *The History of the Decline and Fall of the Roman Empire,* ed. by John Bagnell Bury. 7 vol. Methuen, 1898-1905.

Gide, André Paul Guillaume. *L'école des Femmes.* New ed. Paris: Gallimard, 1928(?).

Gide, André Paul Guillaume. *Incidences.* Paris: Gallimard, 1924.

Gide, André Paul Guillaume. *Montaigne, An Essay in Two Parts,* trans. by S.H. Guest and T.F. Blewitt. Blackamore, 1929.

Gide, André Paul Guillaume. *Les Nourritures Terrestres.*
Paris: Gallimard, 1921.

Gide, André Paul Guillaume. *Pages de Journal (1929-1932).*
Paris: Gallimard, 1934.

Gide, André Paul Guillaume. *Si le Grain Ne Meurt.* Paris:
Nouvelle Revue Francaise, 1924. 3 vol.

Gide, André Paul Guillaume. *Voyage au Congo.* Paris:
Gallimard, 1927.

Gilbert, Sir William Schwenck. *Original Plays. First
Series. Second Series. Third Series.* Chatto and
Windus, 1908. 1909. 1909.

Gillet, Louis. *La Cathédrale Vivante.* Paris: Flammarion,
1936. "A Madame Virginia Woolf ... [from] Louis
Gillet."

*Gillet, Louis. *Londres et Rome.* Paris: B. Grasset, 1936.
Author's presentation copy to Virginia Woolf.

*Gillet, Louis. *Le Trésor des Musées de Province.* Paris:
Firmin-Didot, 1934. Author's presentation copy to
Leonard and Virginia Woolf.

Gissing, George. *The Nether World.* Smith, Elder, 1907.

Gissing, George. *Sleeping Fires.* Unwin, 1927.

Godwin, William. *Caleb Williams.* G. Newnes, 1904(?).

Goethe, Johann Wolfgang von. *Faust.* Stuttgart: T.G.
Cotta, 1860. Belonged to Leonard.

Gogol, Nickolai Vasilevich. *Evenings on a Farm Near Di-
kanka,* trans. by Constance Garnett. Chatto and Windus, 1926.

Goldsmith, Oliver. *Selected Poems,* ed. by Austin Dobson.
Oxford: Clarendon, 1887.

Goncharov, Ivan Aleksandrovich. *Oblomov,* trans. by Nata-
lie A. Duddington. G. Allen and Unwin, 1929. Belonged to Leonard.

Gordon, George. *Shakespeare's English.* Oxford: Clarendon,
1928.

Gore, Catherine Grace Frances. *Romances of Real Life.* H.
Colburn, 1829. 3 vol.

Gorki, Maxim. *Decadence,* trans. by Veronica Scott-Gatty.
Cassell, 1928.

Gorki, Maxim. *The Man Who Was Afraid,* trans. by Herman
    Bernstein. Unwin, 1905.

Gosse, Sir Edmund. *Edmund Gosse.* The Augustan Books of
    Modern Poetry ser. E. Benn, n.d.

[Gosse, Edmund]. *Father and Son: A Study of Two Tempera-
    ments.* William Heinemann, 1907.

Gosse, Edmund. *The Life of Algernon Charles Swinburne.*
    Macmillan, 1917.

Gosse, Edmund. (See Charteris, Evan.)

Gosse, Edmund. *Selected Essays (Second Series).* Travel-
    lers' Library ser. William Heinemann, 1928.

Grafton Galleries. (See [Fry, Roger]. *Catalogue* ... .)

Grant, Elizabeth Raper. *Receipt Book of Elizabeth Raper
    and a Portion of Her Cipher Journal,* ed. by Bartle
    Grant. Soho: Nonesuch, 1924.

Gray, Thomas. *Correspondence of,* ed. by Paget Toynbee
    and Leonard Whibley. Oxford: Clarendon, 1935. 3
    vol.

Gray, Thomas. *The Poetical Works of.* William Pickering,
    1853. Belonged to Julia Jackson, Virginia's mother.

Gray, Thomas. *Poetical Works. English and Latin,* w/in-
    troduction by John Bradshaw. Aldine ed. Bell, 1891.

Gray, Thomas. *The Works of.* William Pickering, 1840. 4
    vol. Belonged to Leslie Stephen.

Green, John Richard. *Letters of,* ed. by Leslie Stephen.
    Macmillan, 1902.

Greene, Robert, and George Peele. *The Dramatic and Poet-
    ical Works of ... with Memoirs of the Authors,* ed.
    by Alexander Dyce. George Routledge, 1874. Belonged
    to Leslie Stephen.

Greene, Robert, and George Peele. *The Dramatic and Poet-
    ical Works of,* ed. by Alexander Dyce. George Rout-
    ledge, 1883.

Grillo, Ernest, ed. *Selections from the Italian Poets.*
    Blackie, 1917. "Virginia from Saxon [Sydney-Turner]
    ... "

Grillo, Ernest, ed. *Selections from the Italian Prose
    Writers.* Blackie, 1917. "Virginia from Saxon
    [Sydney-Turner] ... "

Grimaldi, Joseph. *Memoirs of Joseph Grimaldi,* ed. by
    "Boz," revised by Charles Whitehead. George Rout-
    ledge, 1853.

Grimmelshausen, Hans Jacob Christoffel von. *Simplicissi-
    mus the Vagabond,* trans. by A.T.S. Goodrick; w/intro-
    duction by William Rose. G. Routledge, 1824.

Grote, George. *Posthumous Papers: Comprising Selections
    from Familiar Correspondence During Half a Century;
    ... and Extracts from Authors Ancient and Modern,
    Made by the Same at Various Dates Down to 1871,* ed.
    by Mrs. [Harriet] Grote. William Clowes, 1874. Be-
    longed to Leslie Stephen.

Guedalla, Philip. *Bonnet and Shawl. An Album.* N.Y.:
    Crosby Gaige; London: Hodder and Stoughton, 1928.

Gurney, Hudson. (See Chalmers, George.)

Guthrie, Thomas Anstey. *The Brass Bottle* by F. Anstey.
    Hodder and Stoughton, 1913(?).

Guthrie, Thomas Anstey. *Lyre and Lancet* by F. Anstey.
    Smith, Elder, 1895.

Gwyer, John. *Portraits of Mean Men.* Cobden-Sanderson,
    1938.

Hakluyt, Richard. *Principal Navigations, Voyages, Traf-
    fiques and Discoveries of the English Nation* ... Ev-
    eryman ed. J.M. Dent, 1907. [8 vol.] Vols. II and
    III only.

Hammond, John Lawrence and Barbara. *The Town Labourer,
    1760-1832.* New ed. Longmans, Green, 1925. Be-
    longed to Leonard.

Hammond, L. Barbara. *William Lovett, 1800-1877.* Fabian
    Biographical ser . Fabian Society, 1922. 2 copies of
    this.

Hardy, Florence Emily. *The Later Years of Thomas Hardy,
    1892-1928.* Macmillan, 1930.

Hardy, Thomas. *Collected Poems.* Macmillan, 1920.

*Hardy, Thomas. *The Dynasts.* Macmillan, 1904-09. 3 vol.

*Hardy, Thomas. *Human Shows, Far Phantasies, Songs, and
    Trifles.* Macmillan, 1925. Belonged to Leonard.

Hardy, Thomas. *Poems of the Past and the Present.* Mac-
    millan, 1903.

Hardy, Thomas. *Satires of Circumstances, Lyrics and Reveries, with Miscellaneous Pieces.* Macmillan, 1914. "L.W. from V.W. ... "

*Hardy, Thomas. *Time's Laughingstocks and Other Verses.* Macmillan, 1910.

Hardy, Thomas. *Wessex Poems and Other Verses.* London and N.Y.: Harper, 1898. Belonged to Leslie Stephen.

Hardy, Thomas. *Wessex Poems and Other Verses.* Macmillan, 1903.

Harris, Moses. *The English Lepidoptera: ... Containing a Catalogue of Upward of Four Hundred Moths and Butterflies ...* J. Robson, 1775.

Harrison, Frederick, and James Sharp North. *Old Brighton, Old Preston, Old Hove.* Brighton: n.p., 1937.

Harrison, G.B. *Shakespeare's Fellows: Being a Brief Chronicle of the Shakespearean Age.* John Lane, 1923.

Harrison, William. *Harrison's Description of England in Shakespeare's Youth,* ed. by Frederick J. Furnivall. New Shakespere Society, 1877-81. [3 vol.] Vols. I and II only.

Harte, Francis Bret. *Francis Bret Harte.* The Augustan Books of Modern Poetry ser. E. Benn, n.d.

Hartog, Sir Philip J. *On the Relationship of Poetry to Verse.* (BOUND WITH Sadleir, Michael. *The Northanger Novels*--see Holleyman; and with Roberts, S.C., *q.v.*)

Harvey, Frederick William. *Frederick William Harvey.* The Augustan Books of Modern Poetry ser. E. Benn, n.d.

Haydon, Benjamin Robert. *The Autobiography and Memoirs of ... (1786-1846),* ed. by Thom Taylor; new ed. w/introduction by Aldous Huxley. Peter Davies, 1926. [2 vol.] Vol. I only.

Haynes, Edmund Sidney Pollock. *The Belief in Personal Immortality.* The Inquirer's Library ser. Watts, 1913.

Hazlitt, William. *Lectures on the English Comic Writers.* Temple Classics ser. J.M. Dent, 1900. Belonged to Leonard.

Hazlitt, William. *Political Essays, with Sketches of Public Characters.* 2nd ed. Simpkin and Marshall, 1822. Belonged to Leslie Stephen.

Hazlitt, William Carew. *Memoirs of William Hazlitt. With Portions of His Correspondence*. Richard Bentley, 1867. 2 vol. Belonged to Leslie Stephen.

Headlam, Walter, trans. and ed. *A Book of Greek Verse*. (In Greek and English). Cambridge: University Pr., 1907.

Heine, Henrich. *The Prose Writings of*, ed. by Havelock Ellis. Camelot Classics ser. Walter Scott, 1887.

Heine, Heinrich. *Sammtliche Werke*. Hamburg: Hoffman and Campe, 1867-68. 18 vol. in nine.

Hemingway, Ernest. *The Sun Also Rises*. N.Y.: C. Scribner's, 1927.

Henley, William Ernest. *A Book of Verses*. David Nutt, 1888.

Henley, William Ernest. *Burns: Life, Genius, Achievement*. Edinburgh: T.C. and E.C. Jack, 1898. Belonged to Leslie Stephen.

Herbert, Edward Herbert. *The Poems, English and Latin, of Edward Lord Herbert of Cherbury*, ed. by G.C. Moore Smith. Oxford: Clarendon, 1923.

Herbert, George. *George Herbert*. Augustan Books of English Poetry ser. E. Benn, n.d.

Herodotus, ed. by Joseph William Blakesley. (In Greek). Cambridge: Deighton, Bell, 1870-79. [2 vol.] Vol. I only. Belonged to Leonard.

Herrick, Robert. *Selected Poems*, ed. by G.D.H. and M.I. Cole. Noel Douglas, 1927.

Higgins, M.J. *Papers on Public School Education in England*. Smith, Elder, 1865. (BOUND WITH Stephen, Leslie. *The "Times" ... , q.v.*)

Hitler, Adolf. *Mein Kampf*. Munich: F.E. Nachf, 1934. Belonged to Leonard.

Hogarth, D.G. *The Life of Charles M. Doughty*. Oxford University Pr., 1928.

Hogg, Thomas Jefferson. *Shelley at Oxford*, w/introduction by R.A. Streatfeild. Methuen, 1904.

Holland, Mary Sibylla. *Additional Letters of*. Edinburgh: R.R. Clark, 1899. "Virginia Stephen from F. Helen Holland ... "

Holland, Mary Sibylla. *Letters of,* ed. by Bernard Holland. Edward Arnold, 1898.

Holland, Mary Sibylla. *Letters of,* ed. by Bernard Holland. 2nd ed. Edward Arnold, 1898. "For Vanessa Stephen with Helen Holland's love ... "

Holland, Maud [Maud Walpole]. *Verses.* Edward Arnold, n.d.

Holmes, Oliver Wendell. *Oration ... on the Fourth of July, 1863.* Boston: J.E. Farwell, 1863. (BOUND WITH Stephen, Leslie. *The "Times" ...* , *q.v.*)

Holmes, Oliver Wendell. *Poems.* Boston: Otis Broaders, 1836. Belonged to Leslie Stephen.

Holyoake, George Jacob. *Sixty Years of an Agitator's Life.* T. Fisher Unwin, 1892.

Homer. *The Iliad,* ed. by Walter Leaf. (In Greek). Macmillan, 1886. 2 vol. Belonged to Leonard.

Hookes, Nicholas. *Amanda, A Sacrifice to an Unknown Goddesse, or, A Free-will Offering of a Loving Heart to a Sweet-Heart.* Elkin Mathews, 1923.

Hotson, J. Leslie. *The Death of Christopher Marlowe.* Soho: Nonesuch, 1925.

Howard, Eliot. *The Eliot Marriages: John Eliot (II) and Mariabella Farmborough Briggins, 1734; John Eliot (III) and Mary Weston, 1762,* [comp. by Eliot Howard]. Gloucester: John Bellows, 1894.

Howard, Eliot. *John Eliot of London, Merchant, 1735-1813,* comp. by Eliot Howard. Gloucester: John Bellows, 1893. Belonged to Roger Fry.

Hudson, William Henry. *Idle Days in Patagonia.* J.M. Dent, 1923.

Hudson, William Henry. *Nature in Downland.* J.M. Dent, 1923.

*Hughes, Richard Arthur Warren. *A High Wind in Jamaica.* Chatto and Windus, 1929. Inscribed by author to Virginia Woolf.

*Hughes, Richard Arthur Warren. *In Hazard.* Chatto and Windus, 1938. Inscribed by author to Virginia Woolf.

Hugo, Victor Marie. *Bug Jargal* AND *Le dernier jour d'un Condamné* AND *Claude Geux.* Paris: Charpentier, 1845.

Hugo, Victor Marie. *Cromwell*. *Drame*. Paris: Charpentier, 1844.

Hugo, Victor Marie. *Les Feuilles d'automne* AND *Les Chants du crépuscule*. Paris: Charpentier, 1846.

Hugo, Victor Marie. *Hau d'islande*. Paris: Charpentier, 1845.

Hugo, Victor Marie. *Littérature et Philosophie Mêlées*. Paris: Charpentier, 1850.

Hugo, Victor Marie. *Les Misérables*. Paris: Hachette, 1875. 3 vol.

Hugo, Victor Marie. *Notre-Dame de Paris*. Paris: Charpentier, 1850. 2 vol.

Hugo, Victor Marie. *Odes et Ballades*. Paris: Charpentier, 1845.

Hugo, Victor Marie. *Les Orientales*. Paris: Charpentier, 1845.

Hugo, Victor Marie. *Les Orientales*. Paris: Hachette, 1873. Belonged to Leonard.

Hugo, Victor Marie. *Le Rhin, Lettres à un Ami*. Paris: Charpentier, 1845. 3 vol.

Hugo, Victor Marie. *Théâtre*. Paris: Charpentier, 1844-47. 3 vol.

Hugo, Victor Marie. *Les Voix intérieures* AND *Les Rayons et les ombres*. Paris: Charpentier, 1850.

Hume, David. *An Abstract of a Treatise of Human Nature,* w/introduction by J.M. Keynes and P. Sraffa. Cambridge: University Pr., 1938.

*Huxley, Aldous Leonard. *Point Counter Point*. Chatto and Windus, 1928.

*Huxley, Aldous Leonard. *Texts and Pretexts*. Chatto and Windus, 1932.

Huxley, Henrietta and Thomas Henry. *Poems of Henrietta Huxley with Three of Thomas Henry Huxley*. Privately printed, 1899. Belonged to Leslie Stephen.

Huxley, Julian. (See Wells, H.G., *et al.*)

Huysmans, Joris Karl. *La Cathédrale*. Paris: P.V. Stock, 1903. Belonged to Leonard.

Huysmans, Joris Karl. *L'Oblat*. Paris: P.V. Stock, 1903.
Belonged to Leonard.

Iyengar, K.R. Srinivasa. *Lytton Strachey, a Critical
Study*. Bombay: Allied Publishers, 1938. "Mrs. Virginia Woolf with the author's compliments ... "

James, Henry. *The Better Sort*. Methuen, 1903. Belonged
to Leonard.

James, Henry. *Embarrassments*. W. Heinemann, 1896. (Includes "The Figure in the Carpet," "Glasses," "The
Next Time," "The Way It Came.")

James, Henry. *Maud Evelyn; The Special Type; The Papers
and Other Tales*. Macmillan, 1923. (Includes also
"The Velvet Glove," "Mora Montravers," "Crapy Cornelia,"
"A Round of Visits," "The Bench of Desolation.")

James, Henry. *Partial Portraits*. Macmillan, 1899.

James, Henry. *The Princess Casamassima*. Macmillan, 1886.
3 vol.

James, Henry. *The Sacred Fount*. Methuen, 1901.

James, Henry. *The Spoils of Poynton*. W. Heinemann, 1897.
Belonged to Leonard.

James, Henry. *Terminations*. W. Heinemann, 1895. (Includes "The Death of the Lion," "The Coxon Fund,"
"The Middle Years," "The Altar of the Dead.") Belonged to Leonard.

James, Henry. *The Tragic Muse*. 2nd ed. Macmillan, 1891.

James, Henry. *The Wings of the Dove*. Westminster: A.
Constable, 1902.

James, William. *Human Immortality*. Constable, 1917.

James I. *Demonologie* [1597]. *Newes from Scotland, Declar-
ing the Damnable Life and Death of Doctor Fian, a Notable Sorcerer* ... [1591]. John Lane, 1924.

Jeans, Sir James Hopwood. *The Mysterious Universe*. Penguin Books, 1937.

*Jeffers, Robinson. *Descent to the Dead*. N.Y.: Random
House, 1931. Inscribed by author to Leonard and Virginia Woolf.

Jesse, Captain William. *The Life of Beau Brummell*. Clarke
and Beeton, 1854.

Johnson, Samuel. *Lives of the Most Eminent English Poets: with Critical Observations on Their Works.... With a Sketch of the Author's Life by Sir Walter Scott.* F. Warne, n.d. "To [Virginia], From Nessa and Thoby ... "

*Johnson, Samuel. *London: A Poem, and The Vanity of Human Wishes,* w/introduction by T.S. Eliot. F. Etchells and H. MacDonald, 1930. Presentation copy to Virginia Woolf from T.S. Eliot.

Jonson, Ben. *The Best Plays of the Old Dramatists* [Vol. III]: *Ben Jonson.* Mermaid ser. T. Fisher Unwin, 1894. Belonged to Leonard.

Jonson, Ben. *Timber, or, Discoveries: Being Observations on Men and Manners.* J.M. Dent, 1897.

Jonson, Ben. *The Works of,* ed. by H.C. Hart. Methuen, 1906. [2 vol.] Vol. II only. (Includes *Cynthia's Revels, The Poetaster.*)

Joyce, James. *Haveth Childers Everywhere; Fragment of Work in Progress.* Faber and Faber, 1931.

*Joyce, James. *Ulysses.* Paris: Shakespeare and Co., 1922.

Jusserand, J.J. *A Romance of a King's Life,* trans. by M.R. [*sic*]. Rev. and enl. ed. T. Fisher Unwin, 1896. Belonged to Leslie Stephen.

Kant, Emmanuel. *Prolegomena zu Einer Jeden Kunftigen Metaphysik.* Leipzig: P. Reclam Jun, 1888(?).

Keats, John. *The Letters of,* ed. by Maurice Buxton Forman. 2nd ed. Oxford: Humphrey Milford, 1935.

Keats, John. *Letters of ... to Fanny Brawne Written in the Years MDCCCXIX and MDCCCXX ... ,* ed. by Harry Buxton Forman. Reeves and Turner, 1878.

Keats, John. *Poems,* ed. by G. Thorn Drury. Lawrence and Bullen, 1896. 2 vol.

Keats, John. *The Poetical Works of.* New ed. Edward Moxon, 1851. Belonged to Herbert Duckworth, first husband of Virginia's mother.

Kelleher, D.L. *A Poet Passes.* E. Benn, 1927.

Kenny, Courtney. *The Mystery of Elizabeth Canning.* Stevens, 1907.

Keynes, John Maynard. *Alfred Marshall, 1842-1924, A Memoir.* Offprint from *The Economic Journal,* 34 (Sept. 1924), 311-72.

Keynes, John Maynard. *William Stanley Jevons, 1835-1882: A Centenary Allocution on His Life and Work as Economist and Statistician.* Offprint from *The Journal of the Royal Statistical Society,* 99 (1936). (BOUND WITH next item.)

Keynes, John Maynard, and C.E. Collet. *Herbert Somerton Foxwell, June 17, 1849-August 3, 1936.* Offprint from *The Economic Journal,* Dec. 1936. (BOUND WITH previous item.)

King-Hall, Stephen. *Our Own Times, 1913-1934.* I. Nicholson and Watson, 1934-35. [2 vol.] Vol. I only. Belonged to Leonard.

Kingsley, Charles. *Alton Locke.* Cambridge: Macmillan, 1862. Belonged to Leslie Stephen.

Kingsley, Charles. *Andromeda and Other Poems.* John W. Parker, 1858. Belonged to Leslie Stephen.

Kingsley, Charles. *Poems; Including The Saint's Tragedy, Andromeda, Songs, Ballads, &c.* Macmillan, 1875. Belonged to Leslie Stephen.

Kingsley, Charles. *Yeast.* 7th ed. Macmillan, 1875. Belonged to Leslie Stephen.

Kipling, Rudyard. *Departmental Ditties.* 7th ed. Calcutta: Thacker, Spink, 1892.

Kipling, Rudyard. *Puck of Pook's Hill.* Macmillan, 1906.

Kipling, Rudyard. *Second Jungle Book.* Macmillan, 1906. Belonged to Leonard.

Kirkpatrick, Clifford. *Report of a Research into the Attitudes and Habits of Radio Listeners.* St. Paul, Minn.: Webb, 1933.

Klarwill, Victor, ed. *The Fugger News-letters,* trans. by Pauline de Chary; w/foreword by H. Gordon Selfridge. J. Lane, 1924. Belonged to Leonard.

Krasinska, Francoise. *The Journal of Countess Francoise Krasinska, Great Grandmother of Victor Emmanuel,* trans. by Kazimir Dziekonska. Kegan Paul, 1897. "A.V.S. from D.J.S. [Dorothea J. Stephen]."

Kyd, Thomas. *The Spanish Tragedy,* ed. by Josef Schick. J.M. Dent, 1898.

La Bruyère, Jean de. *Les Caracteres de Theophraste, et de La Bruyère.* Paris: L. Prault and Bailly, 1769. 2 vol. Belonged to Leonard.

Lackington, James. *Memories of the Forty-Five First Years of the Life of James Lackington, the Present Bookseller.* Privately printed, 1810.

La Fontaine, Jean de. *Fables.* Paris: Bossard, 1927. 2 vol.

Lamb, Charles. *The Essays of Elia and the Last Essays of Elia,* w/introduction by Robert Lynd. London and Toronto: J.M. Dent, 1929.

Lamb, Charles. *Miscellaneous Essays and Sketches,* w/introduction by Robert Lynd. London and Toronto: J.M. Dent, 1929.

Lang, Andrew. *Andrew Lang.* The Augustan Books of Modern Poetry ser. E. Benn, n.d.

La Rochefoucauld, Francois, Duc de. *Les Pensées, Maximes, et Réflexions Morales.* Paris: C. Bauche, 1765.

Lawrence, D.H. *Collected Poems.* M. Secker, 1929. 2 vol.

Lawrence, D.H. *England, My England.* M. Secker, 1927.

Lawrence, D.H. *The Ladybird* AND *The Fox* AND *The Captain's Doll.* M. Secker, 1927.

Lawrence, D.H. *St. Mawr* AND *The Princess.* M. Secker, 1930.

Lawrence, D.H. *Sea and Sardinia.* M. Secker, 1930.

Lawrence, D.H. *The White Peacock.* M. Secker, 1927.

Lee, Sidney. *Principles of Biography.* Cambridge: University Pr., 1911. "To Miss Virginia Stephen with Sidney Lee's kind regards.... "

[Lee, Sidney, and Leslie Stephen.] *George Smith, a Memoir, with Some Pages of Autobiography,* comp. by Mrs. E. Smith. Privately printed, 1902.

*Léger, Aléxis Saint-Léger (Saint-John Perse). *Anabasis,* trans. by T.S. Eliot. Faber and Faber, 1930. Inscribed to Virginia Woolf from T.S. Eliot.

Lehmann, John. *New Writing in Europe.* Harmondsworth: Allen Lane, 1940.

Lehmann, John. *Prometheus and the Bolsheviks.* Cresset, 1937. "Virginia ... from John."

Lehmann, Rosamond. *Lettre à Ma Soeur,* trans. from the English by Jean Tolva. Paris: L'artisan du Livre, 1931.

Leith, Mary Charlotte Julia Gordon. *The Children of the Chapel*. AND Algernon Charles Swinburne, *Pilgrimage of Pleasure*. Chatto and Windus, 1910.

Lennox, Sarah. *The Life and Letters of Lady Sarah Lennox, 1745-1826,* ed. by the Countess of Ilchester [Mary Fox-Strangways] and Lord Staverdale [Giles Fox-Strangways]. John Murray, 1901. 2 vol.

Leopardi, Giacomo, Comte. *I Conti,* ed. by Michele Scherillo. 3rd ed. Milano: U. Hoepli, 1911.

Lescure, Pierre de. *Tendresse Inhumaine, Roman*. Paris: Gallimard, 1936. "Pour Virginia Woolf ... [from] Pierre de Lescure."

Lescure, Pierre de. *La Tête au Vent, Roman*. Paris: Gallimard, 1938. "Pour Mrs. Virginia Woolf ... [from] Pierre de Lescure."

Lindsay, Vachel. *General William Booth Enters into Heaven and Other Poems*. Chatto and Windus, 1939.

Lindsay, Vachel. *A Handy Guide for Beggars, Especially Those of the Poetic Fraternity....* N.Y.: Macmillan, 1916.

Lippincott, Benjamin Evans. *Victorian Critics of Democracy: Carlyle, Ruskin, Arnold, Stephen, Maine, Lecky.* Oxford University Pr., 1938.

Litchfield, Henrietta Emma, ed. *Emma Darwin, Wife of Charles Darwin; A Century of Family Letters*. Cambridge: University Pr., 1904. 2 vol. "Virginia Stephen from H.S. Litchfield."

[Llewelyn Davies, Margaret, ed.] *Maternity; Letters from Working-Women, Collected by the Women's Co-operative Guild,* w/preface by the Right Hon. Herbert Samuel. G. Bell, 1915. "For my dear friends Virginia and Leonard, ... [from] Margaret ... "

Locker-Lampson, Frederick. *London Lyrics*. K. Paul, Trench, 1883.

London Library. *Catalogue of,* [ed.] by C.T. Hagberg Wright. Williams and Norgate, 1903. Belonged to Leslie Stephen.

Longfellow, Henry Wadsworth. *Poetical Works*. G. Routledge, 1883.

Longfellow, Henry Wadsworth. *The Poetical Works of*. Frederick Warne, 1891. Belonged to Leonard.

Longus. *Pastoral Loves of Daphnis and Chloe,* trans. by
George Moore. W. Heinemann, 1924.

Lover, Samuel. *Handy Andy.* W. Scott, 1842(?).

Low, Sir Sidney James Mark, and F.S. Pulling, eds. *The
Dictionary of English History.* New ed., rev. and
enl. Cassell, 1928.

Lowell, James Russell. *The Bigelow Papers,* w/preface [by
Thomas Hughes]. New ed. Trubner, 1859. Belonged
to Leslie Stephen.

Lowell, James Russell. *The Bigelow Papers. Second Series.* Boston: Ticknor and Fields, 1867. Belonged to
Leslie Stephen.

Lowell, James Russell. *Last Poems.* Houghton, Mifflin,
1895. Belonged to Leslie Stephen.

Lowell, James Russell. *Poetical Works,* w/introduction by
Thomas Hughes. Macmillan, 1891.

Lowell, James Russell. *The Power of Sound, A Rhymed Lecture.* Privately printed, 1896.

Lowell, James Russell. *Under the Willows and Other Poems.*
Boston: Fields, Osgood, 1869. Belonged to Leslie Stephen.

[Lowell, James Russell, and George William Curtis.] *Memorials of Two Friends.* Privately printed [N.Y.: Gillis-
pie], 1902. (Also includes Charles Eliot Norton.
"Life and Character of George William Curtis.")

Lower, Mark Antony. *A Compendious History of Sussex.*
Lewes: G.P. Bacon; London: J.R. Smith, 1870. 2 vol.
Belonged to Leonard.

Lower, Mark Antony. *The Worthies of Sussex.* Lewes: G.P.
Bacon, 1865.

Lubbock, Percy. *The Craft of Fiction.* Jonathan Cape,
1921.

Lubbock, Percy. *Elizabeth Barrett Browning in Her Letters.*
Smith, Elder, 1906.

Lubbock, Percy. *Samuel Pepys.* Nelson, n.d.

Lucretius Caius, Titus. *De rerum natura,* ed. by H.A.J.
Munro. 4th ed. Cambridge: D. Bell, 1886-93. 2
vol. Belonged to Leonard.

*Lucretius Caius, Titus. *Lucretius on Death,* trans. by
   Robert Calverley Trevelyan. Omega Workshops, 1917.

Lyttelton, Edith. *Alfred Lyttelton: An Account of His
   Life.* Longmans, Green, 1923.

Macaulay, Dame Rose. *And No Man's Wit.* Collins, 1940(?).

Macaulay, Thomas. *Lays of Ancient Rome.* New ed. Longman, Roberts and Green, 1864.

Macaulay, Thomas. *Works of.* Longmans, Green, 1898. 12
   vol.

MacCarthy, Desmond. *The Court Theatre 1904-1907.* A.H.
   Bullen, 1907.

MacCarthy, Desmond. *Remnants.* Constable, 1918. "Virginia from Desmond."

Machen, Arthur. *The Great God Pan.* M. Secker, 1926.

MacKnight, Thomas. *The Life of Henry St. John, Viscount
   Bolingbroke, Secretary of State in the Reign of
   Queen Anne.* Chapman and Hall, 1863.

Macready, William Charles. *Macready's Reminiscences, and
   Selections from His Diaries and Letters,* ed. by Frederick Pollock. Macmillan, 1875. [2 vol.] Vol. I
   only.

Magnus, Laurie. *A Dictionary of European Literature.* G.
   Routledge, 1926.

Maistre, Xavier, Comte de. *Oeuvres Complètes.* Paris:
   Charpentier, 1854. Belonged to Herbert Duckworth,
   first husband of Virginia's mother.

Maitland, Frederic William. *Domesday Book and Beyond:
   Three Essays in the Early History of England.* Cambridge: University Pr., 1897.

Mallarmé, Stéphane. *Poems,* trans. by Roger Fry. Chatto
   and Windus, 1936.

Malory, Sir Thomas. *Le Morte Darthur,* ed. by Sir Edward
   Strachey. London, N.Y.: Macmillan, 1899. Belonged
   to Leonard.

Mandeville, Bernard. *The Fable of the Bees: or, Private
   Vices, Publick Benefits,* ed. by F.B. Kaye. Oxford:
   Clarendon, 1924.

Mann, Thomas. *Buddenbrooks,* trans. by H.T. Lowe-Porter.
   M. Secker, 1930. Review slip.

Mann, Thomas. *Death in Venice,* trans. by H.T. Lowe-
    Porter. M. Secker, 1929.

Manning-Sanders, Ruth. (See Sanders, Ruth Manning.)

Mansfield, Katherine. *The Doves' Nest.* Constable, 1923.

Marlowe, Christopher. *Works of,* ed. by C.F. Tucker Brooke.
    Oxford: Clarendon, 1910.

Marlowe, Christopher, and George Chapman. *Hero and Lean-
    der.* Haslewood Reprints, 1924.

Marryat, Frederic. *Jacob Faithful,* w/introduction by
    George Saintsbury. Constable, 1928. 2 vol.

Martin, Kingsley. *Thomas Paine.* The Fabian Society, 1925.

[Martin, Sir Theodore, ed.] *The Book of Ballads,* ed. by
    Bon Gaultier [pseud. of Theodore Martin]. W.S. Orr,
    1849.

Marvell, Andrew. *Andrew Marvell.* The Augustan Books of
    English Poetry ser. E. Benn, n.d.

Marvell, Andrew. *Poems and Letters,* ed. by H.M. Margoli-
    outh. Oxford: Clarendon, 1927. 2 vol.

Masefield, John. *A Tarpaulin Muster.* M. Secker, 1926.

Massingham, Harold John and Hugh, eds. *The Great Victor-
    ians.* Harmondsworth, Middlesex: Penguin Books, 1937.
    [2 vol.] Vol. I only.

Maugham, William Somerset. *Ah King.* Garden City, N.Y.:
    Doubleday, Doran, 1933.

Maugham, William Somerset. *Cakes and Ale, or, The Skeleton
    in the Cupboard.* Everyman's Library ed. J.M. Dent,
    1936.

Maugham, William Somerset. *Mrs. Dot.* W. Heinemann, 1912.

Maugham, William Somerset. *Of Human Bondage.* W. Heine-
    mann, 1937.

Maupassant, Guy de. *La Maison Tellier.* Paris: P. Ollen-
    dorff, 1905.

Mauriac, Francois. *La Vie de Jean Racine.* Paris: Plon,
    1928.

Maurois, André. *Aspects of Biography,* trans. by S.C. Rob-
    erts. Cambridge: University Pr., 1929. "Pour Virgin-
    ia Woolf/[from] André Maurois."

Mauron, Marie. *Le Quartier Mortisson, Roman*. Paris: Editions Denoël, 1938. "A Virginia ... , [from] Marie Mauron."

Maximilian, Prince Max of Baden. *The Memoirs of*, trans. by W.M. Calder and C.W.H. Sutton. Constable, 1928. 2 vol.

Mazzini, Giuseppe. *Mazzini's Letters to an English Family*, ed. by E.F. Richards. London, N.Y.: J. Lane, 1920-22. 3 vol. Review slip in Vol. I.

McAlmon, Robert. *Village: As It Happened Through a Fifteen Year Period*. [Dijon: Contact Publishing Co., 1924].

McCarthy, Justin. *A History of Our Own Times from the Accession of Queen Victoria to the General Election of 1880*. New ed. Chatto and Windus, 1882. 4 vol. Belonged to Leslie Stephen.

Medwin, T. *Memoir of Percy Bysshe Shelley ... and Original Poems and Papers by Shelley Now First Collected*. The Shelley Papers ser. Whittaker, Treacher, 1833.

Meleager. *Fifty Poems of*, trans. by Walter Headlam. Macmillan, 1890. Belonged to George Duckworth, Virginia's half-brother.

Méléra, Marguerite and Gabrielle. *Six Women and the Invasion*, w/preface by Mrs. Humphry Ward [Mary Augusta Arnold Ward]. Macmillan, 1917. Belonged to Leonard.

Melville, Herman. *Israel Potter*. J. Cape, 1925.

Melville, Herman. *Mardi*. J. Cape, 1923.

Melville, Herman. *Moby Dick*. J. Cape, 1923.

Melville, Herman. *Omoo*. J. Cape, 1923.

Melville, Herman. *Redburn*. J. Cape, 1924.

Melville, Herman. *Typee*. J. Cape, 1923.

Melville, Herman. *White Jacket*. J. Cape, 1923.

Mencken, Henry Louis. *Selected Prejudices*. The Travellers' Library ser. J. Cape, 1926.

Meredith, George. *The Adventures of Harry Richmond*. Westminster: Archibald Constable, 1902.

Meredith, George. *Beauchamp's Career*. Chapman and Hall, 1876. 3 vol.

Meredith, George. *Diana of the Crossways.* Westminster: Archibald Constable, 1902.

Meredith, George. *The Egoist.* C.K. Paul, 1880.

Meredith, George. *Evan Harrington.* Bradbury, Evans, 1866.

Meredith, George. *Lord Ormont and His Aminta.* Westminster: Archibald Constable, 1902.

Meredith, George. *One of Our Conquerors.* Constable, 1924.

Meredith, George. *Poems.* Westminster: Archibald Constable, 1903. 2 vol.

Meredith, George. *Poems.* Westminster: Archibald Constable, 1904. [2 vol.] Vol. I only.

Meredith, George. *Poems and Lyrics of the Joy of Earth.* Macmillan, 1883. Belonged to Leslie Stephen.

Meredith, George. *Poems Written in Early Youth ... Poems from "Modern Love."* Constable, 1909.

Meredith, George. *Rhoda Fleming.* Westminster: Archibald Constable, 1902.

Meredith, George. *Sandra Belloni.* Westminster: Archibald Constable, 1902.

Meredith, George. *The Shaving of Shagpat.* Westminster: Archibald Constable, 1902.

Meredith, George. *Short Stories.* Westminster: Archibald Constable, 1902.

Meredith, George. *Short Stories.* Constable, 1924.

Meredith, George. *The Tragic Comedians.* Constable, 1924.

Meredith, George. *Vittoria.* Constable, 1924.

Milbanke, Ralph. (See [Byron, Lord].)

Milton, John. *Complete Poetical Works,* ed. by H.C. Beeching. H. Frowde, 1900.

Milton, John. *Minor Poems.* Noel Douglas, 1926. Review slip.

Milton, John. *Prose of,* ed. by Malcolm W. Wallace. Oxford University Pr., 1925.

Mirrlees, Hope. *Madeleine.* W. Collins, 1919.

Mitford, Mary Russell. *Our Village*. Whittaker, 1835. 3 vol.

Molière, Jean Baptiste Poquelin, *Oeuvres,* ed. by M. Bret. Paris:Littéraires Associés, 1788. 6 vol.

Molière, Jean Baptiste Poquelin. *Oeuvres complètes*. Paris: Hachette, 1875. 3 vol.

Monro, Harold. *Harold Monro*. Augustan Books of English Poetry ser. E. Benn, n.d.

Monro, Harold. *The Winter Solstice*. Ariel Poems ser. Faber and Gwyer, n.d.

Montaigne, Michel Eyquem de. *Essais,* ed. by H. Motheau and D. Jouarest. Paris: E. Flammarion, 1886-1899. 7 vol.

Montesquieu, Charles Louis de Secondat. *De L'esprit des Lois*. Paris: P. Didot et F. Didot, 1816. 5 vol.

Moore, George. *Celibates*. W. Scott, 1895.

Moore, George. *Esther Waters*. W. Heinemann, 1920.

Moore, George. *Hail and Farewell*. W. Heinemann, 1911-14. [3 vol.] Vols. I and III only.

*Moore, George. *The Making of an Immortal*. Faber and Gwyer, 1927. Author's presentation copy to Virginia Woolf.

Moore, George. *Spring Days*. T. Werner Laurie, 1930(?).

Moore, George Edward. *The Nature and Reality of Objects of Perception*. [Offprint from *Proceedings* of the Aristotelian Society], 1906.

Moore, Marianne. *Selected Poems,* w/introduction by T.S. Eliot. Faber and Faber, 1935.

Moore, Thomas Sturge. *Albert Durer*. Duckworth, 1905.

*Morrell, Ottoline. *A Farewell Message* [s.l.; s.m., 1938]. "To Virginia [from Philip Morrell] ... "

Morris, William. *The Defence of Guenevere and Other Poems,* ed. by Robert Steele. King's Poets ser. Alexander Moring, 1904.

Morris, William. *The Pilgrims of Hope* AND *Chants for Socialists*. Longmans, Green, 1915.

Moultrie, John. *Poems*. 3rd ed. Whittaker, 1852. Belonged to Herbert Duckworth, first husband of Virginia's mother.

Mudie's Select Library. (See *Catalogue*.)

Murasaki, Shikibu. *The Tale of Genji,* trans. by Arthur
    Waley. Vol. I. G. Allen and Unwin, 1925.

Murray, Gilbert. *A History of Ancient Greek Literature.*
    W. Heinemann, 1907.

Murry, John Middleton. *Cinnamon and Angelica, a Play.*
    Richard Cobden-Sanderson, 1920.

Murry, John Middleton. *Countries of the Mind: Essays in
    Literary Criticism.* W. Collins, 1924.

Murry, John Middleton. *God, Being an Introduction to the
    Science of Metabiology.* J. Cape, 1929. Belonged to
    Leonard.

Murry, John Middleton. *The Necessity of Communism.* J.
    Cape, 1932.

Nash, Rosalind. *A Sketch of the Life of Florence Nightin-
    gale.* Society for Promoting Christian Knowledge,
    1937. "To Virginia from H.L.S. ... " [unidentified].

Nation and Athenaeum, The. Volumes 33-44. April 7, 1923-
    March 30, 1929. 12 vol.

Newbolt, Sir Henry John. *Collected Poems, 1897-1907.* Lon-
    don, N.Y.: T. Nelson, 1910.

Newman, John Henry. *An Essay in Aid of a Grammar of As-
    sent.* 2nd ed. Burns, Oates, 1870. Belonged to
    Leslie Stephen.

Newman, John Henry. *Essays Critical and Historical.* Ba-
    sil M. Pickering, 1872. [2 vol.] Vol. II only.

Newman, John Henry. *Fifteen Sermons Preached Before the
    University of Oxford Between A.D. 1826 and 1843.*
    3rd ed. Rivingtons, 1872. Belonged to Leslie Ste-
    phen.

Newman, John Henry. *Historical Sketches: The Church of
    the Fathers* ... 3rd ed. Basil M. Pickering, 1876.
    Belonged to Leslie Stephen.

Newman, John Henry. *Historical Sketches: Rise and Prog-
    ress of Universities* ... Basil M. Pickering, 1872.
    Belonged to Leslie Stephen.

Newman, John Henry. *Historical Sketches: The Turks in Re-
    lation to Europe* ... Basil M. Pickering, 1876. Be-
    longed to Leslie Stephen.

Newman, John Henry. *The Idea of a University Defined and Illustrated.* 4th ed. Basil M. Pickering, 1875. Belonged to Leslie Stephen.

Newman, John Henry. *Loss and Gain: The Story of a Convert.* 6th ed. Burns, Oates, 1874. Belonged to Leslie Stephen.

Newman, John Henry. *Two Essays on Biblical and on Ecclesiastical Miracles.* 4th ed. Basil M. Pickering, 1875. Belonged to Leslie Stephen.

*Nicholson, Celia Anne. *A Boswell to Her Cook: A Cautionary Tale.* Chapman and Hall, 1931. Author's presentation copy to Virginia Woolf.

Nicolson, Sir Harold George. *Why Britain Is at War.* Harmondsworth, Middlesex: Penguin Books, 1939.

Nietzsche, Friedrich. *Thus Spake Zarathustra,* trans. by Thomas Common. G. Allen and Unwin, 1932(?).

*Nijinsky, Romola de Pulszky. *Nijinsky.* V. Gollancz, 1933.

Noailles, Anna Elizabeth, Comtesse de. *Les Eblouissements.* Paris: Calmann-Levy, 1907(?).

Norton, Charles Eliot. (See [Lowell, James Russell, ...]).

Omar Khayyam, *Rubaiyat of Omar Khayyam, the Astronomer-Poet of Persia,* trans. [by Edward Fitzgerald]. 3rd ed. B. Quaritch, 1872. Belonged to Leslie Stephen.

Omar Khayyam. *Rubaiyat of Omar Khayyam the Astronomer-Poet of Persia,* trans. [by Edward Fitzgerald]. Macmillan, 1899. "Virginia Stephen from J.T.S. [Julian Thoby Stephen] ... "

Omar Khayyam, *The Rubaiyat of Omar Khayyam, the Astronomer-Poet of Persia,* trans. [by Edward Fitzgerald]. Macmillan's Golden Treasury ser. Macmillan, 1899. Belonged to Thoby Stephen.

Omar Khayyam. *Rubaiyat of Omar Khayyam, the Astronomer-Poet of Persia,* trans. by Edward Fitzgerald. Noel Douglas, 1927.

Osborne, Dorothy. *The Letters of ... to William Temple,* ed. by G.C. Moore Smith. Oxford: Clarendon, 1928.

Osborne, Dorothy. *The Love Letters of ... to Sir William Temple,* ed. by Israel Gollancz. King's Classics ser. Alexander Moring, 1903.

Oxford and Asquith, Herbert Henry Asquith, Earl of. *Some Phases of Free Thought in England in the Nineteenth Century*. The Lindsey Pr., 1925.

Paget, Sir Richard, H.W. Fowler, and Robert Bridges. *The Nature of Human Speech* by Richard Paget; AND *On the Use of Italic, Fused Participle, &c* by H.W. Fowler; and *Reviews and Miscellaneous Notes* by Robert Bridges. Oxford: Clarendon, 1925.

Pain, Harry. *De Omnibus*. T.F. Unwin, 1901.

The Paston Letters. Written by Various Persons of Rank of Consequence During the Reigns of Henry VI, Edward IV, Richard III and Henry VIII, ed. by John Fenn and Mrs. [Laura] Archer-Hind. Everyman ser. J.M. Dent, 1924. 2 vol.

Patmore, Coventry. *Amelia,* AND *Tamerton Church-Tower, ... with Prefatory Study on English Metrical Law*. George Bell, 1878. Belonged to Julia Stephen, Virginia's mother.

Patmore, Coventry. *The Angel in the House*. 4th ed. Macmillan, 1866. Belonged to Julia Jackson, Virginia's mother.

[Patmore, Coventry]. *Odes*. Savill, Edwards, 1868(?).

[Patmore, Coventry]. (See *The Unknown Eros*.)

Payn, James. *The Backwater of Life, or Essays of a Literary Veteran,* w/introduction by Leslie Stephen. Smith, Elder, 1899.

Payn, James. *Some Literary Recollections*. Smith, Elder, 1884. Belonged to Leslie Stephen.

Peacock, Thomas Love. *The Plays of,* ed. by A.B. Young. D. Nutt, 1910.

Peel, Robert. *Sir Robert Peel from His Private Papers, with a Chapter on His Life and Character by His Grandson, the Hon. George Peel,* ed. by Charles Stuart Parker. John Murray, 1891. 3 vol.

Peele, George. (See Greene, Robert--2 items.)

Pepys, Samuel. *Diary,* transcr. by Mynos Bright; ed. by Henry B. Wheatley. H. Bell, 1923. 8 vol. in three.

Pepys, Samuel. *Private Correspondence and Miscellaneous Papers of ... , 1679-1703,* ed. by J.R. Tanner. G. Bell, 1926. 2 vol. Belonged to Leonard.

Perse, St.-John. (See Léger, Aléxis.)

Pervigilium Veneris: The Eve of Venus. In Latin and in English, ed. and trans. by R.W. Postgate. Grant Richards, 1924.

Philips, John. *The Poems of,* ed. by M.G. Lloyd Thomas. Percy Reprints ser. Oxford: Basil Blackwell, 1927.

Phillips, Stephen. *The Sin of David.* Macmillan, 1904.

Plato. *Cratylus et Theaetetus,* ed. by Martin Wohlrab. (In Greek). Leipzig: B. G. Teubner, 1891. Belonged to Leonard.

Plato. *Dialogi Secondum Thraslli Tetralogias Dispositi,* ed. by Martin Wohlrab. Leipzig: B. G. Teubner, 1887-94(?). [6 vol.] Vol. III only. Belonged to Leonard.

Plato. *Dialogues,* trans. by B[enjamin] Jowett. Oxford: Clarendon, 1871. 4 vol. Belonged to Leslie Stephen.

Plato, *Euthyphro, Apology of Socrates, Crito, Phaedo.* (In Latin). Leipzig: B.G. Teubner, 1897. Belonged to Leonard.

Ploetz, Karl Julius. *Ploetz' Manual of Universal History,* trans. and enl. by William H. Tillinghast. 2nd rev. ed. G.G. Harrap, 1933(?).

Plomer, William. *Cecil Rhodes.* P. Davies, 1933. "For Leonard and Virginia from William ... "

Plomer, William. *Visiting the Caves.* Jonathan Cape, 1936. "Leonard and Virginia ... from William ... "

Poe, Edgar Allan. *Edgar Allan Poe.* Augustan Books of Modern Poetry ser. E. Benn, n.d.

Poems of To-Day. Second Series. Sidgwick and Jackson, 1922.

Polo, Marco. *The Book of Sir Marco Polo, the Venetian,* trans. by Colonel Sir Henry Yule; ed. by Henry Cordier. 3rd ed. J. Murray, 1903. [2 vol.] Vol. II only.

Pope, Alexander. *The Dunciad, An Heroic Poem.* Oxford: Clarendon, 1928.

Pope, Alexander. *Letters of Mr. Pope, and Several Eminent Persons* [W. Wycherley, Sir R. Steele, J. Addison, J. Gay, et al.], *from the Year 1705 to 1711.* Dublin: George Faulkner, 1735. BOUND WITH *Letters of Mr.*

*Pope, and Several Eminent Persons, from the Year 1711
[to 1730].* Dublin, M. Rhames, 1735. This belonged
to Leslie Stephen.

Pope, Alexander. *The Rape of the Lock,* ed. by Hugh MacDonald. F. Etchells and H. Macdonald, 1925. Review
slip.

Portland, the Duke of [William John Arthur Charles James
Cavendish-Bentinck]. *Men, Women, and Things; Memo-
ries.* Faber and Faber, 1937. " ... to Mrs. Virginia
Woolf by ... T.S. Eliot ... "

Potocki de Montalk, Geoffrey, Count. *Surprising Songs:
An Odyssean Tale in Poetry.* Columbia Pr., 1930.

Potocki de Montalk, Geoffrey, Count. *Wild Oats, A Sheaf
of Poems.* Christchurch, N.Z.: Privately printed,
1927.

Pound, Ezra. *Selected Poems,* ed. by T.S. Eliot. Faber
and Faber, 1933.

Power, Eileen Edna. *Medieval People.* Penguin Books, 1937.

Praed, Winthrop Macworth, *Lillian and Other Poems,* [comp.
by Rufus S. Griswold]. N.Y.: Redfield, 1852. Belonged to Herbert Duckworth, first husband of Virginia's mother.

Proust, Marcel. *A l'Ombre des Jeunes Filles en Fleurs.*
Paris: Nouvelle Revue Francaise, 1919-20. 2 vol. in
one.

Proust, Marcel. *Le Côté de Guermantes.* Paris: Nouvelle
Revue Francaise, 1920-21. 2 vol.

Proust, Marcel. *Du Côté de Chez Swann.* Paris: Editions
de la Nouvelle Revue Francaise, 1919. [2 vol.] Vol.
II only.

Proust, Marcel. *Du Côté de Chez Swann.* 79th ed. [*sic*].
Paris: Editions de la Nouvelle Revue Francaise, 1926.
[2 vol.] Vol. II only.

Proust, Marcel. *Du Côté de Chez Swann.* 122nd ed. [*sic*].
Paris: Librairie Gallimard, 1929. [2 vol.] Vol. I
only.

Proust, Marcel. *La Prisonnière (Sodome et Gomorrhe, III).*
Paris: Nouvelle Revue Francaise, 1923. 2 vol. in
one.

Proust, Marcel. *Sodome et Gomorrhe, II.* Paris: Nouvelle
Revue Francaise, 1922. 3 vol. in one.

Proust, Marcel. *Le Temps Retrouvé.* Paris: Nouvelle Revue
    Francaise, 1927. 2 vol. in one.

Pryme, Jane Townley, and Alicia Bayne. *Memorials of the
    Thackeray Family.* Privately printed, 1879. Be-
    longed to Leslie Stephen.

Racine, Jean Baptiste. *Oeuvres.* Paris: C. LeGras, 1750.
    3 vol.

Raleigh, Walter. *The English Novel: A Short Sketch of
    Its History* ... John Murray, 1916.

Reade, Winwood. *The Martyrdom of Man,* w/introduction by
    F. Legge. Watts, 1924.

Reflections Upon Marriage [by Mary Astell]. R. Wilkin,
    1706.

Renan, Ernest. *Souvenirs d'Enfance et de Jeunesse.* Paris:
    Nelson, 1930. Belonged to Leonard.

Rhys, Ernest, ed. *The Prelude to Poetry: Essays and Com-
    ments by the Poets on Their Own Art.* Everyman ed.
    J.M. Dent, 1927.

Richard de Bury [Richard Aungerville]. *The Love of Books:
    The Philobiblon,* trans. by Ernest C. Thomas. King's
    Classics ser. A. Moring, 1902.

Richards, I.A. *Practical Criticism, A Study of Literary
    Judgment.* Kegan Paul, 1929.

Richardson, Samuel. *Clarissa.* 4th ed. S. Richardson,
    1751. 7 vol.

Richardson, Samuel. *The Correspondence of* ... , *to Which
    Are Prefixed a Biographical Account of That Author
    and Observations on His Writings by A[nna] L[aetitia]
    Barbauld.* Richard Phillips, 1804. [6 vol.] Vols.
    II through VI only. Belonged to Leslie Stephen.

Ritchie, Anne Isabella. *Bluebeard's Keys and Other Stor-
    ies.* Smith, Elder, 1882.

Ritchie, Anne Isabella. *Five Old Friends and a Young
    Prince.* Smith, Elder, 1868.

Ritchie, Anne Isabella. *Five Old Friends and a Young
    Prince.* Smith, Elder, 1876. Inscribed by author to
    Julia Duckworth, Virginia's mother.

Ritchie, Anne Isabella. *Miss Angel and Fulham Lawn.* Smith,
    Elder, 1903. Belonged to George Duckworth.

Ritchie, Anne Isabella. *The Story of Elizabeth with Other Tales and Sketches*. Household ed. Boston: Fields, Osgood, 1869.

Ritchie, Anne Isabella. *The Village on the Cliff*. Smith, Elder, 1867.

Ritchie, Anne Isabella. *The Works of*. Smith, Elder, 1875-76. 8 vol.

Ritchie, M.T., ed. *English Drawings, an Anthology*. Chatto and Windus, 1935.

Roberts, S.C. *Lord Macaulay*. English Association, 1927.

Rochester, John Wilmot, Earl of. *Collected Works of John Wilmot, Earl of Rochester*, ed. by John Hayward. Soho: Nonesuch, 1926. Belonged to Leonard.

Ros, Amanda M'Kittrick. *Irene Iddesleigh*. Soho: Nonesuch, 1926.

Rossetti, Christina. *Poetical Works of*, ed. by William Michael Rossetti. Macmillan, 1906.

Rousseau, Jean-Jacques. *Collection Complète des Oeuvres*, ed. by P.A. DuPeyron. Geneva: n.p., 1782. 15 vol.

*Rousseaux, André. *Littérature du Vingtième Siècle*. Paris: Albin Michel, 1938.

*Rowdon, John. *This Book About Painting ... Deals with the Work of Duncan Grant ...* Revaluation ser. [H.J. Marks, 1934].

Rowe, Nicholas. *The Fair Penitent, A Tragedy*. J.R. Tonson and S. Draper, 1750. Belonged to Leonard.

Rozanov, V.V. *Fallen Leaves*, trans. by S.S. Koteliansky; w/foreword by James Stephens. Mandrake Pr., 1929.

Ruskin, John. *Aratra Pentelici. Six Lectures on the Elements of Sculpture*. Smith, Elder, 1872. Belonged to Leslie Stephen.

Ruskin, John. *Munera Pulveris*. Smith, Elder, 1872.

Ruskin, John. *Modern Painters*. Smith, Elder, 1851-68. [5 vol.] Vol. V missing.

Ruskin, John. *Ruskin as Literary Critic*, ed. by A.H.R. Ball. Cambridge: University Pr., 1928. Belonged to Leonard.

Ruskin, John. *Sesame and Lilies*. Smith, Elder, 1871.

Ruskin, John. *Time and Tide*. Smith, Elder, 1872.

Ruskin, John. *Time and Tide*. Oxford University Pr., 1920.

Russell, Bertrand. *The Problems of Philosophy*. N.Y.: H. Holt, 1912.

Russian Tales, trans. by Aylmer Maude [and Louise Maude]. Collins' Clear-type Pr., 1927(?). (Includes 3 stories by Leo Tolstoy, *et al.*)

Rutherford, Mark [pseud. of William Hale White]. *The Autobiography of*, ed. by Reuben Shapcott. 11th ed. T. Fisher Unwin, n.d.

Rutherford, William Gunion. *First Greek Grammar*. [Rev. ed.] Macmillan, 1907.

Sackville-West, Edward. *Piano Quintet*. W. Heinemann, 1925.

Sackville-West, Victoria Mary [a.k.a. Vita]. *Aphra Behn: The Incomparable Astrea*. Representative Women ser. Howe, 1927.

Sackville-West, Victoria Mary [a.k.a. Vita]. *Challenge*. N.Y.: George H. Doran, 1923.

Sackville-West, Victoria Mary [a.k.a. Vita]. *Country Notes*. Michael Joseph, 1939. "V.W. from V.S.W. ... "

Sackville-West, Victoria Mary [a.k.a. Vita]. *The Dragon in Shallow Waters*. W. Collins, 1921.

Sackville-West, Vita. *The Heir*. W. Heinemann, 1922.

*Sackville-West, Victoria Mary [a.k.a. Vita]. *The Land*. W. Heinemann, 1926. Author's presentation copy to Virginia.

*Sackville-West, Victoria Mary [a.k.a. Vita]. *The Land*. Ltd. ed. W. Heinemann, 1926.

Sackville-West, Victoria Mary [a.k.a. Vita]. *Orchard and Vineyard*. John Lane, 1921.

Sackville-West, Victoria Mary [a.k.a. Vita]. *Saint Joan of Arc*. Cobden-Sanderson, 1936. "Virginia from Vita."

Sackville-West, Victoria Mary [a.k.a. Vita]. *V. Sackville-West*. Augustan Books of Poetry ser. E. Benn, 1931.

Sadleir, Michael. *Trollope. A Commentary*. Constable, 1927.

Sainte-Beuve, Charles Augustin. *Nouveaux Lundis*. Paris:
M. Lévy, 1863-72. [13 vol.] Vol. III only.

Saint-Simon, Louis. *Mémoires*, ed. by A. de Boislisle.
Paris: Hachette, 1879-1923. [41 vol.] Vols. I, II,
III only.

Sanders, Ruth Manning. *The City*. E. Benn, 1927.

Sarton, May. *Inner Landscape; Poems*. Cresset, n.d. "To
Virginia Woolf from May Sarton ... "

Sassoon, Philip. *The Third Route*. William Heinemann,
1929. "To Virginia Woolfe [*sic*] ... "

*[Sassoon, Siegfried]. *Recreations*. Chiswick Pr., 1923.
Inscribed by author to Virginia Woolf.

Savage-Armstrong, George Francis. *One in the Infinite*.
Longmans, Green, 1891. Belonged to Leslie Stephen.

Schreiner, Olive. *The Story of an African Farm*. T. Fisher Unwin, 1924.

Scott, Fred Newton. *American Slang*. Oxford: Clarendon,
1926. BOUND WITH Jespersen, O. *Notes on Relative
Clauses*--see Holleyman.

Scott, Walter. *The Journal of*. Edinburgh: David Douglas,
1890. 2 vol. Belonged to Leslie Stephen.

Scott-Moncrieff, C.K., comp. *Marcel Proust. An English
Tribute*. By Joseph Conrad, Arnold Bennett, Arthur
Symons, Compton MacKenzie, Clive Bell, W.J. Turner,
Catherine Carswell, E. Rickword, Violet Hunt, Ralph
Wright, Alex Waugh, George Saintsbury, L. Pearsall
Smith, A.B. Walkley, J. Middleton Murry, Stephen Hud-
son, G.S. Street, Ethel C. Mayne, Francis Birrell,
Reginald Turner, Dyneley Hussey. Chatto and Windus,
1923. "Virginia Woolf from Francis Birrell ... "

Scott-Stokes, Henry Folliott. *Perseus;   Or, Of Dragons*.
K. Paul, Trench, Trubner, 1924.

Sedgwick, Anne Douglas. *Autumn Crocuses*. M. Secker, 1926.

Selected Modern English Essays: Second Series. World's
Classics ser. Oxford University Pr., 1923. (Con-
tains two essays by Virginia Woolf: "Rambling Round
Evelyn" and "The Patron and the Crocus.")

Seligman, Charles Gabriel and Brenda Z. *The Veddas*. Cambridge: University Pr., 1911.

Shakespeare, William. *All's Well That Ends Well,* ed. by Arthur Quiller-Couch and John Dover Wilson. Cambridge: University Pr., 1929.

Shakespeare, William. *As You Like It,* ed. by Arthur Quiller-Couch and John Dover Wilson. Cambridge University Pr., 1926.

Shakespeare, William. *The Comedies of,* ed. by W.J. Craig. London, N.Y.: Oxford University Pr., 1903.

Shakespeare, William. ... *Comedy of Measure for Measure,* ed. by Israel Gollancz. Temple Shakespeare ed. J.M. Dent, 1908.

Shakespeare, William. ... *Comedy of A Winter's Tale,* ed. by Israel Gollancz. Temple Shakespeare ed. J.M. Dent, 1894. Belonged to Leonard.

Shakespeare, William. *Hamlet by William Shake-speare, 1603; Hamlet by William Shakespeare, 1604; Being Exact Reprints of the First and Second Editions ... ,* ed. by Samuel Timmins. Sampson Low, 1860.

Shakespeare, William. *Histories and Poems.* Simpkin, Marshall, Hamilton, Kent, n.d. [192_?].

Shakespeare, William. *The Histories, Poems and Sonnets of,* ed. by W.J. Craig. London, N.Y.: Oxford University Pr., 1903.

Shakespeare, William. *The Life of King Henry V.* N.Y.: American Book Exchange, 1880.

Shakespeare, William. *The Merchant of Venice,* ed. by Arthur Quiller-Couch and John Dover Wilson. Cambridge: University Pr., 1926.

Shakespeare, William. *A Midsummer-Night's Dream,* ed. by Arthur Quiller-Couch and John Dover Wilson. Cambridge: University Pr., 1924.

Shakespeare, William. *Othello: The Moor of Venice.* Bliss, Sands, 1898. Belonged to Leonard.

Shakespeare, William. *Shakespeare's Sonnets,* ed. by Israel Gollancz. Temple Shakespeare ed. J.M. Dent, 1900. Belonged to Leonard.

Shakespeare, William. *The Taming of the Shrew,* ed. by Arthur Quiller-Couch and John Dover Wilson. Cambridge: University Pr., 1928.

Shakespeare, William. *The Tragedies of,* ed. by W.J. Craig. Oxford University Pr., 1903.

Shakespeare, William.   ... *Tragedy of Cymbeline,* ed. by
     Israel Gollancz. Temple Shakespeare ed. J.M. Dent,
     1900. Belonged to Leonard.

Shakespeare, William.   ... *Tragedy of King Lear,* ed. by
     Israel Gollancz. Temple Shakespeare ed. J.M. Dent,
     1902.

Shakespeare, William. *The Works of.* Kegan Paul, 1891.
     Belonged to Leonard.

Shakespeare, William. *The Works of,* ed. by H. Arthur
     Doubleday and T. Gregory Foster. Westminster: A.
     Constable, 1893-98. 12 vol.

Sharp, William. *Romantic Ballads and Poems of Phantasy.*
     Walter Scott, 1888. Belonged to Leslie Stephen.

Shaw, George Bernard. *Arms and the Man: An Anti-romantic
     Comedy in Three Acts.* Constable, 1910.

Shaw, George Bernard. *Candida: A Mystery.* Constable,
     1910.

Shaw, George Bernard. *Love Among the Artists.* Constable,
     1914.

Shaw, George Bernard. *Love Among the Artists.* Constable,
     1924.

Shaw,George Bernard. *Prefaces.* Constable, 1934. Belonged
     to Leonard.

Shaw, George Bernard. *Saint Joan: A Chronicle Play in
     Six Scenes and an Epilogue.* Constable, 1924. Be-
     longed to Leonard.

Shaw, George Bernard. *Saint Joan, a Chronicle, and The
     Apple Cart, a Political Extravaganza.* Constable,
     1932.

Shaw, George Bernard. *An Unsocial Socialist.* Constable,
     1924.

Sheean, Vincent. *The Tide, a Novel.* Garden City, N.Y.:
     Doubleday, Doran, 1933. "For Mrs. Woolf [from] V.
     Sheean ... "

Shelley, Percy Bysshe. *The Complete Poetical Works of,*
     ed. by Thomas Hutchinson. Oxford: Clarendon, 1904.

Shelley, Percy Bysshe. (See Medwin, T.)

Shelley, Percy Bysshe. *The Letters of,* ed. by Roger Ing-
     pen. Isaac Pitman, 1909. 2 vol.

Shelley, Percy Bysshe. *Poetical Works,* ed. by Mrs. [Mary] Shelley. E. Moxon, 1839. 4 vol.

Shelley, Percy Bysshe. *Poetical Works.* G. Newnes, 1902. Belonged to Leonard.

Shelley, Percy Bysshe. *Selected Lyrics,* ed. by G.D.H. Cole and M.I. Cole. Noel Douglas, 1927.

Shelley, Percy Bysshe. *The Shelley Correspondence in the Bodleian Library. Letters of Percy Bysshe Shelley and Others,* ed. by R.H. Hill. Oxford: John Johnson, 1926. Review slip.

Shelley, Percy Bysshe. *Shelley Memorials: From Authentic Sources,* ed. by Lady [Jane] Shelley. *To Which Is Added an Essay on Christianity by Percy B. Shelley: Now First Printed.* Smith, Elder, 1859. This belonged to Anne Isabella Thackeray [m. Ritchie].

Shelley, Percy Bysshe. *Shelley's Lost Letters to Harriet,* ed. by Leslie Hotson. Faber and Faber, 1930.

Sheridan, Richard Brinsley. *An Ode to Scandal,* ed. by R. Crompton Rhodes. Stratford-Upon-Avon: Basil Blackwell, 1927.

Short Stories by Russian Authors, trans. by Rochelle S. Townsend. Everyman ed. J.M. Dent, 1924.

Sidney, Philip. *The Complete Poems of,* ed. by Alexander B. Grosart. Privately printed, 1873. [2 vol.] Vol. I only.

Sidney, Philip. *The Countess of Pembroke's Arcadia.* 11th ed. William Du-Gard, 1662. Belonged to Leslie Stephen.

Sitwell, Edith. *Alexander Pope.* Faber and Faber, 1930. Belonged to Leonard.

Sitwell, Edith. *Collected Poems.* Duckworth, 1930.

Sitwell, Edith. *Edith Sitwell.* Augustan Books of Modern Poetry ser. E. Benn, n.d.

*Sitwell, Edith. *Rustic Elegies.* Duckworth, 1927. Author's presentation copy to Virginia Woolf.

*Sitwell, Edith. *Troy Park.* Duckworth, 1925.

*Sitwell, Osbert. *Dumb-animal, and Other Stories.* Duckworth, 1930. "For Virginia from Osbert."

Sitwell, Osbert. *England Reclaimed: A Book of Eclogues.* Duckworth, 1927. Belonged to Leonard.

*Sitwell, Osbert. *The Man Who Lost Himself*. Duckworth,
      1929. Author's presentation copy to Virginia.

*Sitwell, Osbert. *Out of the Flame*. G. Richards, 1923.
      Belonged to Leonard.

*Sitwell, Sacheverell. *All Summer in a Day, an Autobiograph-
      ical Fantasia*. Duckworth, 1926. Inscribed by author
      to Virginia Woolf.

 Sitwell, Sacheverell. *The Hundred and One Harlequins*.
      Duckworth, 1929.

 Skelton, John. *Complete Poems of,* ed. by Phillip Hender-
      son. J.M. Dent, 1931.

 Smart, Christopher. *A Song to David, with Other Poems,* ed.
      by Edmund Blunden. R. Cobden-Sanderson, 1924. Re-
      view slip.

 Smeaton, Oliphant, ed. *English Satires*. Blackie, 1924.

 Smith, Florence Margaret. *Novel on Yellow Paper: Or, Work
      It Out for Yourself*. N.Y.: W. Morrow, 1937.

 Smith, George. (See Lee, Sidney, and Leslie Stephen.)

 Smith, Goldwin. *England and America*. Manchester: A. Ire-
      land, 1865. (BOUND WITH Stephen, Leslie. *The "Times"*
      ... , q.v.)

 Smith, Goldwin. *The United Kingdom: A Political History*.
      London, N.Y.: Macmillan, 1899. 2 vol. "Adeline Vir-
      ginia Stephen from her loving father ... "

 Smith, Horace. *Poems*. Macmillan, 1889.

 Smith, Logan Pearsall. *English Idioms*. Oxford: Clarendon,
      1923. 2 copies of this, one rebacked and with label
      on spine.

 Smith, Logan Pearsall. *Four Words: Romantic, Originality,
      Creative, Genius*. Oxford: Clarendon, 1924.

 Smith, Miriam. *Poems*. Grant Richards, 1908. "A.V.S.
      from J.W.H. [Jack W. Hills] ... "

 Smollett, Tobias George. *The Adventures of Peregrine Pick-
      le*. J.F. Dove, n.d. Belonged to Leonard.

*Smyth, Ethel Mary. *Beecham and Pharaoh: Thomas Beecham*.
      Chapman and Hall, 1935. Author's presentation copy
      to Virginia.

*Smyth, Ethel Mary. *Impressions That Remained: Memoirs.*
   London, N.Y.: Longmans, Green, 1920. 2 vol. Author's presentation copy to Virginia.

*Smyth, Ethel Mary. *Maurice Baring.* London, Toronto: W.
   Heinemann, 1938. Author's presentation copy to Virginia.

*Smyth, Ethel Mary. *Streaks of Life.* London, N.Y.: Longmans, Green, 1921. Inscribed to Virginia by author.

Smyth, Ethel Mary. *Streaks of Life.* New ed. Longmans,
   Green, 1924.

Somervell, D.C. *Disraeli and Gladstone: A Duo-Biographical
   Sketch.* Jarrolds, 1925. Belonged to Leonard.

*Sophocles. *The Antigone of,* trans. by R.C. Trevelyan.
   Hodder and Stoughton, 1924. Review slip.

Sophocles. *The Oedipus Tyrannus of,* trans. by J.T. Shep-
   pard. Cambridge: University Pr., 1922.

Sophocles. *Plays and Fragments,* trans. by R[ichard] C[la-
   verhouse] Jebb. Cambridge: University Pr., 1892-
   1900. [7 vol.] Vols. V (*The Trachiniae*) and VI (*The
   Electra*) only. Belonged to Leonard.

Sophocles. *Sophocles: For the Use of Schools,* ed. by Lew-
   is Campbell and Evelyn Abbott. New and rev. ed.
   Oxford: Clarendon, 1886-99. 2 vol. Vol. I. (For
   Vol. II, see Holleyman.)

*Spender, Stephen. *Poems.* Faber and Faber, 1933.

*Spender, Stephen. *Trial of a Judge.* Faber and Faber,
   1938.

*Spender, Stephen. *Vienna.* Faber and Faber, 1934. Author's
   presentation copy to Virginia Woolf.

Squire, Sir John Collings, comp. *Selections from Modern
   Poets.* M. Secker, 1921.

Squire, John Collings. *The Survival of the Fittest and
   Other Poems.* George Allen and Unwin, 1916.

Stadtmuller, Hugo, ed. *Eclogae Poetarum Graecorum Scholar-
   um in Usum.* Leipzig: B.G. Teubner, 1883. Belonged
   to Leonard.

Steele, Sir Richard. (See Pope, Alexander. *Letters.*)

Stendhal. (See Beyle, Marie Henri.)

[Stephen, Alfred]. *Jottings from Memory by an Australian Great Grandfather. First Portion--1802 to 1818. Birth and Schoolboy Days; with Some Account of the People, and Life in the West Indies.* Sydney: Robert Bone, 1889. Belonged to Leslie Stephen.

[Stephen, Alfred]. *Jottings from Memory by an Australian Great Grandfather. Second Portion--1818 to 1824. Student-Days and Call to the Bar.* Sydney: Robert Bone, 1891.

Stephen, James Kenneth. *James K. Stephen.* Augustan Books of Modern Poetry ser. E. Benn, n.d.

Stephen, Leslie. (See Green, John Richard.)

Stephen, Leslie. (See Lee, Sidney, and Leslie Stephen.)

Stephen, Leslie. *English Literature and Society in the Eighteenth Century.* Ford Lectures ser. Duckworth, 1904. "Adeline Virginia Stephen from Leslie Stephen ... "

Stephen, Leslie. *Henry Sidgwick.* Offprint from *Mind,* n.s., No. 37, pp. [3]-19. 2 copies of this.

Stephen, Leslie. *Hobbes.* English Men of Letters ser. Macmillan, 1904.

Stephen, Leslie. *The Life of Henry Fawcett.* 3rd ed. Smith, Elder, 1886.

Stephen, Leslie. *The "Times" on the American War.* W. Ridgway, 1865.

Stevenson, Robert Louis. *A Child's Garden of Verses.* Longmans, Green, 1890.

Stevenson, Robert Louis. *Essays of Travel.* Chatto and Windus, 1905. Belonged to Leonard.

Stevenson, Robert Louis. *The Letters of ... to His Family and Friends,* ed. by Sidney Colvin. 4th ed. Methuen, 1901. 2 vol.

Stevenson, Robert Louis. *Poems.* Chatto and Windus, 1906.

Stevenson, Robert Louis. *Robert Louis Stevenson.* Augustan Books of Modern Poetry ser. E. Benn, n.d.

Stevenson, Robert Louis. *Works.* Tusitala ed. William Heinemann, 1924. [35 vol.] Vols. I-V, VII-XV only.

Strachey, Giles Lytton. *Elizabeth and Essex.* Chatto and Windus, 1928.

*Strachey, Giles Lytton. *Eminent Victorians: Cardinal Man-
ning, Florence Nightingale, Dr. Arnold, General Gordon.* Chatto and Windus, 1918. Author's presentation
copy to Virginia.

*Strachey, Giles Lytton. *Landmarks in French Literature.*
Williams and Norgate, n.d. Author's presentation
copy to Virginia.

*Strachey, Giles Lytton. *Queen Victoria.* Chatto and Windus, 1921. Author's presentation copy to Virginia
Woolf.

Strachey, Giles Lytton. *Queen Victoria.* Chatto and Windus, 1937.

Strachey, Ray. *"The Cause": A Short History of the Wom-
en's Movement in Great Britain.* G. Bell, 1928.

Strindberg, August. *Easter and Other Plays.* J. Cape,
1929.

Strindberg, August. *Lucky Peter's Travels and Other Plays.*
J. Cape, 1930.

Surrey, Henry Howard, Earl of. *The Poems of,* ed. by J.
Yeowell. G. Bell, 1902.

Svevo, Italo [pseud. of Ettore Schmidt]. *Confessions of
Zeno,* trans. by Beryl de Zoete. Putnam, 1930.

Swift, Jonathan. *Gulliver's Travels and Selected Writings,*
ed. by John Hayward. Soho: Nonesuch, 1934.

Swift, Jonathan. *Journal to Stella; Together with Other
Writings Relating to Stella and Vanessa,* w/notes by
Sir Walter Scott. G. Newnes, 1904.

Swinburne, Algernon Charles. (See Leith, Mary Charlotte.)

Swinburne, Algernon Charles. *Atalanta in Calydon.* E.
Moxon, 1865.

Swinburne, Algernon Charles. *Atalanta in Calydon, A Tragedy.* Riccardi Pr., 1923.

Swinburne, Algernon Charles. *Bothwell.* Chatto and Windus,
1874.

Swinburne, Algernon Charles. *A Channel Passage and Other
Poems.* Chatto and Windus, 1904. "The Sp[arrow; i.e.,
Virginia] from V.D. [Violet Dickinson] ... "

Swinburne, Algernon Charles. *Collected Poetical Works.*
W. Heinemann, 1924. 2 vol.

Swinburne, Algernon Charles. *Erechtheus: A Tragedy.* 2nd ed. Chatto and Windus, 1876. Belonged to Leonard.

Swinburne, Algernon Charles. *A Note on Charlotte Brontë.* Chatto and Windus, 1877.

Swinburne, Algernon Charles. *Poems.* Chatto and Windus, 1904. 6 vol.

Swinburne, Algernon Charles. *Poems and Ballads.* John Camden Hotten, 1866.

Swinburne, Algernon Charles. *Selections from the Poetical Works of.* 9th ed. Chatto and Windus, 1904. Belonged to Thoby Stephen.

Swinburne, Algernon Charles. *Swinburne's Hyperion and Other Poems. With an Essay on Swinburne and Keats by Georges Lafourcade.* Faber and Gwyer, 1927. Belonged to Leonard.

Taylor, Henry. *Notes from Books, in Four Essays.* 2nd ed. John Murray, 1849. Belonged to Anne Isabella Thackeray [m. Ritchie].

Taylor, Henry. *The Virgin Widow: A Play.* Longmans, 1850.

Tchekoff, Anton. *Plays by ... , Second Series,* trans. by J. West. Duckworth, 1920. (Includes *On the High Road; The Proposal; The Wedding; The Bear; A Tragedian in Spite of Himself; The Anniversary; The Three Sisters; The Cherry Orchard.*)

Tchekoff, Anton. [See also Chekhov.]

Tennyson, Alfred. *Alfred Tennyson.* Augustan Books of Modern Poetry ser. E. Benn, n.d.

Tennyson, Alfred. *Ballads and Other Poems.* C.K. Paul, 1880.

Tennyson, Alfred. *The [Complete] Works of Alfred Lord Tennyson.* Macmillan, 1894. Belonged to Thoby Stephen.

Tennyson, Alfred. *Demeter and Other Poems.* Macmillan, 1889. Belonged to Leslie Stephen.

Tennyson, Alfred. *Enoch Arden,* [etc.]. Edward Moxon, 1864. Belonged to Harriet Marian Thackeray, first wife of Virginia's father.

Tennyson, Alfred. *The Holy Grail and Other Poems.* Strahan, 1870. Belonged to Herbert Duckworth, first husband of Virginia's mother.

Tennyson, Alfred. *Idylls of the King.* Edward Moxon, 1859.

[Tennyson, Alfred]. *In Memoriam.* Macmillan, 1894. Belonged to Thoby Stephen.

Tennyson, Alfred. *The Lover's Tale.* C. Kegan Paul, 1879.

Tennyson, Alfred. *The Princess: A Medley.* 8th ed. Edward Moxon, 1858.

Tennyson, Hallam, ed. *Tennyson and His Friends.* Macmillan, 1912.

Terry, Dame Ellen. *Ellen Terry and Bernard Shaw,* ed. by Christopher St. John. 2nd ed. Constable, 1931.

Thackeray, William Makepeace. *A Collection of Letters of William Makepeace Thackeray, 1847-1855,* [ed. by Mrs. J.O. Brookfield]. Smith, Elder, 1887. Belonged to Leslie Stephen.

Thackeray, William Makepeace. *Contributions to "Punch."* Smith, Elder, 1886.

Thackeray, William Makepeace. *Miscellaneous Essays, Sketches, and Reviews.* Smith, Elder, 1885.

Thackeray, William Makepeace. *Miscellanies: Prose and Verse.* Bradbury and Evans, 1854-57. [4 vol.] Vol. III only. (Includes *The Memoirs of Barry Lyndon, Esq.,* etc.)

Thackeray, William Makepeace. *Pendennis.* Ward, Lock, 1910.

Thackeray, William Makepeace. *Roundabout Papers* AND *The Four Georges* AND *The English Humourists* AND *The Second Funeral of Napoleon.* Smith, Elder, 1877.

*Thomas, Edward. *Collected Poems.* Faber and Faber, 1936.

Thompson, Francis. *Francis Thompson.* Augustan Books of English Poetry ser. E. Benn, n.d.

*Thompson, Francis. *Poems.* Elkin Mathews and John Lane, 1894.

Thomson, James ("B.V."). *Poems, Essays and Fragments,* ed. by John M. Robertson. A. and H. Bradlaugh Donner, 1892.

Thomson, James ("B.V."). *Poems, Essays and Fragments,* ed. by John M. Robertson. A.C. Fifield, 1905.

Thucydides. *The Peloponnesian War,* trans. by Richard Crawley. J.M. Dent, 1903. [2 vol.] Vol. I only.

Thucydides. *The Peloponnesian War,* Book II, ed. by E.C. Marchant. (In Greek). Macmillan, 1893. Belonged to Leonard.

Tolstoi, Leo. *Plays,* trans. by Louise and Aylmer Maude. Oxford University Pr., 1923.

Tolstoi, Leo. *Tolstoy on Art and Its Critics,* ed. by Aylmer Maude. Oxford University Pr., 1925.

Tolstoi, Leo. *What I Believe,* ed. by V. Tchertkoff and A.C. Fifield. Free Age Pr., 1906(?).

Tolstoi, Leo. *What Then Must We Do?,* trans. by Aylmer Maude. Oxford University Pr., 1925.

Trelawny, Edward John. *The Adventures of a Younger Son,* ed. by F. Collins. J.M. Dent, n.d.

*Trevelyan, Robert Calverly. *An Epistle.* Dorking: A.A. Tanner, 1940. Author's presentation copy to Virginia and Leonard Woolf.

Trollope, Anthony. *An Autobiography,* w/introduction by Michael Sadleir. World's Classics ser. Oxford University Pr., 1928.

Trollope, Anthony. *Framley Parsonage.* Collins' Clear-Type Pr., n.d. Belonged to Leonard.

Trotsky, Leon. *The History of the Russian Revolution,* trans. by M. Eastman. Gollancz, 1934.

Trotsky, Leon. *The History of the Russian Revolution to Brest-Litovsk.* Allen and Unwin, 1919. Belonged to Leonard.

Trotsky, Leon. *Literature and Revolution,* trans. by Rose Strunsky. George Allen and Unwin, 1925. Belonged to Leonard.

Turner, W.J. *W.J. Turner.* Augustan Books of Modern Poetry ser. E. Benn, n.d.

Tutt, James William. *British Moths.* G. Routledge, 1896.

Twain, Mark. (See Clemens, Samuel Langhorne.)

Twelve Poets. A Miscellany of New Verse. Selwyn and Blount, 1918. "V.W. from R.M.S. [Ruth Manning Sanders]."

The Unknown Eros and Other Odes.   Odes I-XXXI [by Coventry Patmore]. G. Bell, 1877.

Untermeyer, Louis, ed. *The Albatross Book of Living Verse: English and American Poetry from the Thirteenth Century to the Present Day.* W. Collins, 1933.

Vanbrugh, John. *Plays Written by Sir John Vanbrugh.* J. Rivington, 1776. 2 vol. "To V.S. ... [from Clive Bell]."

Vanbrugh, John. (See Centlivre, Susannah. Also Wycherley, William.)

*Vigny, Alfred, Victor. *Journal d'un Poète.* New ed., rev. and enl. by Fernand Baldensperger. The Scholartis Pr., 1928.

Virgil. *Bucolica et Georgica.* Leipzig: B.G. Teubner, 1904. Belonged to Leonard.

Wallas, Graham. *Men and Ideas,* w/preface by Gilbert Murray. G. Allen and Unwin, 1940. Belonged to Leonard.

Walpole, Horace. *Letters,* ed. by C.B. Lucas. G. Newnes, 1904(?).

*Walpole, Sir Hugh. *The Apple Trees: Four Reminiscences.* Berkshire, England: Golden Cockerel Pr., 1932. Inscribed by author to Virginia.

*Walpole, Sir Hugh. *Hans Frost: A Novel.* Macmillan, 1929. Inscribed by author to Virginia.

*Walpole, Sir Hugh. *Judith Paris: A Novel.* Macmillan, 1931. Inscribed by author to Virginia.

*Walpole, Sir Hugh. *The Old Ladies.* Macmillan, 1924. Inscribed by author to Virginia.

*Walpole, Sir Hugh. *Rogue Herries: A Novel.* Macmillan, 1930. Inscribed by author to Virginia Woolf.

*Walpole, Sir Hugh. *Roman Fountain.* Macmillan, 1940. Inscribed by author to Virginia.

*Walpole, Sir Hugh. *Vanessa: A Novel.* Macmillan, 1933. Inscribed by author to Virginia Woolf.

Ward, Alfred Charles, ed. *A Book of American Verse.* World's Classics ser. Oxford University Pr., 1935.

Watson, Sir William. *Ode on the Day of the Coronation of King Edward VII.* John Lane, 1902. Belonged to Leslie Stephen.

Watson, Sir William. *Selected Poems*. London, N.Y.: John
    Lane, 1903.

Webb, Sidney and Beatrice. *Soviet Communism: A New Civi-
    lization*. 2nd ed. Longmans, Green, 1937. 2 vol.
    "To Leonard and Virginia Woolf ... from ... Sidney
    Webb [and] Beatrice Webb ... "

Webster, John. *Complete Works,* ed. by F[rank] L[awrence]
    Lucas.   Chatto and Windus, 1927.   4 vol.   Belonged
    to Leonard.

*Wellesley, Dorothy, Duchess of Wellington. *Genesis, an
    Impression*. W. Heinemann, 1926. Author's presenta-
    tion copy to Virginia Woolf.

Wellesley, Dorothy, Duchess of Wellington. *Poems of Ten
    Years: 1924-1934*. Macmillan, 1934. "Virginia Woolf
    from Dorothy Wellesley ... "

Wellesley, Dorothy, Duchess of Wellington. *Selections
    from the Poems of,* w/introduction by W.B. Yeats.
    Macmillan, 1936.

Wells, Herbert George. *Mr. Belloc Objects to "The Outline
    of History."* Watts, 1926.

Wells, Herbert George. *Mr. Britling Sees It Through*.
    London, N.Y.: Cassell, 1916. 2 copies of this.

*Wells, Herbert George. *The Outline of History, Being a
    Plain History of Life and Mankind*. Cassell, 1920.
    Belonged to Leonard.

Wells, Herbert George. *A Short History of the World*. La-
    bor Publishing Co., 1924.

Wells, Herbert George, *et al.* [Julian Huxley and G.P.
    Wells]. *The Science of Life*. Waverley, n.d. 3
    vol.

White, Antonia. *Frost in May*. D. Harmsworth, 1933.

White, Gilbert. *The Natural History of Selborne ... to
    Which Are Added, The Naturalist's Calendar, Miscella-
    neous Observations, and Poems*. New ed. C. and J.
    Rivington, 1825. 2 vol. Belonged to Leslie Stephen.

Whitman, Walt. *Criticism, an Unpublished Essay*.   Amenia,
    N.Y.: Troutbeck Pr., 1924.

Whitman, Walt. *Leaves of Grass*. Philadelphia: D. McKay,
    1884.

Wilde, Oscar. *The Picture of Dorian Gray*. Leipzig: B.
    Tauchnitz, 1908.

Wilson, Harriette. *Harriette Wilson's Memoirs of Herself and Others,* w/preface by James Laver. P. Davies, 1929. Review slip.

Wolfe, Humbert. *Humbert Wolfe.* Augustan Books of Modern Poetry ser. E. Benn, n.d.

Wollstonecraft, Mary. *Letters Written During a Short Residence in Sweden, Norway and Denmark.* 2nd ed. J. Johnson, 1802.

Women's Co-operative Guild. (See [Llewelyn-Davies, Margaret].)

Wood, Ellen. *East Lynne.* T. Nelson, 1906(?).

Woolman, John. *The Journal of,* w/introduction by John G. Whittier. Glasgow: Robert Smeal, 1882. Belonged to Leslie Stephen.

Wordsworth, William. *Poetical Works.* Edward Moxon, 1836-37. [6 vol.] Vol. VI missing.

Wordsworth, William. *The Prelude.* Edward Moxon, 1850.

Wordsworth, William. *The Sonnets of.* Edward Moxon, 1838.

Wycherley, William. (See Pope, Alexander. *Letters.*)

Wycherley, William, *et al. The Dramatic Works of Wycherley, Congreve, Vanbrugh, and Farquhar,* ed. by Leigh Hunt. Routledge, Warne, 1860. Belonged to Leslie Stephen.

Xenophon. *Memorabilia,* w/notes by Percival Frost. New ed. Whittaker, 1867.

Yeats, John Butler. *Early Memories: Some Chapters of Autobiography.* Churchtown, Dundrum: The Cuala Pr., 1923.

Yeats, William Butler. *Autobiographies: Reveries Over Childhood and The Trembling of the Veil.* Macmillan, 1926.

Yeats, William Butler. *Collected Plays.* Macmillan, 1934.

Yeats, William Butler. *Poems.* T. Fisher Unwin, 1927.

Yeats, William Butler. *Selected Poems, Lyrical and Narrative.* Macmillan, 1929.

*Yeats, William Butler. *The Tower.* Macmillan, 1928.

Yeats, William Butler. *W.B. Yeats.* Augustan Books of English Poetry ser. E. Benn, n.d.

Yeats, William Butler. *Wheels and Butterflies*. Macmillan, 1934.

*Yourcenar, Marguerite. *Denier du Rêve, Roman*. Paris: B. Grasset, 1934. Author's presentation copy to Virginia Woolf.

*Yourcenar, Marguerite. *Les Songes et les Sorts*. Paris: B. Grasset, 1938. Author's presentation copy to Virginia Woolf.

[The intended terminal date on this list is 1941, the year of Virginia Woolf's death. Literary works printed after then which may have been acquired by her husband, are not included.]

AMBIGUOUS ITEMS AS LISTED BY HOLLEYMAN

INCOMPLETE LISTINGS

"Herodotus. *History*. 1857." (Index, p. 28)
Herodotus. *Halicarnassensis Musae,* edited by G.F. Creuzer and J.C.F. Baehr. (In Greek). Leipzig: Hahnian, 1856-61. [4 vol.] Vol. II only. ["Monks House Catalogue," Sec. 7, p. 5]

"Massinger, Ford, Green &c. *Dramatic Works of*. 1883." (Index, p. 39). I.e., 3 vol.:
The Dramatic and Poetical Works of Robert Greene and George Peele, edited by Alexander Dyce. London, N.Y.: G. Routledge, 1883.

The Dramatic Works of Massinger and Ford, w/introduction by Hartley Coleridge. New ed. London, N.Y.: G. Routledge, 1883.

The Dramatic Works of Wycherley, Congreve, Vanbrugh, and Farquhar, edited by Leigh Hunt. London, N.Y.: G. Routledge, 1883.

These belonged to Leonard Woolf. ["Monks House Catalogue," Sec. 3, p. 4]

LISTED UNDER "ANON." (Index, p. 2)

"*Mr. Dooley in Peace and War*. 1899."
[Dunne, Finley Peter]. *Mr. Dooley: In Peace and in War.* Grant Richards, 1899. ["Victoria Square Catalogue," Sec. 5, p. 55]

"*Paris for Every Man. 1924.*"
Griggs, Arthur Kingsland. *Paris for Everyman.* Dent,
1924. ["Victoria Square Catalogue," Sec. 5, p. 57]

"*Voyages Round the World from the Death of Capt. Cook to
the Present Time. 1843.*"

[Kippis, Andrew]. *Voyages Round the World from the Death
of Capt. Cook to the Present Time.* Edinburgh: Oliver
and Boyd, 1843.

This belonged to Leslie Stephen. ["Victoria Square Catalogue," Sec. 1, p. 5]

"*Woodland Moor and Stream. 1899.*"
[Jordan, Denham]. *Woodland, Moor and Stream.* Smith, Elder, 1889.

This belonged to Leslie Stephen. ["Victoria Square Catalogue," Sec. 1, p. 36]

LISTED UNDER "VARIOUS AUTHORS" (Index, pp. 61-62)

"*Diary Illustrative of the Times of George the Fourth.*
Vol. I. 1838."

[Bury, Lady Charlotte (Campbell)]. *Diary Illustrative of
the Times of George the Fourth.* New ed. Henry Colburn, 1838. [2 vol.] Vol. I only.

This belonged to Leslie Stephen. ["Victoria Square Catalogue," Sec. 1, p. 58]

"*Jungle Tales.* Vol. 8. 1933."
Tales from the Outposts, ed. by L.A. Bethell. (*Jungle
Tales,* Vol. VIII). William Blackwood, 1933.

This belonged to Bella Southorn, Leonard Woolf's sister.
["Victoria Square Catalogue," Sec. 5, p. 11]

* "Various" = "several in one work"

INDEX OF AUTHORS AND WORKS
NAMED IN THE COLLECTED ESSAYS
AND IN THE CHARTS, PART III, ABOVE

(Roman numerals indicate the 4 volumes of *Collected Essays*
[1966-67]; italicized numbers refer to pages of the appro-
priate charts [pp. 42-271, above]. *Women and Writing* is
indexed only for essays uncollected elsewhere.)

"A"

Abaelardus, Petrus--IV:42; *213*
Adam, Alexander--IV:106; *162*
Adam Bede (G. Eliot)--I:200, 201;
 102
Adams, Henry--*149*
Addison, Joseph--I:4, 85-94, 132,
 158; II:45, 136; III:72, 82;
 *42-43, 110, 150, 153, 164, 198,
 248, 268*
Adeline (S. Wilkinson)--*110*
Aeschylus [see also *Agamemnon*]--
 I:1, 7, 12, 213; II:45, 181,
 244, 274, 275; IV:52; *52, 124,
 144, 164, 171, 197, 207, 259*
Affectation (Sheridan)--BP50; *238*
Agamemnon (Aeschylus)--I:1, 7-8,
 11, 320; II:10; *124, 171, 197*
Aksakoff, Serge--CW94, 98; BP101-
 05; *173, 229-30*
A la Recherche du Temps Perdu
 (Proust)--II:55, 86, 89, 95,
 96-97; *50, 209*
Alice in Wonderland (Carroll)--
 I:255; *150*
All's Well That Ends Well
 (Shakespeare)--*244*
Almayer's Folly (Conrad)--*171,
 172*
Ambassadors, The (James)--II:128-
 29; *200*
Anabasis, The (Xenophon)--I:118;
 116
Anderson, Sherwood--II:112-14,
 115, 117, 119; *45, 46*

"Angel in the House, The" (C.
 Patmore)--I:215; BP38; *51, 207*
Angelica (*sic*; i.e., *Miss Angel*
 [A. Thackeray])--IV:74; *91*
Anima Poetae (Coleridge)--BP31;
 59
Ann Veronica (Wells)--CW62; *55*
Anna Karenina (Tolstoy)--I:57-
 59; II:269-70, 272; *104, 184,
 229*
Anson, George--III:184; *66*
Anstey, Christopher--*253*
Antigone (Sophocles)--I:4, 56;
 II:127; *184, 197, 200*
Antiquary, The (Scott)--I:139-43;
 47-48
Antony and Cleopatra (Shake-
 speare)--II:39, 151, 250; IV:
 200; *67, 88, 120, 196*
Arabian Nights, The--I:128; *221*
Arcadia, The (Sidney)--I:19-27,
 34, 40, 69; II:4; BP46; *64, 72,
 123, 224, 239*
Ardath (Corelli)--IV:98; *78*
Ariel (Maurois)--*180*
Aristophanes--I:12; III:225, 226;
 198, 232
Aristotle--I:260; III:37, 39;
 BP35, 37; *166, 206, 246*
Arnold, Matthew--I:272; II:32,
 41, 42, 46, 139, 154, 160, 165,
 205, 211, 214; IV:20, 58, 84;
 CW29; BP114, 163; WW75; CDB66;
 *47, 59, 76, 82, 96, 112, 120,
 127, 130, 144, 156, 162, 163,
 183, 191, 217, 223*
Arnold, Edwin--I:209-10; *52*